MINERVA SERIES OF STUDENTS' HANDBOOKS

NO. 5

General Editor
BRIAN CHAPMAN
MA, D.PHIL (*Oxon*)

The Use of Economic Statistics

The Use of
Economic Statistics

BY

CONRAD BLYTH

Fellow of Pembroke College
Cambridge

GEORGE ALLEN & UNWIN LTD
Ruskin House
Museum Street London

PRINTED IN GREAT BRITAIN
in 10 *on* 11-*pt. Times type*
BY SIMSON SHAND LTD
LONDON, HERTFORD AND HARLOW

PREFACE

This is an elementary introduction to the sources of economic statistics and their uses in answering economic questions. It is intended primarily for students studying elementary economics in their first or second year at university, but who are not necessarily going to be either economic or statistical specialists. No mathematical knowledge is assumed, and no mathematical symbols are used.

Some knowledge of the sources of economic statistics, and some facility in presenting and interpreting statistics, are nowadays amongst the qualifications which university students of economics may be expected to attain. The object of this book is to show—by asking and answering a number of typical questions of applied economics—what the most useful statistics are, where they are found, and how they are to be interpreted and presented. By this quantitative approach to economics, the reader is introduced to the major British, European and American official sources, to the social accounts, to index numbers and averaging, and to elementary aids to inspection such as moving averages and scatter diagrams.

Because the main feature of the book is the detailed working through of examples, the reader is expected to have close at hand some of the British sources—in particular, the *Monthly Digest of Statistics*, *National Income and Expenditure*, and the *Annual Abstract of Statistics*. Exercises using these sources are provided at the end of each chapter.

The book is based on a course I have given to Cambridge students during the last five years, and I acknowledge the help given by those students who have been my raw materials.

Permission to reproduce official statistics has been kindly granted by the Controller of HM Stationery Office, the Organisation for European Economic Co-operation and the US Department of Commerce.

C. A. B.

December 1959

CONTENTS

LIST OF TABLES

LIST OF CHARTS

WARNING

This book contains frequent reference to tables of statistics contained in the official publications *National Income and Expenditure*, the *Monthly Digest of Statistics* and the *Annual Abstract of Statistics*. Unless otherwise stated the references are to the 1959 edition of *National Income and Expenditure*, the 1958 edition of the *Annual Abstract of Statistics* and the September 1959 *Monthly Digest of Statistics*.

The arrangement of the tables in these publications differs in different editions, and if the student is using editions different from those referred to in this book he should make use of the indexes and tables of contents of his editions to make certain he finds the correct statistics.

All official United Kingdom statistical publications are published by Her Majesty's Stationery Office (HMSO).

The following abbreviations for titles of sources are used:

MDS   *Monthly Digest of Statistics*
AAS   *Annual Abstract of Statistics*
NIE   *National Income and Expenditure*
ET   *Economic Trends*
MLG   *Ministry of Labour Gazette*
BTJ   *Board of Trade Journal*
SCB   *Survey of Current Business* (United States)

A reference table of United Kingdom economic statistics is included after Chapter 12.

CHAPTER ONE

Production and Employment in the Cotton Industry Since the War

(A) STATING THE FACTS

1. COLLECTIONS OF OFFICIAL STATISTICS

What have been the changes in production and employment in the cotton industry since the war? What have caused these changes? These two questions are typical of those asked about industries. In this chapter we intend to introduce the major official sources of statistics and the methods adopted in using the sources to answer such questions.

There are four United Kingdom Government publications which are basic sources of economic statistics:

The Annual Abstract of Statistics (published annually);
The Monthly Digest of Statistics (published monthly);
Economic Trends (published monthly);
National Income and Expenditure (published annually).

We shall refer to these respectively as AAS, MDS, ET and NIE. All are prepared by the Central Statistical Office in collaboration with the Statistics Divisions of Government Departments. The first three present a wide range of statistics of employment, production, incomes, prices, wages, balance of payments, etc. AAS in general gives annual figures for about ten consecutive years, MDS gives recent annual and monthly figures, and ET also gives recent annual and monthly figures (but less comprehensively) and includes charts as well. Statistics dealing with new subjects are frequently first introduced in ET with explanatory articles. NIE is a comprehensive collection of income, expenditure and output statistics organized on distinctive principles (see Chapter 4 below).

The British student of economic statistics is advised to possess copies of a recent AAS and a recent MDS, and to develop the habit of regularly browsing through new issues of MDS and ET as they appear monthly. Most university and public libraries will make these publications available.

B

2. PRODUCTION STATISTICS

It is an unfortunate necessity, but we must ask 'what is the cotton industry'. Before we can examine the production statistics of any industry we must know what its principal products are. Firms sometimes produce a wide range of products. For example, a cotton weaving firm may weave cotton cloth, and also cloth made from a mixture of cotton yarn and man-made fibre yarn. Or a cotton spinning firm may spin yarn from both cotton and a man-made fibre such as rayon. If by the term 'cotton industry' we mean firms producing products made only from cotton, and if by the term 'man-made fibre industry' we mean firms whose products are made from man-made fibres alone, we will inevitably leave a large number of firms unclassified outside these groupings. We thus adopt the method of classifying firms according to their 'principal products', i.e. if a cotton weaving firm's product with the highest value is cloth made from cotton alone, it is classified as being in the cotton industry. Thus the definition of the cotton industry which we adopt is that it is a number of firms whose principal products are made from cotton alone. A similar type of definition based upon principal products applies to all other industries, although the common feature may sometimes be a raw material (the cotton industry), sometimes a final product (the motor industry), and sometimes a method (the engineering industry).

It follows from this type of definition of an industry that the production (or output) of the industry may consist of a number of different objects. For example, we know that the cotton industry produces mainly cotton goods. But it is likely to produce some goods which are mixtures of cotton and man-made fibres. So the answer to a question about the production of the cotton industry cannot rely on statistics of the production of purely cotton goods alone (unless we have good reason to neglect the production of other goods).

In most industries there are natural sub-divisions which depend upon related, although distinct, activities. In the case of cotton there are the activities of spinning, doubling, weaving, finishing, etc. Here again we have the problem of classification of firms, and here again we use the criterion of principal products—a firm is a cotton spinning firm if its principal product is single cotton yarn. If we are ignorant of the organization of the industry we are concerned with, we should refer to some authority. Useful reference books covering a wide range of British industries are those by G. C. Allen and Duncan Burn.[1] If we are not clear as to what the principal products of an industry are,

[1] Allen: *British Industries and their Organization* (4th Ed., London, 1959). Burn: *The Structure of British Industry* (London, 1958).

we should refer to the reports of the Censuses of Production, which give brief definitions of industries and lists of their principal products. Descriptions of the Censuses and the industrial classification they adopt are given in the note at the end of this chapter.

Thus the first steps in the examination of the production statistics of an industry is to find out something about its organization, its principal products and any other products that it produces. The essential facts regarding the cotton industry are (1) it is conventionally regarded as consisting of spinning, doubling and weaving sections, whose principal products are respectively single cotton yarn, doubled cotton yarn and woven cotton cloth; (2) cotton spinners produce large quantities of man-made fibre yarn and mixture yarn, and cotton weavers produce man-made fibre cloth and cloth from mixtures of cotton and man-made fibre yarn, as well as their principal products. These facts are partly reflected in the production statistics contained in the AAS and the MDS. The student is advised to refer to these publications now, using the index at the end of each to find the tables giving figures for production of cotton goods. The 1958 AAS contains annual production statistics from 1947 to 1957 in Table 180; the September 1959 MDS contains annual figures for 1937 and 1953-8, and monthly figures from April 1957 to July 1959, in Table 83. *In the MDS both the monthly and the annual figures are presented in the form of weekly averages*—this is usual and care must be taken when the AAS and the MDS are being used together. The MDS figures for single yarn support what was stated about the products of cotton spinners above: in 1957 the weekly average of single yarn spun in the cotton industry was 16.85 million lb., of which 2.87 million lb. was spun rayon and mixture yarns. Both the MDS and the AAS give separate figures for cotton cloth and man-made fibre and mixture cloth, but in this case there is no indication as to what proportion of each type comes from the cotton industry and what from the man-made fibre industry. In this case the safest thing we can do is to keep in mind all types of cloth in considering cotton weavers' production, even though we may suspect that their man-made fibre cloth production is small.

The second stage of our inquiry comes when, having obtained information about the main types of activity and product, we ask whether the variety of types of product within each activity is important. Need we retain the detail, or can we safely neglect it? An answer depends largely upon the problem that is under investigation, but there are two principles worth considering. (1) If the individual components of a total are small it is usually safe to neglect them.

Consider the weight of total yarn production. Between 1947 and 1957 the proportion of yarn spun from man-made fibres and mixtures increased. But in 1957 this was still a small proportion of total yarn spun, and whatever effects this increasing proportion may have had upon total production it is likely they would have been small. Hence we would neglect this detail unless we had special reasons for thinking it important. (2) The second principle refers to the objects of our inquiry. If we are interested in an industry as a unit or as a whole, we may neglect detail in the first stages of an inquiry. But if we are interested from the start in individual firms or products (i.e. in the structure of the industry) we may not safely neglect detail. For example, it may be that certain firms specialize in spinning some man-made fibre yarn. Then the statistics we have just quoted show the growing importance of these firms. Obviously we cannot neglect this. In what follows in this chapter we shall take the view (for reasons of space) that we are not specially interested in the structure of the industry and in individual types of product. We are interested in the industry as a whole and in its broad outlines. But the student must always be ready to ask whether it is safe to neglect detail, to answer the question by reference to the objects of the investigation, and to omit detail if he decides it is not required. Note that examination of the statistics will often show complexities of detail where none were suspected, and a general question about an industry as a whole may have to be answered in terms of its structure. All these points will be discussed in later chapters, and some exercises on the structure of the cotton industry are given at the end of this chapter.

The last consideration of production statistics in general is concerned with the method of presenting the statistics after we have decided that we may safely neglect detail. There are three approaches:

(a) If the units of measurement of the individual items are the same, we may simply add. For example, we would add pounds of single cotton yarn to pounds of single mixture yarn and call the result 'single yarn production'. Can we safely add pounds of single yarn to pounds of doubled yarn? Once again the answer depends upon the detail that is required. Normally spinning and doubling are considered such distinct activities that the two products are not added. But if the distinction does not interest us, there is no reason why we should not add them.

(b) If the units of measurement are different, or if we doubt the wisdom of adding products with similar units of measurement, we may combine the measurements of the different products into an *index*, weighing each product by a measure (usually its value) of its importance. Indexes of production are described below in Chapter 4. The 1958 AAS in Table 152 presents the figures of an index of production of Textile industries as a whole, but not for Cotton separately.

(*c*) As an alternative to method (*b*), we may select the output of one product as an *indicator* of changes in output as a whole. This method can be justified if the selected product or group of products is both important and representative. By representative we mean that changes in the output of the majority of the products are similar to the change in the output of the product selected as indicator. By selecting the indicator, we omit superfluous information.

3. INTERPRETATION OF THE PRODUCTION STATISTICS

We are now ready to give an answer to the question 'what have been the changes in the production of the cotton industry since the war?' Our selection of the appropriate statistics proceeds as follows. (1) We commence by distinguishing spinning from weaving. (2) There is no need to distinguish the separate activity of doubling as the production of doubled yarn appears to change over the years in much the same way as single yarn. (3) We measure the production of the spinning and doubling activities by the total weight of single yarn spun, i.e. as an indicator of production we use the sum of the outputs of different types of single yarn. (4) Weaving presents the problems discussed above. We shall take as our measure woven cotton cloth, but we shall also consider man-made fibre and mixture cloth because some cotton weavers may produce some of this. (5) We shall examine the annual statistics of the products mentioned under (3) and (4), for the years 1947-58. 1947-57 are in the 1958 AAS, and the 1958 figure can be obtained from the MDS. These statistics are presented in Table 1.1. (6) From inspection of Table 1.1 we give the following statement which is an answer to our question. '*Production of yarn increased every year after 1947 until 1951 when it attained its post-war peak. It fell sharply in 1952; rose again in 1953 and 1954; and fell again in 1955 and 1956. In 1957 it rose slightly; in 1958 it fell again. Although production fluctuated in the years 1952-8, the over-all impression is one of a decline since 1951 as compared with the rise between 1947-51.*' We shall not give a statement for woven cotton cloth production: the student can verify that its changes are the same as those of yarn production. In fact, *either yarn production or woven cloth production is a suitable indicator of the production of the entire cotton industry.* For this reason, when below we consider the causes of these changes in production we shall consider only cloth production.

TABLE 1.1

Output of Cotton Industry Products, 1947-58

Annual Totals

Year	Single Yarn*	Woven cloth: cotton	Woven cloth:† man-made fibres and mixtures
	million lb.	*million linear yards*	*million linear yards*
1947	787·7	1,632	388·7
1948	962·2	1,933	507·3
1949	989·8	2,005	587·2
1950	1,052·1	2,123	706·6
1951	1,077·0	2,202	758·7
1952	770·7	1,691	600·9
1953	952·5	1,864	768·7
1954	996·9	1,994	780·8
1955	879·3	1,781	698·1
1956	849·4	1,612	702·0
1957	876·6	1,628	659·5
1958	782·7	1,429	601·0

* Including man-made fibres spun in the cotton industry.
† Woven mainly in the man-made fibre industry.
Sources 1947-57: 1958 AAS, Table 180.
          1958: February 1959 MDS, pp. v & vi.

The statistics of man-made fibre and mixture cloth in Table 1.1 show some movements different from those of cotton cloth. The increased production after 1952 caused output to reach a post-war maximum in 1954. But over the whole period the changes resemble those of cotton cloth sufficiently closely to make it unnecessary to pay special attention to them even though some cotton weavers may have produced this sort of cloth. In the following section we shall consequently neglect man-made fibre products (an exercise on the statistics of the man-made fibre industry is given at the end of the chapter). Of course if the object of our inquiry was the textile industry as a whole, this difference in experience of cotton weavers and man-made fibre weavers would be a fact worth stressing.

Note on statistical tables

Table 1.1 above is what is called a *summary* (or *text*) table. It shows the statistics which we have decided are useful in answering our question, and is presented so that the reader can follow our conclusions. It is our evidence. To be a help and not a hindrance to the reader, all summary tables must have:

(1) a title
(2) headings for all columns and rows
(3) a note describing the source of the statistics

(4) a statement of the units of measurement (e.g. 'thousands of tons' or 'percentage of 1948 figure')

(5) a clear separation of columns.

In presenting tables in an essay or report it is best to draw them up first on separate pages. Later, if the essay or report is being typed or printed, they can be inserted in the text. Do not squeeze a table on to a small piece of paper simply because a small piece of paper is the first thing that comes to hand: allow plenty of space between columns, between rows, and between headings and figures.

If a figure is not available for inclusion in a table, or if it is so small as to be negligible, do not leave a blank space. Use the conventional signs which are:

.. meaning 'not available'

— meaning 'negligible or zero'.

4. EMPLOYMENT STATISTICS

What have been the changes in employment in the cotton industry since the war? This is such a common type of question that it is necessary to consider what we mean by *employment*. (1) It can mean what is loosely described as the labour force, or—as it is officially styled—*working population*. This includes all persons actually working, all persons available for employment (i.e. the unemployed who want work) and the armed forces. It includes employers, employees and self-employed, and also part-time workers. (In the United Kingdom it refers to persons aged fifteen years and over.) Monthly statistics of the working population are given in Table 15 of the September 1959 MDS and (for June of each year) in Table 131 of the 1958 AAS. (2) It can mean total civilian employees, whether at work or not. Annual statistics (for May of each year) are given for 164 industries in Table 134 of the 1958 AAS. (3) It can refer to the numbers of persons employed, i.e. on the books (the payrolls) of firms. These figures *include* most of those persons who are temporarily out of work but who expect to be taken on again, and *exclude* the wholly unemployed. These figures for Great Britain only are given every month for all manufacturing industries (and a few others) in Tables 15-26 of the September 1959 MDS. It is these statistics, i.e. employees actually at work, that we usually require when we talk about employment without qualification. (The unfortunate inclusion of most of the temporarily unemployed is due to the method of collecting the statistics.)

Table 15 of the September 1959 MDS gives the numbers of people employed in textiles as a whole for some recent months and for June of some recent years. Table 23 gives the same figures (distinguishing males and females) for the individual textile industries, e.g. 'cotton spinning, doubling, etc.'; 'cotton weaving, etc.'; 'textile finishing'; 'rayon and nylon production and weaving and silk.' By reference to earlier editions of the MDS we can extract a series of figures of employment from 1948 to 1958 in textiles as a whole, and in the two sectors which interest us, viz. cotton spinning, doubling, etc., and cotton weaving, etc. These figures (for the month of June each year) are shown in Table 1.2.

TABLE 1.2

Employment in the Cotton Industry (Great Britain only), 1948-58

June figure: thousands

Year	Total Textiles	Cotton spinning, doubling etc.	Cotton weaving etc.
1948	922	168·9	122·4
1949	965	173·6	131·4
1950	1,004	179·5	133·8
1951	1,025	183·8	135·1
1952	892	149·8	119·5
1953	963	161·8	122·0
1954	985	169·0	122·4
1955	946	150·7	117·1
1956	926	145·3	105·5
1957	925	146·9	103·9
1958	862	132·4	96·8

Source: MDS.

Why do we select June? The statistics are monthly statistics. Such statistics may be affected by seasonal influences, e.g. employment in the building industry may decline in the winter months as building activities are hindered by the cold weather. We are interested in the change in employment from year to year. Thus a comparison of, say, December 1954 and July 1955 would leave us undecided as to what part of the change is due to the effect of differences in the seasons on production and hence on employment. To eliminate as far as possible these complicating seasonal influences we compare figures referring to similar dates. Also, it is as well to avoid those months such as July and August when holidays are usually taken—complications may arise if the holiday pattern shifts (e.g. from August to July)—and also to avoid the winter months because of the irregularity of the winter seasonal factors. Thus because of the peculiarities of the English climate the best months for the purposes of yearly comparisons would appear to be May, June and October. June was selected in

Table 1.2 because the June statistics are most easily obtained from the MDS. (The problem of eliminating seasonal factors in monthly and quarterly statistics is considered again in Chapters 2 and 9 below.)

Note that due to changes in the method of collecting the employment statistics there exist no figures before 1948 satisfactorily comparable with that for 1948 and subsequent years.

Table 1.2 shows what we expect, viz. employment in cotton spinning and weaving changed in much the same way as did production over the years 1948-58. It rose until 1951; then fell sharply, and despite small increases in 1953-4 has subsequently fallen below the 1952 level. In fact between 1951 and 1958 employment in cotton spinning and weaving fell by about 90,000 persons. This is over half of the fall in total textile employment of 163,000.

Remember one feature of these statistics. They include those people who although temporarily out of work are still on the books of the firms. They also include people working part-time and short-time. Hence in a bad year like 1952, the employment statistics may underestimate the seriousness of the situation. Unfortunately, by how much we cannot easily say (see exercise 12.6 at the end of this chapter).

5. UNEMPLOYMENT STATISTICS

It is natural at this point to ask what happened to the 90,000 people who left the cotton industry between 1951 and 1958. Are they all unemployed? The official unemployment statistics refer to the number of *registered* unemployed, i.e. people who have registered at Employment Exchanges as seeking work. They include both the wholly unemployed, i.e. those out of a job, and the temporarily stopped, i.e. those suspended from work on the understanding that they will shortly return to their former employment. Note, as has been remarked in the previous section, that many of the temporarily stopped will also be included in the employment statistics. The basic source for all unemployment statistics is the monthly *Ministry of Labour Gazette*. This publication classifies the monthly statistics by industry, by area, by sex, and into the two types of wholly unemployed and temporarily stopped. The AAS and the MDS provide summaries of this information. Very often neither the AAS nor the MDS give the figures we want, and this is so in our present problem. It is such a common problem that we shall examine it in some detail.

The AAS figures for unemployment refer to the United Kingdom, i.e. Great Britain and Northern Ireland. The MDS figures refer only to Great Britain. This problem of geographical coverage arises so frequently in British statistics that the student must at all times be in the habit of checking the geographical coverage which will usually be indicated either in Table headings or in footnotes. How do we cope with this complication in the present inquiry? Let us retrace our steps. We have employment statistics for cotton weaving and spinning *which refer to Great Britain. Similar statistics are not available for Northern Ireland in any source.* We need comparable unemployment statistics. Normally we would choose the United Kingdom for our geographical area as most statistics refer to this wider area (including the production statistics used above). But in this important case the detailed monthly employment statistics we wish to use are available only for Great Britain: thus Great Britain is the appropriate geographical coverage for both employment and unemployment statistics. However, comparable unemployment statistics for cotton spinning and weaving are not available in either the AAS or the MDS (the student should verify this). They are available in the *Ministry of Labour Gazette*, and our correct procedure would be to extract the June figures from issues of the *Gazette*.

Without going to the *Gazette* we can obtain some guidance about the fate of the 90,000 by using the United Kingdom figures in the AAS (these are for the month of June and so are comparable in respect of time). The figures are presented in Table 1.3.

TABLE 1.3

Employment and Unemployment in Cotton Spinning, Doubling and Weaving
1951 and 1958

June figure: thousands

	1951	1958	Change between 1951 and 1958
Employment (in Great Britain)	318·9	229·2	−89·7
Unemployment (in United Kingdom)	1·1	19·1	+18·0

Source: Employment: MDS, September 1958, Table 22.
Unemployment: 1958 AAS, Table 135.

It is clear that the reduction in employment of about 90,000 people in cotton spinning and weaving (in Great Britain) between 1951 and 1958 has by no means entailed an increase in unemployment of that amount. For the United Kingdom as a whole the increase was only 18,000. On this evidence we can say that most of the people who left the industry either found employment in other industries, or—although unemployed—have not registered for employment at an Employment Exchange. The latter possibility may refer to the position of married women. A more detailed study of the unemployment situation requires the use of the more appropriate statistics mentioned above.

6. STATEMENT OF THE FINDINGS

We are now ready to give a short statement of our findings. '*The post-war period of rising production and employment ended in 1952. In that year production of cotton cloth fell by about one fifth and employment in cotton spinning and weaving by at least one sixth (compared with 1951). There was some recovery in the following two years, but the decline in production and employment persisted and was particularly noticeable in 1958. As judged from the official unemployment statistics, persistent unemployment has not been very high, although it is not known how many of those leaving jobs in the industry have found other work.*' This statement is intended to show the form of the summary usually attempted in this type of investigation where detail is not required (or is judged to be unnecessary).

(B) CHOOSING AN EXPLANATION

7. CHOICE OF AN EXPLANATION WHICH FITS THE FACTS

The second question this chapter posed was: what has caused the changes in production and employment? Our method of answering is to choose an explanation which fits the facts. It involves two steps.

(1) We choose an explanation (or hypothesis). At this stage the student must rely upon his knowledge of economics and of the industrial background to the problem under consideration. (Some standard explanations which are frequently useful are listed below.) An explanation will usually be of the form: a change in X causes a change in Y.

(2) We compare the changes in X with the changes in Y to find out whether these changes are of the type suggested by the explanation. If they are, we accept the explanation which now becomes an answer to the question.

In a problem such as our present cotton industry example, there is a routine procedure we can adopt in choosing our explanations. We start from the commonsense principle that products are made to be sold. A fall in sales will cause a fall in production. First of all we ask: in what markets have sales fallen (or risen)? Is it sales in home markets, i.e. in the United Kingdom? Or is it sales overseas, i.e. exports, which have decreased? When we have answered these questions we are ready to ask why sales have fallen (or risen) in these particular markets. Here are some possible explanations:

i.   The fall in sales has been caused by a fall in consumers' incomes (i.e. the ability to buy or consume has declined).

ii.   The fall in the sales of a product is due to a rise in its price, this being due to either (*a*) increased cost of production or (*b*) the imposition of a tax.

iii.   The fall in the sales of one product is due to the fact that consumers are buying more of an alternative product.

iv.   The fall in the sales is due to the imposition of some legal restrictions on the conditions of sale, e.g. an increase in the minimum downpayment (if it is sold on credit).

Note that these explanations are not mutually exclusive (e.g. sales may fall both because incomes fall and because consumers buy more of an alternative product—the economics student may be able to provide a single comprehensive explanation of all three of these events). Also, an explanation may need to be cast in more precise terms than those in which it originally appears (e.g. in explanation iii above we should attempt to name the alternative product or products).

The procedure we shall adopt in the case of changes in the production of the cotton industry is:

(*a*) Examination of the statistics of home consumption, and of exports, of the products of the cotton industry to find out in which markets sales have fallen.

(*b*) Selection of the explanation that sales of the products of the British cotton industry have declined because of competition from the textile industries of other countries, i.e. home and overseas customers are increasing their purchases of other countries' textile products and reducing their purchases of British cotton products.

(*c*) The explanation is then tested. What we shall do here as an illustration is to compare the imports of British cotton cloth with the total imports of cotton cloth into those countries in which sales of British exports have declined. In fact, both for reasons of space and for more weighty reasons discussed below we shall narrow the investigation even further and consider imports of cotton cloth into British colonies only.

8. EXPORT AND IMPORT STATISTICS

The basic sources of export and import statistics of values and quantities of commodities are the monthly *Accounts relating to Trade and Navigation of the United Kingdom*, and the *Annual Statement of Trade*.

Totals and details of the most important commodities are given in the AAS and the MDS. Usually we look in the AAS and the MDS for the figures we need, but if they are not available there we must be prepared to refer to the basic sources.

What statistics are we in fact interested in? The first step is to see what types of cotton products are exported. Table 271 of the 1958 AAS under the headings 'cotton yarns and woven fabrics' and 'artificial silk' gives the figures for 1957 reproduced here in Table 1.4. Note that the names of products and classes of products do not always follow those adopted in the production statistics. In fact,

TABLE 1.4

Exports of Certain Textile Products, 1957

Type of Export	Quantity		Value
			£ million
Cotton yarns	million lb.:	37·6	16·8
Finished thread for sewing, etc.	million lb.:	10·0	10·8
Cotton woven fabrics	million sq. yards:	455·5	59·9
Man-made fibre yarns	million lb.:	44·1	16·2
Man-made fibre and mixture woven fabrics	million sq. yards:	112·2	16·5

Source: 1958 AAS, Table 271.

woven fabrics are the same as woven cloth, and artificial silk is the same as man-made fibre. If we are in doubt as to the correspondence of definitions and names there is only one thing to do: ask someone who knows. It is clear from Table 1.4 that woven cotton fabrics form the major part of cotton textile exports. In examining production changes we had decided that we need only consider cloth, and as cotton cloth is the major export we shall keep to the rules of disregarding unnecessary detail and choose exports of woven cotton fabrics as the indicator of exports of cotton goods.

9. ESTIMATION OF HOME SALES OF CLOTH

Where do we find statistics of sales of cloth in the United Kingdom? There are no statistics as such. Woven cloth is sold (after finishing) to the housewife, and is also sold as a raw material to the clothing and furnishing industries (amongst others) whence it appears as clothes and covers, etc. It is not impossible to examine the sales statistics of these different types of goods, but in this case their interpretation is difficult. A simple, although crudely approximate, approach is to estimate the *cloth available for consumption in the United Kingdom*. This is frequently a useful calculation and is based upon the formula:

production+imports=exports+available for consumption in the United Kingdom. The left hand side of the equation is Total Supplies; the right hand side is Total Disposals. By adding imports to production, and subtracting exports, we obtain the quantity available for consumption at home. The quantity available for home consumption is a *rough measure*, or indicator, of home sales, and includes both sales and changes in stocks (inventories). We may expect that this rough measure will reflect changes in actual sales because weavers will alter their production as sales change. (It is a rough measure for another reason. If production, exports and imports all refer to cloth, then part of what we call quantity available for home consumption may actually be exported in the form of clothing. The student would normally attempt to estimate the importance of this. We shall not bother about this difficulty here.)

We have already obtained production statistics; we know where to find the export and import figures. Before we make our estimates there is one final difficulty. Exports and imports are measured in square yards while production is in linear yards. For our purposes, can we treat a linear yard of cloth as the same as a square yard of cloth? The answer to this type of question must always be obtained from someone who knows. In this case, the answer is yes, so we proceed to ignore the difference in units.[1] The statistics are presented in Table 1.5.

Exports reached their post-war maximum in 1949, although they recovered again to reach another high figure in 1951. In 1952 both exports and home sales fell sharply. Despite the rough nature of the estimates of home sales, the figures strongly suggest that in 1952 the fall in home sales was the more important. Exports continued their fall after 1952. Home sales recovered in 1954 and from 1954-7 were at levels similar to those of 1949-50. Our statistics show small falls in 1955 and 1956, but we can hardly attribute much significance to these in view of the roughness of the estimates. The important facts are that home sales recovered from the 1952-3 slump and reached their earlier level in 1954, since when there has been little or no change. Since 1954 home sales have not risen to offset the continued decline in exports. We need explanations of three main sets of facts: (1) the rise in sales both at home and overseas from 1947-51; (2) the fall in sales both at home and overseas in 1952; and (3) the continued fall in exports since 1953.

---

[1] For most purposes linear yards of United Kingdom cotton cloth can be converted to square yards by adding 10 per cent. The student can verify that if we do this the conclusions of the following paragraphs are unaffected.

TABLE 1.5

Production, Exports and Imports of Woven Cotton Cloth, 1947-57

Year	Production	Imports	Total Supplies (Production plus Imports)	Exports	Available for Consumption in UK (Total Supplies less Exports)
	million linear yards	*million sq. yards*	*million yards*	*million sq. yards*	*million yards*
1947	1,623	155·1	1,778	532·9	1,245
1948	1,933	222·7	2,156	761·5	1,394
1949	2,005	347·9	2,353	903·6	1,449
1950	2,123	286·8	2,410	822·5	1,587
1951	2,202	375·5	2,578	865·2	1,713
1952	1,691	179·6	1,871	710·8	1,160
1953	1,864	98·8	1,963	709·9	1,253
1954	1,994	267·2	2,261	637·3	1,624
1955	1,781	299·5	2,081	554·5	1,526
1956	1,612	305·6	1,918	474·3	1,444
1957	1,628	416·3	2,044	455·5	1,588

Note: Exports and Imports are of 'woven cotton fabrics'. Export and Import figures have been rounded to nearest million sq. yards before addition or subtraction.

Source: 1958 AAS, Tables 180, 270, 271.

We shall not attempt to explain all these facts here. As an example of our methods we shall limit the scope of the inquiry and ask why export sales continued to fall after 1953. But before we answer this we shall draw attention to one feature of the import statistics. Imports of cloth quadrupled between 1953 and 1957 (or almost trebled between 1952 and 1957). When we examine the import statistics in detail (in the *Trade and Navigation Accounts*) we find that the major part of these cloth imports was of the kind called 'grey, unbleached', i.e. cloth which requires finishing. This means that although this imported cloth was competing with the products of United Kingdom spinners and weavers, it was providing employment for the United Kingdom textile finishers. (The student should examine the employment statistics and verify that employment in 'textile finishing' fell negligibly between 1953 and 1957.) Some of these imports, after being finished in the United Kingdom, may have been exported. Imports of grey, unbleached cloth have been recognized as being important competitors of the products of United Kingdom weavers and for this reason monthly import figures of this type of cloth have been shown in recent years in the MDS (see September 1959 MDS, Table 126).

Note on rounding and errors

Many of the figures in the sources are presented in 'rounded' form.

For instance, in Table 180, 1958 AAS, figures for woven cloth production are given in millions of linear yards. The 1957 figure of 1,628 million linear yards means that the true figure lies between 1,627,500,001 and 1,628,499,999 linear yards. In choosing 1,628 million linear yards the official statisticians have rounded off the true figure to the nearest million linear yards. This means that the rounded figure has a possible error of anything up to plus or minus half a million yards (written as ±half a million).

We used the rounded production figures in Table 1.5. In the sources the import and export figures are given to the nearest hundred thousand square yards, and in using them in Table 1.5 to estimate cloth available for consumption in the United Kingdom we rounded them further to the nearest million square yards. Thus the import and export figures in Table 1.5 also have a possible error of ±half a million.

When figures are added or subtracted the rule is to add the possible absolute errors. Thus the possible error of our estimate of cloth available for consumption in the United Kingdom in any year is ±1½ million yards. If we calculate the change between any two years the possible error is ±3 million yards. The importance of this is that any change between two years *less* than 3 million yards must be regarded as insignificant. We can attach importance to changes only if they are greater than 3 million yards. Clearly, the changes in Table 1.5 are much greater than this and hence we can disregard the errors of rounding in this case.

Errors of rounding should be avoided whenever possible by making calculations with unrounded figures. Where this is not possible (because the sources provide only rounded figures) we should estimate the possible error so as to allow for it, if necessary, in our conclusions.

Errors of rounding may arise in division and multiplication. For example, suppose the output of a steel mill in a certain month is 22,498 tons of steel, and the number of employees at work during the month in the mill is 1,121. The average output per employee is $\frac{22498}{1121} = 20.069$ tons (three decimal places, unrounded). Rounded to one decimal place this is 20·1 tons. If the output and employment figures were first rounded to the nearest thousand tons of steel, and hundred employees, before the division was made, average output per employee would be $\frac{22}{1.1} = 20.0$ tons. The error due to rounding in this case is 0·5 per cent.

If only the rounded figures for output and employees were available, we would estimate the average output per employee as being approximately between $\frac{22 \cdot 5}{1 \cdot 05} = 21 \cdot 4$ tons (highest possible output figure divided by lowest possible employment figure) and $\frac{21 \cdot 5}{1 \cdot 15} = 18 \cdot 7$ tons (lowest possible output figure divided by highest possible employment figure). Thus average output per employee is about $20 \cdot 0 \pm 1 \cdot 4$ tons, or $20 \cdot 0 \pm 7$ per cent of 20 tons.

The student should note that it is possible to estimate approximately the possible percentage error of a quotient of two rounded figures by adding the percentage errors in the separate figures: output is 22,000 tons with a possible error of 500 tons which is about 2 per cent of 22,000; employees number 1,100 with a possible error of 50 which is about 5 per cent of 1,100; the average output per employee calculated from the rounded figures is $20 \cdot 0$ tons with a percentage error of about 7 per cent of 20 tons. Thus our remarks on errors of rounding can be summarized in two rules: (1) the error in sums and differences is the sum of the separate errors; (2) the percentage error in quotients (and products) is the sum of the separate percentage errors.

10. THE CAUSE OF THE FALL IN EXPORTS SINCE 1953

The final problem we have set ourselves is to find out why exports fell since 1953. As we stated earlier, we choose the explanation that this is due to competition from other countries' textile products. The most straightforward approach is to examine the textile imports of

TABLE 1.6

United Kingdom Exports of Woven Cotton Fabrics, 1954 and 1957

Destination	million sq. yards 1954	1957	Fall between 1954 and 1957
British Colonies	200,490	132,639	67,851
British Dominions	254,025	172,986	81,039
India Pakistan and Ceylon	17,757	13,881	3,876
Rest	165,106	136,254	28,852
TOTAL	**637,378**	**455,760**	**181,618**

Source: Trade and Navigation Accounts.

those countries to which Britain exports textiles to find out whether imports from Britain were being displaced by other imports, i.e.

C

whether imports from Britain were declining while some other country's sales were rising. We first find out in what overseas markets British exports were declining. The *Trade and Navigation Accounts* give figures for exports to individual countries. These figures have been used in Table 1.6 which classifies exports of cloth according to whether they are destined for British Colonies; British Dominions (South Africa, Australia, New Zealand, Canada); India, Pakistan and Ceylon; and the Rest (all foreign countries including Ireland and Sudan). It appears that the fall in exports was almost entirely due to roughly equal falls in exports to the first two groups—British Colonies and British Dominions.

Trade statistics of the British Commonwealth are presented in two official British publications: the *Statistical Abstract of the Commonwealth and the Sterling Area* (published annually), and the *Digest of Colonial Statistics* (published quarterly). We wish to examine the origin of imports of cotton cloth into British Colonies and British Dominions. Here we shall consider only imports into British Colonies (leaving the student to examine the cases of other cloth imports and the case of imports into the British Dominions). The *Digest of Colonial Statistics* (No. 39; October-December 1958; Table 38) presents statistics of imports of *cotton piece goods* into British colonial territories. A summary of these statistics suitable for our purposes is given in Table 1.7. Note that the figure for all colonial territories

TABLE 1.7

Imports of Cotton Piece Goods into British Colonial Territories,* 1954 and 1957

million sq. yards

Origin	1954	1957
United Kingdom	127	82·6
Japan	162	307
USA	11·1	14·6
Germany	12·4	5·98
India	335	251
Other Countries†	74·7	218
TOTAL	722	879

* Figures exclude imports into Federation of Malaya, Northern Rhodesia and Nyasaland.
† Including the British Colonies of Hongkong and Singapore.
Source: Digest of Colonial Statistics (No. 39; Table 38).

excludes the Federation of Malaya, Northern Rhodesia and Nyasaland, but includes Singapore. Total imports increased by 157 million square yards between 1954 and 1957. Of the supplying countries, British exports declined as we already knew, Indian exports also declined, while Japanese and 'Other Countries' exports increased. The explanation that we chose thus fits the facts: British exports have declined in the face of competition from the exports of other countries. We conclude that *in the case of exports to British Colonies* our explanation is acceptable.

11. NOTE ON CENSUSES OF PRODUCTION AND THE STANDARD INDUSTRIAL CLASSIFICATION

The Census of Production is a periodical inquiry undertaken by the Board of Trade. The industries covered are mining, manufacturing, building and public utilities. The first Census was taken in 1907, followed by others in 1912, 1924, 1930 and 1935. From 1948 on, a Census has been taken every year. The Censuses of 1952-3 and 1955-7 were taken on a sample basis (i.e. only a representative selection of firms were questioned) and the present procedure is that a full Census is taken periodically, the Censuses in the intervening years being on the sample basis. Full Censuses have been taken in 1951, 1954, and 1958. The results of the Censuses are published in *Reports* by HMSO and are usually not available for several years after the Census year. Summaries are published more promptly in the *Board of Trade Journal* and in the AAS.[1] The Reports contain introductory notes which explain the scope and coverage of the Census, and the differences between the Censuses: the student should always refer to these notes when using the results.

The questions which firms are asked differ in different Censuses, but the standard questions asked in recent Censuses include:
number of working proprietors
persons employed
wages and salaries
expenditure on plant, machinery and vehicles
expenditure on new building work
materials and fuel purchased
amount paid for work given out
stocks at beginning and end of period
output in value and quantity
transport payments.

The 1948 Census was taken only in Great Britain, but subsequent Censuses refer to the United Kingdom as a whole. The term 'larger establishments' in the post-war Censuses means firms employing more than ten people and most Censuses refer only to such firms (the

[1] The 1958 AAS, Table 153, gives a summary up to and including the 1956 Census.

student must examine the difference in coverage when comparing Census results). The term 'gross output' used in the *Reports* means the selling value of the output of an industry; the term 'net output' is gross output *less* the value of the materials and fuel used in production.[1]

The Censuses provide economists with a considerable amount of information not available in other sources. For instance, the *Reports* of the full Censuses classify firms in an industry according to numbers employed. For the statistician, the Censuses provide the basis of statistical information from which many types of statistics are derived. In particular the estimates of national income and the indexes of industrial production (see Chapter 4) are largely based on the information provided by the Censuses.

The classification of firms and their products into industries in the Census *Reports* follows the *Standard Industrial Classification* (SIC), first adopted in 1948 and revised in 1957. The object of this classification is to secure uniformity and comparability in the statistics published by different Government Departments. The thing which is classified is the establishment—farm, mine, factory, shop or office at a particular address. The criterion of classification is principal industrial activity, e.g. 'the manufacture of metal-working machine tools, engineers' small tools for use with machine tools, and welding machinery of all descriptions', or 'the spinning or doubling of yarn or cotton or cotton waste, the manufacture of cotton sewing thread, and the spinning of rayon, nylon, etc., staple fibre on cotton spinning machinery'. Each activity defined in this way is called a trade or industry with a short title such as 'Machine Tools' or 'Cotton Spinning and Doubling'. These trades are classified into orders which represent the common industrial groups. In the 1957 classification there are twenty-four orders covering 152 trades or industries.[2]

The orders are:

    I   Agriculture, forestry, fishing
    II   Mining and quarrying
    III Food, drink and tobacco
    IV Chemicals and allied industries
    V   Metal manufacture
    VI Engineering and electrical goods

[1] For the various distinctions between net and gross see further in Chapter 4 below.

[2] The difference between the 1948 and 1957 classifications as far as the orders is concerned is a difference in names. In the case of trades the 1957 SIC reduced the number from 163 to 152 and made some rearrangements in activities.

VII	Shipbuilding and marine engineering
VIII	Vehicles
IX	Metal goods not elsewhere specified
X	Textiles
XI	Leather, leather goods and fur
XII	Clothing and footwear
XIII	Bricks, pottery, glass, cement, etc.
XIV	Timber, furniture, etc.
XV	Paper, printing and publishing
XVI	Other manufacturing industries
XVII	Construction
XVIII	Gas, electricity and water
XIX	Transport and communication
XX	Distributive trades
XXI	Insurance, banking and finance
XXII	Professional and scientific services
XXIII	Miscellaneous services
XXIV	Public administration and defence.

The term 'industrial production' usually refers to the output of mining, manufacturing, construction, gas, electricity and water, i.e. to orders II-XVIII,[1] but frequently any of the orders is referred to as an industry or industry group. The fourteen orders III-XVI are called the manufacturing industries.

Most official statistics that the student uses are classified on this basis. Where there is any doubt as to the comparability of different sets of statistics, e.g. whether employment statistics are comparable with output statistics, the student should refer to the *Standard Industrial Classification* (HMSO, 1957) or to the detailed description of industries given in the *Reports* on the Censuses of Production.

The differences between the 1948 and 1957 classifications may cause some small complications when pre-1957 statistics are compared with post-1957 statistics—if back numbers of AAS or MDS are being used to get a series of figures over a lengthy period of time. The main differences between the two SIC's are explained in an article in ET, October 1958.

12. EXERCISES
(N.B. Most of the statistics referred to in these exercises are in tables in the 1958 AAS or the September 1959 MDS. Other issues of the AAS and the MDS contain the same statistics, although the table numbers may be different.)

[1] These orders, II-XVIII, are those covered by the Censuses of Production.

(1) Compare the production of the cotton industry before and after the 1939-45 war. What part of the change in production can be explained by a change in exports? [HINT: Compare the years 1935-8 with the years 1948-51. The 1958 AAS does not contain pre-war production statistics, but these can be obtained from an earlier edition. Table 271 of the 1958 AAS gives pre-war export statistics; import statistics are in Table 270.]

(2) Table 228 of the 1958 AAS gives figures of sales of 'wholesale textile houses'. Table 18 of the 1959 National Income and Expenditure (NIE) contains consumer expenditures on various types of household goods. Do these statistics confirm the view adopted in section 9 above that home sales of cloth from 1954-7 were roughly constant and at a level similar to that of 1949-50?

(3) In what *textile* industries did employment fall less than the fall in cotton spinning and weaving between 1951 and 1957? [HINT: Employment statistics are in Table 23 of the Spetember 1959 MDS.] Can you explain the differences between the changes in the various industries? [HINT: Compare the employment statistics with the production statistics in Tables 180 and 199 of the 1958 AAS. The most important textile industries besides cotton to consider are: Woollen and worsted, Rayon and nylon production and weaving, and Hosiery.]

(4) Have sales of cotton cloth suffered at the expense of man-made fibre cloth in the United Kingdom in recent years? [HINT: From Tables 180, 270 and 271 in the 1958 AAS estimate quantities of man-made fibre (and mixture) cloth available for home consumption between 1947 and 1957. Compare with estimates of cotton cloth given above in section 9, Table 1.5.]

(5) Have sales of British man-made fibre cloth in British Colonies suffered the same fate as sales of cotton cloth in recent years? [HINT: If you have the sources cited in section 10 above available, apply the methods outlined in that section.]

(6) The following statistics (from the *Ministry of Labour Gazette*) are unemployment numbers for Great Britain comparable with the employment statistics in the MDS (see section 5 above). Were the unemployed of 1952 re-employed in the textile industries in 1953? [HINT: Compare the changes in unemployment between 1951 and 1952, and 1952 and 1953, with the corresponding changes in employment (MDS, September 1959, Tables 15 and 23). Note the discrepancies between the set of figures: e.g. between 1951 and 1952 employment in cotton spinning and doubling fell by 34,000, but registered unemployment rose by 51,000. This discrepancy is explained by the

fact that the employment statistics *include* many of those temporarily unemployed. Extend your comparisons to the separate male and female statistics.]

TABLE 1.8

Registered Unemployed in Textiles, 1951-3
Great Britain. *June number*

		1951	**1952**	**1953**
Textiles	*Males*	1,868	44,176	4,505
	Females	3,119	92,536	7,201
Cotton spinning,	*Males*	230	15,961	1,027
doubling, etc.	*Females*	442	36,177	1,451
Cotton weaving,	*Males*	120	7,812	332
etc.	*Females*	253	20,719	1,054

Note: Numbers include both wholly unemployed and temporarily stopped.
Source: Ministry of Labour Gazette.

(7) From the *Ministry of Labour Gazette* of July 1951, 1952 and 1953 extract the numbers of wholly unemployed in Great Britain in the textile industries for the month of June in these years (note that the *Gazettes* do not distinguish wholly unemployed and temporarily stopped for the United Kingdom as a whole). Use these figures to make the calculations suggested in the previous exercise. Do these figures remove the discrepancies discovered in that exercise?

(8) Between June 1951 and June 1957 civil employment in the United Kingdom increased by 1,228 thousands of people (see Tables 131 and 132 of the 1958 AAS: sum of Great Britain and Northern Ireland). Where did the increased labour force come from? To what extent was it due to (i) a fall in the numbers of wholly unemployed; (ii) a reduction in the size of the military forces; (iii) an increase in the population aged between 15 and 64; (iv) an increase in the number of women at work; (v) an increase in the number of people aged over 64 at work? [HINT: for (i) and (ii) see Tables 131 and 132 in the 1958 AAS; for (iii) see Table 7 (age distribution of the home population) in the 1958 AAS; for (iv) see Table 131 of 1958 AAS for 1957 figure— an earlier AAS or MDS will give the 1951 figure (note that this is available for Great Britain only); can you discover sources to answer (v)?].

PRODUCTION AND EMPLOYMENT IN THE COTTON INDUSTRY 39

fact that the employment statistics exclude many of those seeking employment. Extend your comments on the economic state and
onal statistics.]

CHAPTER TWO

The Slump in the Motor Industry
1956-7

1. THE PROBLEM: EFFECT OF HIRE PURCHASE CONTROLS UPON CAR SALES

During 1955 controls were imposed by the British Government upon
the hire purchase of motor cars along with other durable consumer
goods. In February the minimum deposit was made 15 per cent of
the price, with a maximum repayment period of twenty-four months.
The minimum deposit was increased to $33\frac{1}{3}$ per cent in July, and to
50 per cent in February 1956. (The purchase tax on cars had been
increased from 50 per cent to 60 per cent in October 1955.) It was not
until December 1956 that the minimum deposit was reduced (to 20
per cent). It was increased again to $33\frac{1}{3}$ per cent in May 1957, and in
October 1958 these controls on minimum deposit and maximum repayment period were taken off completely.

Let us suppose (correctly) that we remember reading in the newspapers that the motor industry suffered a decline in production
during 1956 and 1957. Was this caused by the imposition of controls
on the conditions of hire purchase? What effect did the progressive
relaxation of the controls have? Here we have a problem similar to
those discussed in Chapter 1, but made slightly easier because we
have a suggestion as to one possible influence upon sales, viz. varying
degrees of control over the conditions of sale.

In one important respect the motor industry problem differs from
that of cotton. Controls were varied at different times of the year.
The effect of the increase in the minimum deposit imposed in July
1955 we would expect to be shown in a lower level of sales after July
as compared with the level before July. Hence we shall require
statistics relating to periods shorter than one year—monthly or
quarterly statistics. The problems raised by these sorts of statistics
will be discussed in section 3.

As in all exercises of this type the first step is to remind ourselves
of the structure of the motor industry. Firms in the industry produce
not only cars and commercial vehicles (and their parts and acces-

sories) but also agricultural tractors, trailers, marine engines and many other types of vehicles and equipment. In both popular and official usage the term 'motor industry' consists of those firms producing cars or commercial vehicles as their principal product. (The expression 'vehicle industry' is used to cover the wider classification.) Cars (or automobiles) are sold both to private individuals and to firms. Commercial vehicles—generally divided into goods transport vehicles such as vans and trucks, and passenger transport vehicles such as omnibuses—are bought almost exclusively for business purposes. The purchase of cars and commercial vehicles by firms is considered to be part of business investment, i.e. an addition to the stock of productive wealth (see Chapters 4 and 6 below). The industry sells its products both in the United Kingdom and abroad. The hire purchase controls discussed above refer to sales of cars in the United Kingdom on terms of credit involving hire purchase. Such sales (estimated to be about 20 per cent of all car sales) will normally be to private individuals and small firms (large firms will either pay cash or use trade or bank credit). Thus a slump in the motor industry could be caused not only by the imposition or tightening of hire purchase controls on private purchases of cars, but also by a fall in business investment or a fall in exports.

2. THE SOURCES

Let us now survey the available statistical sources. (*a*) *Production*. The 1958 AAS, Table 158, contains for the years 1948 to 1957 numbers of passenger cars and commercial vehicles produced. The unit of measurement is either a finished vehicle or a chassis, i.e. the figures given are numbers of vehicles including chassis. The figures of cars are classified according to horsepower rating; the figures of commercial vehicles are classified according to whether they are 'public service vehicles', i.e. buses, trolley-buses, etc., 'goods vehicles', i.e. vans, trucks, etc., and 'battery driven vehicles'. The MDS (September 1959, Tables 77-8) gives monthly figures from April 1957 to August 1959 classified according to whether the vehicles (and chassis) are intended for export or for the home market.

(*b*) *Exports and imports*. Table 271 of the 1958 AAS gives annual figures (from 1949-57) of exports of cars and commercial vehicles. Numbers of chassis are given separately. Table 270 gives figures of imports of all motor vehicles (unclassified). Table 128 of the MDS gives monthly export figures. There is a difference between the statistics of exports and the production statistics of vehicles intended for export. The main reasons for this are a difference in the dates at which the same type of information is collected, the fact that cars bought by overseas buyers from the export quota of production may be used in the United Kingdom for some time before they are exported, and some small differences in coverage in types of vehicles.

(c) *Home sales.* First, there are new registrations of vehicles (for purposes of taxation). Tables 234 and 241 of the 1958 AAS give the figures for Great Britain and Northern Ireland respectively. Table 136 of the September 1959 MDS gives similar monthly figures for Great Britain alone. Statistics of new registrations refer not only to new models, both British and foreign, but also to used vehicles which have not been previously registered in the United Kingdom (e.g. because they have been imported after use in a foreign country). The reasons for the difference between the statistics of new registrations and the production statistics of vehicles intended for the home market are the same as those given above for the export statistics.

As a second measure of home sales there are statistics of the value of sales and vehicles in the United Kingdom. Table 18 of the 1959 NIE gives personal (household) expenditures on 'motor cars and motorcycles, new and second hand' for 1948 to 1958. Table 19 gives the same information *but expressed in 1954 prices*. Table 4 of the September 1959 MDS presents the same statistics (both in current and 1954 prices) for the years 1952-8, and quarterly from 1956 to the second quarter of 1959. (The MDS does not contain these particular expenditure statistics for quarters before 1955.) Tables 49 and 50 of the 1959 NIE entitled 'gross fixed capital formation by type of asset' give business expenditures on various types of vehicles annually for 1948-58, at current and 1954 prices. Of these various types of expenditure statistics it is the value of expenditures at 1954 prices which are most useful for our purposes. The reason is quite straightforward. Suppose ten cars are bought in 1949, and eight in 1950; and suppose the average price of a car is £500 in 1949 and £700 in 1950. Then the value of expenditures at current prices is

1949: $10 \times £500 = £5,000$
1950: $8 \times £700 = £5,600$

The value of expenditures at constant (1949) prices is

1949: $10 \times £500 = £5,000$
1950: $8 \times £500 = £4,000$

It is clear that the value of expenditures at current prices is a poor indicator of the number of cars sold *if prices are changing*. We eliminate the variable price factor by calculating the value of expenditures at a constant price, and hence represent the purely volume change more accurately. The reason why this roundabout way of obtaining an indicator of volume is adopted is that if we started with the quantities, e.g. numbers of cars and numbers of motorcycles, there are the difficulties discussed above in Chapter 1 of adding them together: in effect we are constructing a *volume index*, and for a fuller discussion of these matters, relating them to national income accounting and indexes of prices and production, the student is referred to Chapters 3 and 4 below.

This list of the major sources of statistics of the motor industry is a varied one. We have figures for production, imports and exports of vehicles, and three different types of statistics for home sales: (i) new registrations, (ii) the expenditure statistics and (iii) the production statistics of vehicles intended for the home market. Type (iii), because it refers to production and not sales, is likely to be the least reliable indicator of sales—especially from month to month or quarter to quarter (the difference between production and sales is of course changes in stocks). Consequently we shall not use these figures. The consumers' expenditure statistics, although they include both new and second-hand cars, and also motorcycles, are otherwise appropriate—although a word of warning is required here: these figures are derived by guessing the proportion of all cars sold which are purchased privately, i.e. for non-business reasons. The official statisticians who make these guesses admit that the calculation is somewhat arbitrary. The student is advised to read what they say in the official reference book.[1] New registrations are usually considered the best comprehensive indicator of sales of new cars (without distinguishing household from business purchases). The wisest thing to do is to examine both types (i) and (ii). The production, import and export statistics present no problems. In fact, we can neglect imports in our investigation—from the AAS we find that the number of motor vehicles of all types imported in 1957 was about 17,000, which is negligible compared with the 1957 production of cars alone of 861,000.

It is useful at this stage to bring together the figures of production, exports and home sales for the years to be covered by our investigation. We include 1953-4 also for comparison, and the annual statistics are shown in Tables 2.1 and 2.2. These statistics show four things. First, production of both cars and commercial vehicles reached peaks in 1955 (actually, examination of figures before 1953 shows that production increased from the end of the war until 1955). Second, in 1956 exports of both kinds fell, rising in 1957 in the case of cars alone.

[1] Central Statistical Office: *National Income Statistics. Sources and Methods* (Studies in Official Statistics No. 3, HMSO London, 1956), pp. 124-5.

TABLE 2.1

Production, Exports and Home Sales of Cars, 1953-7

Year	Production*	Exports*	New Registrations	Consumers' Expenditure†	Gross Fixed Capital Formation: cars
				£ million	£ million
	thousands	*thousands*	*thousands*	1954 *prices*	1954 *prices*
1953	594·8	308·6	302·1	161	81
1954	769·2	373·5	395·3	221	90
1955	897·6	390·6	512·8	295	107
1956	707·6	335·8	408·6	227	97
1957	860·8	426·3	434·3	249	95

* Including chassis.

† New and second-hand, including motor cycles.

Sources: AAS, MDS and NIE (New registrations: sum of Great Britain and Northern Ireland).

Third, consumers' expenditures on cars, etc., fell considerably in 1956 and rose slightly in 1957. Fourth, business expenditures on vehicles stopped rising in 1956—on cars it fell—and fell in 1957. Clearly, motor production and sales were expanding until 1956, when they suffered reductions in all markets, home and overseas, business and private. In 1957 sales of cars abroad and to household consumers at home rose again, the increase being particularly large abroad.

TABLE 2.2

Production, Exports and Home Sales of Commercial Vehicles, 1953-7

Year	Production*	Exports*	New Registrations	Gross Fixed Capital Formation: road goods vehicles, buses and coaches
	thousands	*thousands*	*thousands*	£ million 1954 *prices*
1953	239·5	103·9	109·3	110
1954	268·7	118·6	123·2	126
1955	339·5	139·9	167·2	157
1956	297·0	126·1	165·0	157
1957	288·3	122·5	153·9	142

* Including chassis.

Sources: AAS, MDS and NIE. (The descriptions of commercial vehicles in the different sources differ slightly.)

Our investigation so far illustrates the slump in the industry in 1956 (a fall in car production of over 20 per cent is considerable) and to a lesser degree in 1957; and suggests that the slump was not due to a single cause—obviously hire purchase controls did not cause the fall in exports of commercial vehicles. The influence of hire purchase controls was only one of a number of factors which could have caused the slump, and we now turn to a more detailed examination of the controls and the home sales of cars.

3. QUARTERLY STATISTICS AND SEASONAL FACTORS

If we are to examine the effects of hire purchase controls on car sales we can not rely on annual statistics. For example, to examine the effect of controls imposed in March of any year, we would compare the sales of cars in the months after March with sales before March. Of course, controls imposed early in any one year might have the effect of reducing annual sales compared with those in the previous year. But if there are other influences as well as controls affecting sales, such an annual comparison may not be revealing. Furthermore, if controls have merely a delaying effect on sales—while prospective buyers save up the extra down payment—annual comparisons may be useless. It is normally better to study the effects of a specific influence, acting or commencing to act at a certain date, by comparing the situation shortly before and shortly after the date.

In the present problem, how long should be the period of time that we use for comparison? To some extent this is a matter of trial and error and will depend upon the particular influence and the things it is influencing. A change in Bank Rate, for instance, will affect short-term interest rates in a day or two. But the so-called 'credit squeeze' of 1957 may take several years for its full effects upon fixed investment to be felt. In the first instance daily statistics would be needed; in the second instance annual figures may be sufficient. The imposition or stiffening of hire purchase controls might be expected to make their effect on sales felt within a month. As the statistics of new registrations are available in the MDS for each month, it is possible to compare these figures the month before and the month after.

Table 136 in the September 1959 MDS gives new registration statistics (for Great Britain) for cars from April 1957 to August 1959. Consider the year 1958. August was the lowest month with 31,716 registrations. February (38,770) and December (38,332) are also low. March with 58,714 and May (57,265) are the highest. The monthly average for the year is 46,371. It is clear that there is a considerable monthly variation, and we suspect (correctly) that this is due to fairly regular seasonal influences. For example, people tend to buy cars in the spring in anticipation of summer holidays. These seasonal influences are likely to make month to month comparisons of new registrations very difficult: it will be difficult to separate the influence of the seasonal buying habits from the influence of the hire purchase controls. It is impossible to avoid this difficulty completely, but we can remove some of the difficulty if we use quarterly statistics instead of monthly (i.e. take the sum of January, February and March for the first quarter). If we do this we eliminate some of the seasonal influences, and some of the uncertain effects of variable seasonal influences. Also, we expect that a comparison of the quarter before the imposition of hire purchase controls with the quarter after gives us a period of time long enough for most of the effects to appear, but short enough to be uninterrupted by too many other influences. Thus, as a general working rule, we use quarterly statistics for investigations of this type, i.e. of the effects of influences upon sales which are expected to make themselves felt within the course of a year, although we recognize that we can not expect that seasonal influences will be excluded completely.

Table 2.3 presents quarterly statistics of new registrations of cars. Note that these are available only for Great Britain, and include both private and business owned cars. The consumers' expenditure statistics discussed above, which are only available on a quarterly basis from 1955, are also shown. We first see if there are any regular seasonal changes in the new registration figures. (This is the reason for considering a period of six years—if there is a regular seasonal pattern it will usually show itself in a period of this length.) (1) Consider the change between the 1st and 2nd quarters each year. In every year included in the table new registrations were higher in the 2nd quarter than the 1st, e.g. in 1956 123,988 cars were registered in the 2nd quarter compared with 119,158 in the 1st. (2) Also, excluding 1953, new registrations were lower in the 3rd quarter of each year than the 2nd—and if we omit 1957 as well, 3rd quarter registrations were lower than either those in 1st and 2nd quarters. (3) There appears to be nothing so systematic about the 4th quarter: in 1953, 1954 and 1958 it was above the 3rd quarter; from 1955-7 it was below it. However, in every year except 1955 the 4th quarter was below the following 1st quarter, e.g. new registrations in 4th quarter 1956 (72,198) were lower than the 81,022 in the 1st quarter 1957.

Thus the seasonal pattern appears to be (starting from the 4th quarter) a rise in the 1st quarter followed by another rise in the 2nd quarter, and a fall in the 3rd quarter. As far as the 4th quarter is concerned, the safest thing to say at this stage is that the pattern may have varied. However, in what follows it is worth keeping in mind that in 1956 and 1957, when the 4th quarter was below the 3rd quarter, total annual registrations had fallen below the 1955 peak, while in 1953, 1954 and 1958 total annual registrations had increased over the previous year. If there is an increase between the 3rd and 4th quarters when registrations are increasing, and a fall when they are declining, it would imply that a normal seasonal pattern, i.e. one

TABLE 2.3

Home Sales of Passenger Cars, 1953-8

Quarter	New Registrations: Great Britain	Consumers' Expenditure* £ million 1954 prices
1953.1	58,924	..
2	75,169	..
3	75,369	..
4	86,333	..
1954.1	97,464	..
2	98,922	..
3	86,441	..
4	104,454	..
1955.1	124,307	75
2	137,589	82
3	120,373	73
4	119,996	65
1956.1	119,158	70
2	123,988	73
3	85,584	51
4	72,198	33
1957.1	81,022	44
2	124,639	78
3	115,297	71
4	105,505	56
1958.1	141,400	86
2	155,708	98
3	128,920	76
4	130,420	76

* New and second-hand, including motor cycles. 1953 and 1954 figures not available.
Sources: MDS and ET.

which would be evident if annual registrations were constant, would be one with little change one way or the other between these quarters. Of course this is no more than a speculation, but it is worth keeping it in mind when we consider the effects of the controls.

We shall not consider here the consumers' expenditure figures of Table 2.3. The period is not really long enough to interpret a seasonal pattern, but the student should make an attempt—keeping in mind what we have found out about new registrations.

4. GRAPHICAL PRESENTATION

The next stage in the inquiry is to find out when new registrations stopped increasing in the 1955-6 period, and when they started to rise again. We know there was a slump, and we know there was a recovery. When did the slump commence and when did it stop? The way to go about this is to prepare a graph of the quarterly new registration statisitcs. This is shown in Chart 2.1.

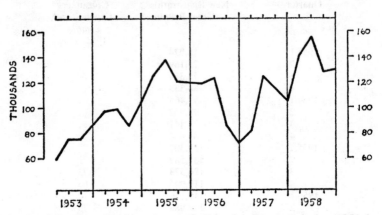

CHART 2.1. New Registrations of Cars in Great Britain, 1953-8. Quarterly, in thousands.
Source: Table 2.3.

The rules for drawing charts or graphs are as follows: (i) Use graph paper, ruled in squares, and make all marks with a sharp pencil so that they can be erased if necessary.

(ii) Decide on the unit of measurement to be used on the vertical axis. In our present inquiry, our knowledge of the seasonal pattern is not very good and small quarterly changes of less than 1,000 cars can not mean anything to us. (In fact, it is doubtful if changes less than 5,000 cars mean anything.) A change of 1,000 cars represents a change of between 1 and 2 per cent, and as a general rule we disregard changes less than 2 per cent. So our unit of measurement would be 1,000 cars, and we plot our graph using figures to the nearest thousand. Thus for 1953 we plot

1st quarter 59
2nd quarter 75
3rd quarter 75
4th quarter 86.

(iii) We represent the unit of measurement by a length on the vertical axis (this representation being known as the 'scale'). The length of the unit of measurement must be able to be observed clearly, and the smallest lengths that can be easily seen are between one millimetre (1 mm.) and one tenth of an inch. So we would represent 1,000 cars by 1 mm. or $\frac{1}{10}$ inch depending how our graph paper is ruled. It would do no harm to choose a larger scale, but it would be unwise to choose a smaller one.

(iv) The unit of measurement of the horizontal axis (the axis on which time is measured in our type of chart) is already chosen by the nature of the statistics we are dealing with—it is one quarter of a year. We represent this by a length which shows changes clearly. Usually, if the unit on the vertical axis is represented by 1 mm., the time unit can be safely represented by 5 or 10 mm.

(v) The graph paper should be chosen to suit the exercise and the units of measurement (*not* the other way round). For example, if we decide to represent 1,000 cars by 1 mm., and the figures to be plotted range from 50,000 to 150,000, we need graph paper whose vertical length is at least 100 mm. (and probably a bit more to permit titling).

(vi) The figures (of thousands of cars) should be plotted by points marked in pencil, and adjacent points joined by a straight line. (No attempt should be made to draw a curved line through all or a number of the points.)

(vii) Finally, when the plotting has been checked, and any alterations made, the lettering and titling is done, with the units of measurement and a description of the graph clearly shown as in Chart 2.1. If the graph is required as a permanent record it is useful to draw over the pencil lines and lettering in ink.

The use of charts is an aid to the simple inspection of a table of figures. Features of changes often stand out clearly in a chart while in a table they may be difficult to see. Chart 2.1 shows the tendency for car registrations to rise until early 1955; the sharp fall in the second half of 1956 with the subsequent sharp rise in the second half of 1957; and the tendency for further rises in 1958. It is obvious also that the changes are not smooth: the seasonal pattern with the high 2nd quarter is marked.

The graph shows that registrations fell in the 3rd quarter of 1955. This however, is what we expect from our knowledge of the seasonal pattern—compare this fall on the graph with the other 3rd quarter falls. Between the 3rd and 4th quarters of 1955 there is little or no change, while between these quarters in 1953 and 1954 there were increases in each case of more than 10,000 cars. It would seem that

D

either a more-than-seasonal increase had stopped, or the quarterly change was below the normal seasonal increase. Whichever way we interpret this, it appears that sales of cars had experienced a set-back. Whether it was a reduction in the rate of growth, or an absolute decline, we can not say. But now consider the change between the 4th quarter of 1955 and the following 1st quarter. In 1953-4, and 1954-5, there were increases of 10,000 and 20,000 cars respectively. In 1955-6 there was a fall of about 1,000. We noted above that the usual seasonal pattern contained a rise in registrations in the 1st quarter. Here we have strong evidence of a large fall, i.e. not just a smaller-than-usual rise, but an absolute fall.

In the 2nd quarter of 1956 registrations rose slightly, but by less than in previous or subsequent 2nd quarters. Similarly, the fall in the 3rd quarter is obviously partly seasonal but the amount of the fall—about 40,000 cars—is much larger than in previous or subsequent 3rd quarters. The same sort of argument points to the 4th quarter fall as being unseasonal.

The rise in the 1st quarter of 1957 follows the seasonal pattern, and the amount—about 10,000 cars—is the same size as in 1954. We hazard the guess that *leaving out seasonal factors* the fall in registrations had ceased by the 1st quarter of 1957. This is confirmed by the large rise in registrations in the 2nd quarter which was clearly much greater than usual—in this quarter a strong recovery in registrations is apparent.

On this evidence we date the cycle in new registrations as follows: registrations, which had been increasing ever since early 1953, stopped increasing in the 4th quarter of 1955. They fell during the first three quarters of 1956, the fall stopping in the 4th quarter. By 1st quarter, 1957, they were rising again and the rise continued into the 2nd quarter. Again on this evidence, we say that the hire purchase controls, introduced in February 1955 and strengthened by stages until February 1956, had no clearly defined effect until the last quarter of 1955 and the 1st quarter of 1956, and it is by no means obvious that the changes in registrations in these quarters were due entirely or even mainly to the controls. However, the reduction in the minimum downpayment from 50 per cent to 20 per cent in December 1956 was followed by a large increase in registrations in the following six months.

In May 1957 this minimum downpayment was increased again to $33\frac{1}{3}$ per cent where it stayed until October 1958. Chart 2.1 clearly shows a seasonal 3rd quarter fall in 1957 followed by an unseasonal fall in the last quarter. The general appearance of the graph suggests a *check* to the recovery following the re-strengthening of the controls in May. What is interesting, however, is that the rise in registrations re-asserted itself in early 1958—without any relaxation of controls. This leads to the hypothesis that when demand for cars is strong, hire purchase controls can only temporarily curb sales: buyers need a little time to save or search out other forms of finance. From this it might follow that during 1956 when sales of cars did fall for about a year, i.e. when there was something more than a temporary curb to sales, hire purchase controls were not the cause. This, of course, is speculation on the basis of very little evidence. One way of testing this is to see whether there were falls in the sales of other consumer durable goods also sold on hire purchase whose terms were regulated by the same controls as those on cars. If the sales of these goods— such as refrigerators, washing machines, television sets, etc., show the same pattern as those of cars the evidence would support the explanation that changes in hire purchase controls affected car sales. In the following section we examine one of these pieces of evidence, leaving the others as exercises at the end of the chapter.

5. SUPPLEMENTARY EVIDENCE: TELEVISION SETS

In February 1955, when hire purchase controls were imposed, amongst the articles discriminated against in this way were television sets. The minimum downpayment was set at 15 per cent and the maximum repayment period was twenty-four months. In July the

TABLE 2.4
Home Sales of Television Sets, 1953-8
thousands

1953.1	209·6	1956.1	184·2
2	315·4	2	225·8
3	242·0	3	360·1
4	362·0	4	662·6
1954.1	158·8	1957.1	319·6
2	208·1	2	303·8
3	331·8	3	499·5
4	509·4	4	677·3
1955.1	249·6	1958.1	290·9
2	340·9	2	262·9
3	400·1	3	509·1
4	614·3	4	937·0

Source: MDS.

minimum downpayment was increased to 33⅓ per cent and in February 1956 it went to 50 per cent. In October 1955 the purchase tax rate had been increased to 60 per cent. All these changes were the same as those applied to cars. However, unlike cars, television sets experienced no further changes until October 1958.

Monthly statistics of home sales of television sets are contained in Table 74 of the September 1959 MDS. From earlier issues of the MDS we can obtain quarterly figures from 1953 to 1958. These are shown in Table 2.4 and are presented as a graph, along with car registrations, in Chart 2.2.

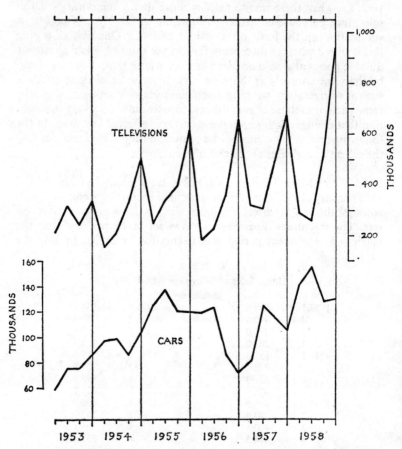

CHART 2.2. New Registrations of Cars in Great Britain and Home Sales of Television Sets in the United Kingdom, 1953-8. Quarterly, in thousands.
Source: Tables 2.3 and 2.4.

In preparing a chart including two or more sets of statistics, the rules given above (section 4) apply. Also, the following rules should be observed. (i) Avoid including so many sets of statistics that the chart becomes confusing or unintelligible. If in doubt, place some of the sets of figures on separate charts. (ii) The scales should be chosen so that a given percentage change in each of the sets of figures is represented approximately by the same height. For example, car registrations range from about 50,000 to about 150,000 a quarter, and in Chart 2.1 this trebling was represented by a height on the vertical scale of about 50 mm. Sales of television sets range from about 150,000 to 900,000, i.e. a six-fold increase. So the scale should be chosen so that this six-fold increase is represented by a vertical height of about 100 mm. A convenient scale would be to represent 10,000 sets by 1 mm. Note that there is no hard and fast rule here: the object is to avoid as far as possible deceiving the eye.

Inspection of Chart 2.2 shows that there is a pronounced seasonal peak in sales of television sets in the 4th quarter, a seasonal trough in the 1st quarter, a rise in the 2nd quarter in four years out of the six, and a rise in the 3rd quarter each year except 1953. The normal seasonal pattern would appear to be a rise from the 1st to the 4th quarter, and a fall in the 1st quarter—obviously people buy television sets before the long winter nights set in.

A comparison of the quarters of 1954 and 1955 shows no difference in pattern: the sales in the 1955 quarters are all higher than those in 1954. Hire purchase controls appear to have had little effect in 1955. But the fall in the 1st quarter, 1956, is clearly more than seasonal— we might suspect that the stiffening of controls in February 1956 caused this as it may have caused the similar fall in car registrations in this quarter. Subsequently, however, the quarterly increases appear to be seasonally normal, and in the 3rd and 4th quarters the increases are above the levels of the previous year—it suggests that people had saved up the money for the increased deposit and were buying the set they had previously planned to buy. This then is evidence that hire purchase controls had an effect, although the effect was in the nature of a delaying action.

There seems to be enough evidence here to support the view that the controls imposed on the hire purchase of cars and television sets in 1955 and 1956 did play some part in causing sales to fall in early 1956. It is doubtful whether we should conclude more than that. The fall in sales was separated by about a year from the first instalment of controls, and this lengthy delay makes the existence of a strong cause-and-effect relationship doubtful. On the other hand sales in 1955 may have been even higher than they were in the absence of controls, but there is no simple way of testing that guess.

In this section and the previous one we have been discussing one of the possible influences upon the level of car sales. In section 2 above we saw that overseas demand and business investment demand were important influences upon the level of sales of the motor industry during the period we are concerned with. The student who is also a reader of crime fiction will have realized that the statistical analysis of economic problems has several parallels with crime detection. In particular, statistical evidence is often highly circumstantial. However, while in a murder story the evidence normally points to a single unknown murderer, in economic problems the evidence normally points to several coincidental influences. The problem, after they have been identified, is to assess their relative importance and their inter-relationships. In this chapter we have not studied all the influences upon the motor industry in the years 1955-7 in a comprehensive manner. We have tried to estimate the relative importance of seasonal influences upon sales and the effects of hire purchase controls largely because the seasonal problem is such a common problem. But we have not attempted to examine the connections between the fall in business investment in motor vehicles and the fall in car sales to households.

6. NOTE ON STATISTICS OF HIRE PURCHASE AND OTHER INSTALMENT CREDIT

In this chapter we have tried to find out whether changes in sales of cars were likely to have been caused by changes in hire purchase controls. We inspected quarterly sales of cars to see whether the periods of changing sales coincided with periods when changes in controls were likely to be effective. There is another profitable line of inquiry: the amount of hire purchase credit given to car buyers can be compared with both changes in sales and changes in controls. The reasons that we have not followed this line in this chapter are, first, that the use of hire purchase statistics presents some special problems; and second, because it is a useful investigation for the student to make himself (see exercise 5 at the end of this chapter). Here we shall briefly describe the hire purchase statistics.

The collection of these figures in the United Kingdom is a recent venture reflecting a recent awareness of the importance of this type of finance. The Board of Trade started inquiries in 1956 and the results are published every month in the *Board of Trade Journal*. The inquiry refers to both household and business durable goods (cars, commercial vehicles, farm equipment and tractors, industrial and building plant and equipment, furniture, radio and television, etc.), and the statistics include credit granted by household goods shops and finance houses. The original estimates which started for the month of October 1955 referred mainly to hire purchase credit. More complete estimates including other types of instalment credit began to be collected in July 1957.

The estimates (both pre- and post-July 1957) are presented as:

(i) Debt: hire purchase and other credit instalments outstanding at the end of each month owing directly to
  (a) household goods shops
  (b) finance houses
(ii) New business:
  (a) hire purchase and other instalment credit sales of household goods shops
  (b) new hire purchase and other instalment credit extended by finance houses direct to hirers.

Every month the *Board of Trade Journal* publishes these estimates in a summary form; every three months they are given in considerable detail—distinguishing, for example, credit extended by finance houses both for new private cars and used private cars. MDS and ET give the monthly summaries but not the details. Until July 1957 the estimates of new business were shown as an index with December 1955=100. Since July 1957 they are shown with July 1957=100. Thus in the September 1959 MDS the index of new business of household goods shops in January 1959 is 147: meaning that this new business was 47 per cent above that in July 1957. The *Board of Trade Journal* also shows credit sales as a percentage of total sales, and the average amount of credit extended on each agreement (classified by type of article); the latter figure is not given in MDS or ET.

What in fact is available is thus a monthly series of estimates of total debt and new business since October 1955, with a wider coverage since July 1957, and with details of types of articles given only in the *Board of Trade Journal*. The main points about the use of the statistics to note are (i) that as sales of durable goods are influenced by seasonal buying habits, so the hire purchase statistics will reflect these seasonal factors; (ii) there is a break and change of coverage in the series at July 1957—this means that the determination of the seasonal pattern, a procedure which usually requires examining several years' figures, is difficult; and (iii) the estimates do not include that part of credit given to households represented by the ordinary unpaid bill—probably of no importance in the case of cars but of some importance in the purchase of the smaller household goods.[1]

7. EXERCISES

(1) In what countries did British exports of motor vehicles fall in 1956? [HINT: use the *Trade and Navigation Accounts* for December 1956 which give annual figures for 1955 and 1956.]

(2) The figures for the production of cars in the MDS divide cars into three classes according to horsepower rating. Do the statistics of production for the home market (total production less production for export) of the three classes show any different features in 1955-7, and if so, might the different features be related to different effects of hire purchase controls upon different classes of cars? [HINT: draw graphs of the quarterly home production of the three classes of cars.]

(3) Did other durable consumer goods experience the fall in sales in 1956 and the rise in 1957 found in the cases of cars and television sets? [HINT: the MDS and the AAS give statistics of domestic electrical washing machines, vacuum cleaners and domestic refrigerating machinery, amongst other durable goods.]

(4) What evidence is available to support the view that the advent of television has had an adverse effect upon cinema attendances? [HINT: the 1958 AAS, Table 89, gives annual number of cinema admissions. Table 262 gives television receiving licences current. Draw graphs of these two sets of figures and compare them.] What else might have affected cinema attendances?

(5) Is there any evidence that the removal of hire purchase controls on cars, television sets and other durable goods in October 1958 caused an increase in the amount of hire purchase and other instalment credit granted? [HINT: the total amount of new hire purchase business is shown in MDS; amounts for different types of goods in the *Board of Trade Journal* (e.g. May 22, 1959, p. 1200). As the series of monthly statistics is not long enough to clearly distinguish the seasonal pattern the simplest procedure is to compare the same months of different years, e.g. January 1959 with January 1958.] Can you find any evidence that any increase in hire purchase credit that did occur reflected an increased volume of sales and not just more credit for each sale? [HINT: use the *Board of Trade Journal's* figures of average value of credit extended per agreement. Compare the change in this with the change in credit extended in all agreements.]

[1] Regular customers of household goods shops whose financial circumstances are considered satisfactory may be allowed periods up to three months before they are required to settle their accounts. This type of credit is uncontrolled and is not recorded in the statistics.

CHAPTER THREE

How Much Have Prices Risen
Since Before the War?

1. COMMODITY PRICES

Everyone knows that the subject of price increases—or decreases—is no mere academic matter but something which affects everyone's welfare. To put the matter in its simplest terms, if a family man in Britain today, earning a low income of about £10 a week, finds that the prices of all the things he buys for his family—food, clothing, housing, fuel, etc.—increase by about 10 per cent in the next year, then he will be forced to buy about 10 per cent less of those things. Unless his income increases, or unless he borrows or steals, he will be worse off. Because prices do change we are interested in both the reasons why prices change and in the measurement of the changes. In this chapter we are not concerned with the reasons why prices change; it is the measurement of price changes that concerns us.

How much have prices risen since before the war? We must first decide what sort of prices we are interested in. Most people who ask this question and who wish to compare the change in their wages or salary with price changes think of *retail prices:* prices of groceries in the grocer's shop, of clothes in the clothing shop—in other words the prices the ordinary consumer pays to the retailer for goods and services. *Wholesale prices*, on the other hand, are not so clearly defined. They are the prices fetched by goods sold by a producer to a wholesale merchant, by one wholesaler to another, or by a wholesaler to a retailer. Normally the difference between the wholesale price of a commodity and the retail price of the same article will include costs of transport, insurance, handling, storage and packaging together with the profit margin of the retailer. Whether a wholesale price is quoted inclusive of the transport, insurance, etc., charges will depend upon the normal conditions under which the commodity is sold. Of course, many commodities—such as copra—which are sold wholesale will not have a retail price because nobody buys copra retail. But bottles of coconut oil are bought retail.

There are two especially important groups of commodities which are sold wholesale—the industrial raw materials such as tin, rubber and coal, and the agricultural foodstuffs such as wheat, meat and butter. (Some commodities, such as vegetable oils, fall into both groups.) These commodities are important for several reasons : all of them are traded internationally, the receipts from their production form the major part of the incomes of many countries, most industrial countries import at least some of the commodities in large quantities, and many are sold in internationally recognized competitive markets. The wholesale prices of these commodities are important to many producers and consumers and they are a major influence in the lives of hundreds of millions of people. Changes in the prices of

TABLE 3.1

British Wholesale Price Ratios of Representative Commodities

Ratio of 1957 *Price to* 1938 *Price*

		Description	Ratio
Foods, etc.			
1	Wheat	Eng. Gazette	3·21
2	Wheat	Manitoba	3·11
3	Flour		3·33
4	Barley	Eng. Gazette	2·28
5	Oats	Eng. Gazette	3·02
6	Oats	American mixed	3·60
7	Potatoes	Good English	3·58
8	Rice	Burma, No. 2	6·02
9	Beef	Prime	3·30
10	Beef	Middling	3·28
11	Mutton	Prime	3·27
12	Mutton	Middling	3·40
13	Pork	Large and small, av.	3·33
14	Bacon	Home, Grade 1	2·85
15	Butter	Average	2·55
16	Sugar	Java floating	7·58
17	Sugar	Cont. white	9·91
18	Coffee	Ceylon plant. Low middling	5·87
19	Coffee	Rio good	15·77
20	Tea	Average import price	3·88
21	Cocoa	Accra ff.	7·65
Metals, etc.			
22	Iron	Scott pig and Cleveland pig (average)	3·81
23	Iron bars	Common	3·39
24	Copper	Standard	5·23
25	Tin	Straits	3·89
26	Lead	English pig	5·67
27	Aluminium	Virgin ingot	2·02
28	Zinc		5·54
29	Coal	Yorkshire house	3·09
30	Coal	Average export price	5·44

Textiles, etc.

31	Cotton	Middling Am.	5·13
32	Cotton	East Ind.	7·56
33	Flax	Medium Grade cont. retted and Belgium import price (average)	3·68
34	Hemp	Manila for roping and Italian S.B. (average)	6·04
35	Jute	L.J.A. firsts	5·90
36	Wool	Merino P.P. average of fleece and greasy	6·25
37	Wool	English Lincoln half hogs	5·78
38	Silk	Japanese	4·23
39	Rayon	Viscose staple. 1½ denier	2·35
40	Sisal	British E.A. No. 1	4·05
41	Hides	Average of R.P. dry and salted, and average import price	3·36
42	Leather	Dressing hides and average import price (average)	3·44

Oils, etc.

43	Tallow	Town	4·61
44	Oil	Palm	6·21
45	Oil	Olive	5·04
46	Oil	Cottonseed	7·33
47	Oil	Soya bean	7·11
48	Oil	Whale No. 1	6·52
49	Linseed	Oil and seeds (average)	4·21

Miscellaneous

50	Petroleum	Motor spirit (c.i.f.)	3·15
51	Petroleum	Kerosine (c.i.f.)	3·69
52	Petroleum	Gas oil (c.i.f.)	2·93
53	Soda	Crystals	2·22
54	Sodium Nitrate		3·73
55	Indigo	Bengal, good consuming	2·62
56	Timber	Hewn, sawn or split (average import price)	3·65
57	Cloves	Zanzibar	5·50
58	Ginger	Africa	4·10
59	Rubber	No. 1 R.S.S.	2·89
60	Tobacco	Flue cured. United States	2·58
61	Tobacco	Flue cured. Southern Rhodesia	3·17

Sources: Journal of the Royal Statistical Society (Series A); Commonwealth Economic Committee Commodity Reports; MDS.

the industrial raw materials and the agricultural foodstuffs are a large element both in the retail price changes of the goods and services the ordinary consumer buys, and in the changes in the incomes of the producers of the commodities.

Because of their importance, and because of the existence of markets with regularly quoted prices, records of these wholesale commodity prices have been collected by financial journals for several decades. A useful collection is that of the Editor of the *Statist* journal, published annually in the *Journal of the Royal Statistical Society* (*Series A*). Journals such as the London *Financial Times* publish daily price quotations. The MDS and AAS both give statistics of the wholesale prices of a wide range of commodities (see September 1959 MDS, Table 169; 1958 AAS, Table 350). We shall now use some of this information to answer the question of the extent of the rise in prices between 1938 and 1957. We obtain the average price of a certain commodity in a certain market during a certain year by averaging the daily or weekly price quotations. The ratio of the price of a commodity at one date to its price at another date is called a *price ratio*. Thus if the average wholesale price of one pound of Danish butter in 1958 was 3s 6d, and the average price in 1957 was 2s 6d, the price ratio for 1958 is $\dfrac{\text{3s 6d}}{\text{2s 6d}}=1\cdot40$ which means that the price of Danish butter in 1958 was 40 per cent above its level in 1957. The reason why information about price changes is commonly presented in the ratio form is that the reader can immediately interpret the relative changes. The date to which the divisor (the bottom line in the ratio) refers is called the *base* of the price ratio. We thus measure percentage changes from the base date.

In Table 3.1 price ratios for 1957, based on 1938, are shown for sixty-one industrial raw materials and foodstuffs. The table contains most of the major internationally traded commodities, although not all the various grades and types are shown. The price changes range from the doubling of the price of aluminium to the sixteen-fold increase in the price of Brazilian coffee. In the twenty year period to which the ratios refer the prices of the sixty-one commodities experienced a large variety of increases. The question that arises is: amidst this variety of price increases, is there a typical or average increase? Averages of one sort or another are continually used in summarizing masses of statistical information and we shall pause to consider what an average is before we rush to calculate it.

2. AVERAGES AND FREQUENCY DISTRIBUTIONS

The things we investigate in most sciences have two related features: diversity and uniformity. Diversity is the feature which strikes the most casual observer—Table 3.1 witnesses the variety of price changes between 1938 and 1957. The search for uniformity always involves processes of simplification and summarizing: the disregarding of irregular features, the isolation of common characteristics and patterns. The scientist simplifies and summarizes at his own risk—too much simplification and valuable knowledge is lost; too little and the information or collection of statistics is an unintelligible morass. Averaging is an ancient and respectable method of summarizing information. But at all times it must be related to the diversity of the information—an average is of no value whatsoever unless we know how diverse is the information from which it is calculated.

To see the characteristics of diverse information, such as is contained in Table 3.1, the information is best organized in a distinctive form known as a *frequency distribution*. If we run our eye down the price ratios of Table 3.1 we find that there are no ratios below 2·00, there are 10 in the class between 2·01 and 3·00 (inclusive), 24 in the class between 3·01 and 4·00, 5 in the class between 4·01 and 5·00, and so on. The interval we have chosen for this classification, i.e. the difference between 3·00 and 2·01, between 4·00 and 3·01, etc., is called the *class interval*, and the numbers of ratios contained in each class—10, 24, 5, etc.—are called the *frequencies*. The set of frequencies is called a frequency distribution. This sort of classification itself is a summary, for we lose information about individual commodities and have instead information about groups of commodities—such as that there are twenty-four commodities with price ratios between 3·01 and 4·00. How much information can we afford to lose in this way? In other words, how large should we choose our class interval? There is a convenient rule of thumb: to establish the main features of a frequency distribution, the class interval should be chosen so that the number of classes lies between twelve and twenty. In our case, if we select a class interval of 0·50, i.e. classes of 2·01 to 2·50, 2·51 to 3·00, etc. (all inclusive), we shall have twenty-eight classes which is not too great as we shall have several zero frequency classes. This frequency distribution is shown in Table 3.2. Note that because there are two isolated large ratios there are a number of zero classes. It would be more usual to save space by having after 8·00 one class labelled '8·01 and greater' with a frequency of 2.

The graphical version of this frequency distribution, called a *histogram*, is shown in Chart 3.1. The classes are marked on the horizontal axis, and for each frequency a rectangle is drawn with its base equal to the length representing the class interval, and with its height proportional to the frequency. The reason for drawing the histogram is that some of the features of the frequency distribution stand out more clearly when they are seen on a graph.

The frequency distribution of the sixty-one price ratios illustrates

TABLE 3.2

Frequency Distribution of Price Ratios of Table 3.1

Class Interval=0·50

Range	Frequency	Range	Frequency
2·01—2·50	4	9·01— 9·50	0
2·51—3·00	6	9·51—10·00	1
3·01—3·50	15	10·01—10·50	0
3·51—4·00	9	10·51—11·00	0
4·01—4·50	4	11·01—11·50	0
4·51—5·00	1	11·51—12·00	0
5·01—5·50	5	12·01—12·50	0
5·51—6·00	5	12·51—13·00	0
6·01—6·50	4	13·01—13·50	0
6·51—7·00	1	13·51—14·00	0
7·01—7·50	2	14·01—14·50	0
7·51—8·00	3	14·51—15·00	0
8·01—8·50	0	15·01—15·50	0
8·51—9·00	0	15·51—16·00	1
		TOTAL	61

the twin features of uniformity and diversity. As was apparent from Table 3.1 the ratios range from 2 to 16. But we now see clearly that there is a tendency for the values of the ratios to cluster about 3·5—the greatest frequency in fact is in the class 3·01 to 3·50. This tendency to cluster is the evidence of a uniformity which is called the *central tendency*. Besides this, the distribution has two other characteristics: first, it has a tail stretching to the right of Chart 3.1—evidence of the diversity or of the dispersion about the central tendency; and second, it shows irregularities—there is no smooth falling-off in frequency as we move from left to right (i.e. from low ratios to high ratios). Note that of the twenty-one foodstuffs in the list nine have ratios in the class 3·01 to 3·50—the marked central tendency in this class is largely, but not entirely, due to the food price ratios.

We use the characteristic of a central tendency to answer our question about a typical or average price ratio. We locate the typical or average price ratio in the range or class where the central tendency occurs—about 3·5. The type of summarizing statement we make is 'on the average, commodity prices rose between 1938 and 1957 about three and a half-fold (250 per cent), although the range of rises was between two- and sixteen-fold'. We can make this statement more precise by defining an average. There are three commonly used types of averages:

(1) *arithmetic mean*. This is the common average used in ordinary speech. It is the sum of the sixty-one price ratios divided by sixty-one.

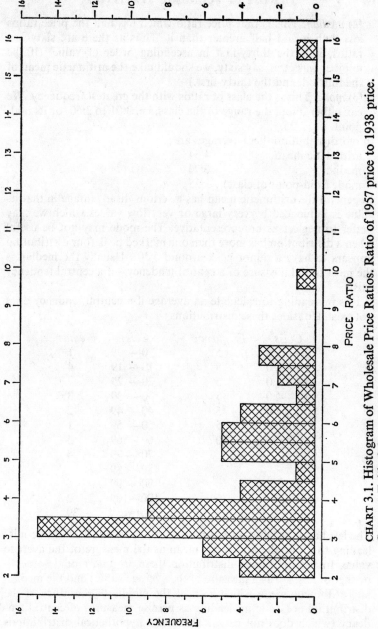

CHART 3.1. Histogram of Wholesale Price Ratios. Ratio of 1957 price to 1938 price.
Source: Table 3.2.

(2) *median*. This is that price ratio which has half the price ratios less than it and half greater than it. Thus as there are sixty-one ratios, it is the thirty-first in ascending order of value. (If the number was even, say sixty, we should take the arithmetic mean of the thirtieth and the thirty-first.)

(3) *mode*. This is the class of ratios with the greatest frequency. We can either quote the range of the class, i.e. 3·01 to 3·50, or its mid-point, i.e. 3·25.

In our distribution these averages are:

arithmetic mean   4·54
median   3·73
mode (mid-point of class) 3·25

In general the arithmetic mean has a serious disadvantage in that its value is influenced by very large or very low values which we may prefer to neglect as unrepresentative. The mode may not be useful when a distribution has more than one marked peak (our distribution appears to have a minor peak around 5·50). Usually the median is the most useful measure of a central tendency—if a central tendency exists.

It is misleading to calculate an average if a central tendency does not exist. Consider these distributions:

Class	Frequency	Class	Frequency
0·1—1·0	5	0— 9	1
1·1—2·0	5	10— 19	4
2·1—3·0	5	20— 29	7
3·1—4·0	5	30— 39	3
4·1—5·0	5	40— 49	2
5·1—6·0	5	50— 59	1
TOTAL	30	60— 69	3
		70— 79	4
		80— 89	7
		90— 99	5
		100—109	2
		TOTAL	39

The left hand distribution has no central tendency; it might be misleading to quote the arithmetic mean as the measure of the average value. In the right hand distribution there are two modal values—neither of any use as a measure of the average value; and the median and arithmetic mean which lie near the middle of the range of the distribution are quite misleading as precise measures of central tendency (which does not exist). These two hypothetical distributions are extreme cases and are intended to warn the student about the possible difficulties that can be encountered in attempting to give a meaningful figure for the average value of a set of numbers. Remember that the idea of an average is a summarizing idea, and by no means can every body of statistical information—such as a frequency distribution—be usefully summarized by a single, unambiguous number. When a central tendency can not be discerned from the frequency distribution or its histogram this fact should be clearly stated. When a central tendency is discernable, an average value can be measured, but in quoting the average in argument or discussion the range of the distribution should be indicated and any irregularities noted.

In the present example, we choose the median (3·73) as the measure of the average price ratio, and would say that, on the average, wholesale commodity prices increased by about 270 per cent between 1938 and 1957.

3. PRICE INDEXES

We have estimated the average wholesale commodity price increase between 1938 and 1957. What are the uses of the calculations we have made? If a merchant in 1938 with a capital of £10,000 held a stock of the commodities listed in Table 3.1, we can tell him that he would need about £37,000 to hold the same stock in 1957. Again, if we are interested in the prices of individual commodities, it is useful to have some standard of reference against which to judge their changes. For example, it is not very illuminating to consider the price of aluminium in isolation from other prices; but it is quite illuminating to say that the price of aluminium has not risen as much as the average level of commodity prices, i.e. the price of aluminium has *fallen* relative to the average price level—aluminium has become cheaper in terms of other commodities. This idea can be made precise by dividing the aluminium price ratio by the median price ratio: $\frac{2\cdot02}{3\cdot73}=0\cdot54$, which says that the price of aluminium in terms of other commodities has fallen by about one half.

The commonest use of averages of price ratios is by economists and financial commentators who are attempting to explain past trends or predict those of the future. Clearly, too great an emphasis upon the cases of individual commodities will be misleading: an indicator of typical tendencies is required, and this is where the use of an average is useful. For these purposes the average of the price ratios is expressed as a *price index*. The price index is the average value of the

E

ratios multiplied by 100 (in some cases by 1,000). The index number at the base date is then 100, and in the case of our commodity prices (using the median as average) we have

1938=100
1957=373

from which we conclude that commodity prices increased on the average by 273 per cent between 1938 and 1957. We could calculate an index number for any day, week, month or year in the same way, keeping 1938=100. For example, if we found that the median 1958 ratio was 4·15, we would have

1938=100
1957=373
1958=415 (hypothetical figure)

meaning that in 1958 prices were 315 per cent above the 1938 level, and $\dfrac{415-373}{373} \cdot 100 = 11·3$ per cent above the 1957 level. Note that the multiplication of the ratios by 100 to arrive at the index number form is the usual way of expressing these calculations, and is adopted as a simple device to avoid the appearance of too many decimal points which may confuse the reader.

Several regularly used wholesale commodity price indexes are calculated by this method. The student will find useful the *Statist* index calculated from the arithmetic mean of forty-five commodity prices, monthly and yearly, with average 1867-77=100, published in the *Journal of the Royal Statistical Society, Series A;* and the *Economist* Sensitive Commodity Price Indicator, calculated weekly from the arithmetic mean of seventeen commodity prices, with 1952=100, published in the London *Economist.*

These indexes are useful as indicators of trends in commodity prices, but the method of calculation has one defect: it gives equal importance to each commodity. For the purpose for which these indexes are used, this is not an important defect, but if the method is applied to retail prices it does need to be modified.

4. RETAIL PRICE INDEXES AND THE COST OF LIVING

Suppose the ordinary British household buys the following basket of foodstuffs each week:

6 ¼ lb. packets of tea
4 lb. stewing steak
8 cabbages
1 bottle tomato sauce

and suppose that the retail prices of these articles (which we imagine are the same in all shops) are:

	Week 1	Week 2	Price ratio (base is week 1)
1 packet tea	10d	1s 0d	1·200
1 lb. steak	3s 0d	3s 3d	1·083
1 cabbage	1s 0d	9d	0·750
1 tomato sauce	1s 3d	9d	0·600

Let us average the price ratios: the arithmetic mean is the most appropriate average when the number of items is too small to be arranged in a frequency distribution. We find that the arithmetic mean ratio is 0·908, showing that the retail prices of foods, on the average, fell by 9 per cent between week 1 and week 2 $\left[\left(\dfrac{1\cdot000 - 0\cdot908}{1\cdot000} \right) \right.$ ·100=9·2 per cent $\left. \right]$. As an index, based on week 1, this is written as

week 1=100·0
week 2= 90·8

But this calculation does not take into account the fact that the importance of the four articles differs considerably—importance measured by the expenditure on the article. In week 1, 60d was spent on tea, 144d on meat, 96d on cabbages and only 15d on sauce. An index of retail prices which treats each article as important as another will give a misleading result if it is used to estimate the changed cost of buying a basket of goods and services. The 8 per cent rise in the price of steak is a much more important event in the life of our ordinary family than the 40 per cent fall in the price of sauce: the family saves 6d on sauce but if it keeps on buying the same amount of steak it spends 12d more.

There are several ways of avoiding the difficulty, and they all involve *weighting* each ratio by the importance of the article as measured by the expenditure on it. We thus calculate a *weighted average* price ratio. In our hypothetical food price example we find the weighted arithmetic mean price ratio:

$$\frac{(1\cdot200 \times 60d) + (1\cdot083 \times 144d) + (0\cdot750 \times 96d) + (0\cdot600 \times 15d)}{60d + 144d + 96d + 15d}$$

=0·981, i.e. we multiply each price ratio by its weight—the expenditure on the article in the base date—and divide by the sum of the weights. Our new index is thus:

week 1=100·0
week 2= 98·1

which shows that retail prices of food, on the average, fell by about 2 per cent and not 9 per cent as estimated previously.

Most retail price indexes—and many other price indexes—are calculated in this way. The practical problem of the statisticians is the choice of the appropriate weights. In the example, we used as weights expenditures in week 1; we could have used expenditures in week 2. To see what is involved in the choice of weights we shall consider the price index from the point of view of the cost of buying a basket of goods. We expand the example by assuming that the composition of the basket differs slightly in week 2 from week 1. Our information is given in Table 3.3. The data for week 1 and the price data for week 2 are the same as before. We assume that the households spend the same amount on food each week, but they reduce their consumption of tea when its price rises, and increase their consumption of cabbages when their price falls. There are thus two baskets of food—that bought in week 1 and that bought in week 2. Each basket actually cost 315d. *Each would have cost something different if it had been bought in the other week.* How much would the week 1 basket have cost if it had been bought at the week 2 prices? The answer is given in column (7) of Table 3.3. We value week 1 quantities at week 2 prices and add. The cost would have been 309d, and the ratio of this cost to what the basket actually did cost in week 1 (i.e. week 1 quantities at week 1 prices) is $\frac{309d}{315d} = 0.981$. Expressed as an index this is:

week 1 = 100·0
week 2 = 98·1

and we see that this index of the cost of a given basket of goods is the same thing as our weighted index of retail prices.

How much would the week 2 basket have cost if it had been bought at week 1 prices? The answer is in column (8) of Table 3.3. We value week 2 quantities at week 1 prices and add: the cost would have been 329d. The ratio of the actual cost of the week 2 basket (week 2 quantities at week 2 prices) to its cost at week 1 prices is $\frac{315d}{329d} = 0.957$. As an index this is

week 1 = 100·0
week 2 = 95·7.

So if we are interested in the changing cost of a basket, it all depends upon what basket we are interested in. If we are interested in the week 1 basket, we know its cost at week 2 prices would be about 2 per cent less than at week 1 prices; if we consider the week 2 basket,

TABLE 3.3
Prices and Quantities of Baskets of Foodstuffs
(Hypothetical data)

	Week 1			Week 2			Week 1 Quantities valued at Week 2 Prices	Week 2 Quantities valued at Week 1 Prices
	Price (1)	Quantity (2)	Expenditure d (3)	Price (4)	Quantity (5)	Expenditure d (6)	d (7)	d (8)
Tea ¼ lb. packet	10d	6	60	1/-	5	60	72	50
Stewing steak 1 lb.	3/-	4	144	3/3	4	156	156	144
Cabbage 1 lb.	1/-	8	96	9d	10	90	72	120
Tomato sauce 1 bottle	1/3	1	15	9d	1	9	9	15
TOTALS			315			315	309	329

its cost at week 2 prices would have been about 4 per cent less than at week 1 prices.

It is customary to call the cost of that large basket of all goods and services which the ordinary household buys the *cost of living*. The idea of the cost of living can be meaningless unless we are clear as to what and whose basket we are considering. The costs of different baskets are likely to change in different ways.

Let us now return to the food retail price index calculated above. We chose week 1 expenditures as weights and the index we obtained is identical with the first of our cost indexes (based on the week 1 basket). The second of our cost indexes (based on the week 2 basket) is identical to a food retail price index whose weights are the expenditures on week 2 quantities valued at week 1 prices, i.e. the expenditures in column (8) of Table 3.3.[1] So we see that a weighted retail price index is the same thing as an index of the cost of buying a basket of goods, and the choice of weights is the same problem as the choice of the composition of the basket of goods.

The practical usefulness of retail price indexes is based on the fact that in normal times (no rationing, no wars, no violent price changes) over periods of up to between five and ten years the composition of the bundle of goods and services which the ordinary household buys does not change enough to lead to ambiguities. But over longer periods of time the composition of the basket changes and different weights give considerably different results. In any case there is not much point in examining the changing cost of a bundle of goods between the present day and, say, the middle of the nineteenth century as many goods available in the middle of the nineteenth century are not purchased today while many goods bought today were not available in the nineteenth century. For instance, red flannel underwear and kerosine were important items in the budgets of working-class families at the end of the nineteenth century, but who buys such articles today? The change in their prices since the end of the nineteenth century is not a very interesting fact to know. This is not to say that a rough idea of the change in the level of retail prices over lengthy periods of time can not be obtained—what is dangerous is, in view of the difficulty of knowing just what the changes mean, to attach too much importance to precise measurements and small changes.

But over shorter periods of time the shifting sands are more stable and greater reliance can be attached to properly constructed retail

[1] It is left as an exercise for the student to construct this index by weighting the price ratios by these expenditures, and to compare the result with the cost index.

price indexes. Official indexes are of two types. First, there are those whose weights are based on a special study of household expenditures in a period of time considered to be normal (we should perhaps say, with no obvious abnormalities). The index is calculated periodically (usually monthly) and each time the same set of weights is used. Such an index is called a *fixed weight* index. Note that the base date of the index need not be the same as the date to which the expenditures refer. The second type of index has weights which are altered on each occasion that the index is calculated. For example, if the index is based on 1954, the 1955 index number—measuring the percentage change in prices since 1954—is calculated with 1955 weights. The 1956 index number is calculated with 1956 weights, and so on. This type of index, which requires a large quantity of information each time the index is calculated is not usually calculated more frequently than once a year or at most once a quarter.

Finally, mention must be made of a device frequently used in the comparison of price changes between two dates when the baskets of goods of the two dates differ significantly. If the baskets differ sufficiently, indexes using different weights based on the two different baskets will differ. In the example of Table 3.3 (week 1=100) week 1 weights give an index number for week 2 of 98·1 and week 2 weights give 95·7. If we are trying to obtain a convenient rough indicator of the average change in prices we take an average of these two index numbers. In practice we take as an average the *geometric mean*, which is the square root of their product, i.e. $\sqrt{(98\cdot1\times95\cdot7)}$ which is approximately 96·8, indicating that the level of retail prices has fallen by about 3·2 per cent. Note that in taking this average we have lost touch with that sub-stratum of reality which is a basket of goods which someone bought at some time. For this reason we can not expect the device to show more than the direction of average price changes and their order of magnitude.

5. OFFICIAL BRITISH RETAIL PRICE INDEXES

(a) *Index of Retail Prices*. This index is prepared by the Ministry of Labour and is the latest of a number of indexes the earliest of which were calculated before the first world war. It covers a wide range of household goods and services—food, alcoholic drink, tobacco, housing, fuel and light, durable household goods, clothing and footwear, transport and vehicles, and services. Table 167 of the September 1959 MDS gives a classification of the articles included, and a complete list is to be found in the pamphlet *Method of Construction and Calculation of the Index of Retail Prices* (HMSO, London). The weights are based upon the results of a survey of the budgets of about 13,000 households during 1953-4 and reflecting the expenditure pattern of nearly nine-tenths of all households in the United Kingdom. The excluded households are those whose head had a weekly gross income of £20 or more, and those in which at least three-quarters of the income came from pensions or similar grants. This means that changes in the index reflect changes in the cost of buying the household goods and services of all British households except the wealthiest and the poorest—broadly speaking, all with wage or salary earners receiving up to £20 a week.[1]

The base date is January 1956, i.e. January 1956=100, and the weights are the 1953-4 expenditures revalued at January 1956 prices. Table 167 of the September 1959 MDS shows the weights expressed as proportions, i.e. adjusted so as to add up to 1,000, for the main classes of goods and services. Food, for example, is allocated 350 points out of 1,000, which is the same thing as saying that expenditures on food are 35 per cent of total expenditures.

Tables 165-6 of the September 1959 MDS give index numbers for the total and for the major groups, monthly from April 1958 to August 1959, with annual monthly averages also. For example, the index number for housing in February 1959 is 126·2 showing that between January 1956 and February 1959 the cost of housing (rent, rates, etc.) for the ordinary household rose by 26·2 per cent. Again, for example, the food index number in February 1959 is 109·1 and in February 1958 is 103·9 showing that between these dates the retail price of food rose by $\left(\dfrac{109\cdot1-103\cdot9}{103\cdot9}\right)\cdot100=5\cdot0$ per cent. Table 167 of the MDS gives indexes for various sub-groups, e.g. meat and bacon. These sub-group indexes are published only for January, April, July and October each year.

Every type of article which falls into a particular group is not priced in the construction of the index. For one reason the task would be very great; for another, it is unnecessary—the prices of representative articles which will act as indicators of the price changes of a class of articles are sufficient. Details of the methods of collecting the information about prices are given in the official pamphlet mentioned above.

---

[1] The evidence of the 1953-4 budget survey (whose results are discussed below in Chapter 10) is valuable statistical information itself. The fact that nine-tenths of British households have similar consumption patterns (which means that the proportions of income spent on the same classes of goods are similar) shows that the old-fashioned division of styles of living into 'working class' and 'middle class' iis nappropriate or at least needs to be revised nowadays.

Between 1947 and 1956 the Ministry calculated two indexes called *Interim Indexes of Retail Prices*. The first, based on June 1947, ran until January 1952, had weights derived from a pre-war budget inquiry revalued at 1947 prices. The second, based on January 1952, had weights based on 1950 consumption estimates revalued at 1952 prices. Annual monthly averages of these indexes and their groups are shown in Table 165 of the September 1959 MDS, which also gives the weights used in these two indexes.

There is an overlap in all three retail price indexes—the first interim index is calculated for January 1952 and the second for January 1956. It is thus possible to link or chain the three indexes to obtain a consecutive monthly series from 1947 to the present time. The earlier interim index (June 1947=100) for January 1952 (all items) is 132. The later interim index (January 1952=100) for January 1956 is 115·8. (These index numbers are given in the first and second columns of Table 165 of the MDS.) The index number of the present retail price index for February 1959 is 110·3. This information means that the cost of a certain basket increased by 32 per cent between June 1947 and January 1952, the cost of another basket increased by 15·8 per cent between January 1952 and January 1956, and the cost of yet another basket increased by 10·3 per cent between January 1956 and February 1959. *Provided the three baskets do not differ too greatly in composition* it is reasonable, to get a rough indicator of the movement in retail prices, to add these percentage increases to get the overall increase from June 1947 to February 1959. The answer to this sum is obtained by multiplying the indexes:

$$\frac{132 \times 115 \cdot 8 \times 110 \cdot 3}{100 \times 100} = 169 \cdot 2$$

showing that the overall increase is about 70 per cent.

Such a linked index for the years 1948 to 1955 is given in the first column of Table 165 of the MDS, and by using the present Index of Retail Prices in Table 166 the linked index can be continued to the present. This type of linked index, calculated over a lengthy period of time, can not be used to provide precise calculations or undisputable evidence in economic argument. It gives a rough indicator of the movement in retail prices. Remember that if expenditure patterns have altered considerably, or if the kinds of goods and services bought differ substantially, then the measurement of average price changes becomes merely a piece of arithmetic without economic significance. We interpret the figure of 70 per cent increase estimated in the previous paragraph to mean *not* that the cost of living has increased by 70 per cent—rationing and the unavailability of goods in the early part of the period mean that expenditure patterns have changed considerably over the twelve year period—but simply that the typical increase in retail prices has been of the order of 70 per cent.

(b) *Index of Market Prices of Goods and Services.* This is an index calculated by the Central Statistical Office in connection with their estimates of national income and expenditure (see Chapter 4). The index is of the variable weight type described above (section 4): each time the index is calculated the weights are those based on the prevailing basket of goods and services purchased. These weights refer to the expenditure of all consumers on all goods and services, i.e. they represent the average expenditure pattern of all classes of households. The index for all goods and services—'Total consumers' expenditure' —and for the major classes is published in NIE. In 1957 NIE, Table 21, there are annual index numbers for 1938 and for 1946-56 with 1948=100. In 1959 NIE, Table 20, there are index numbers for 1948-58 with 1954=100.

The strict interpretation of the index is as follows: according to Table 20 of the 1959 NIE the index of market prices of total consumers' expenditure in 1957 was 111 (1954=100). This means that between 1954 and 1957 the cost of all the goods and services bought by consumers in *1957* increased by 11 per cent. The same type of statement applies to the index number for any other year with reference to the basket of goods bought in that year. This interpretation is unambiguous and meaningful. But when we compare the index numbers of two consecutive years (one of which is not the base year) the interpretation, strictly speaking, is not clear. The 1957 index number of 111 refers to the 1957 bundle of goods; the 1956 index number of 108 (also from Table 20 and based on 1954) refers to the 1956 bundle of goods. The increase in the index between 1956 and 1957, $\left(\dfrac{111-108}{108}\right)\cdot 100 = 2\cdot 8$ per cent, has meaning only if the 1956 and 1957 bundles of goods are similar. In this case they are similar enough, and we can meaningfully say that the cost of living rose by about 3 per cent. It is customary to interpret this index as we interpret a linked index, i.e. as an indicator of the change in retail prices giving a rough idea of the order of magnitude of the relative change. The remarks made above about the Index of Retail Prices and the care that needs to be taken in its use in comparisons over lengthy periods of time apply to this index also.

The actual construction of the index proceeds in a roundabout way: it is derived from the estimates of expenditure at constant prices (see section 2, Chapter 2; and Chapter 4). If we divide a money value by a volume we obtain a price, e.g. £1,000 spent on buying five motor cars gives us an average price per car of £200. Similarly an index of money expenditures divided by an index of money expenditures at constant prices (which is a volume index) gives a price index. The consumers' expenditure figures in Table 18 of 1959 NIE have been divided by the consumers' expenditures at 1954 prices in Table 19 to obtain the 1954 based price indexes in Table 20. Such indexes are called implicit price indexes or average value indexes.

The MDS gives quarterly estimates of consumers' expenditure (see Table 4, September 1959) both at current prices and at average 1954 prices. By dividing the former by the latter we can obtain a quarterly market prices index (1954=100). Such an index is not published officially (see exercises at the end of this chapter).

6. THE CHANGE IN RETAIL PRICES BETWEEN 1938 AND 1957

We are now ready to give an answer to the question about the change in retail prices between 1938 and 1957, and—what is important—we can appreciate what the question and its answer mean. The 1957 NIE, Table 21, has indexes (1948=100) for 1938 and 1946-56. An index number for 1957 can be found in Table 29 of the 1958 NIE. Note that in some of the indexes in the tables the 1955 and 1956 numbers in the 1958 NIE are different from those given in the 1957 NIE. The reason is that the 1958 NIE figures are revised figures: what we do is use the 1958 NIE figures for as many years back as they are given, which is back to 1948, and use the 1957 NIE figures for 1938, 1946 and 1947. Table 3.4 shows the indexes for market prices of total consumers' expenditure and total food expenditures (the other two indexes in the table are described below).

Remembering that these are variable weight indexes, and that their meaningful use depends upon the absence of too large a change in the composition of the baskets of goods and services bought, we find that between 1938 and 1957 the price level of all items increased by $\left(\dfrac{141-51}{51}\right) \cdot 100 = 176$ per cent, and of foods by $\left(\dfrac{171-59}{59}\right) \cdot 100 = 190$ per cent.

The student will remember that we have called these calculations 'rough indicators', and it is natural to ask: how rough? The best way to answer this is to calculate another index using different weights to

TABLE 3.4

Retail Price Indexes, 1938-57

	Market prices of consumers' expenditure 1948=100		Retail prices 1938=100. Monthly averages	
	Total	Total food	All items	Food
1938	51	59	100	100
1946	87	87	..	..
1947	93	94	..	..
1948	100	100	173·9	151·9
1949	102	105	178·9	160·0
1950	106	112	184·5	171·9
1951	115	122	201·8	190·9
1952	121	136	220·3	220·8
1953	124	142	226·5	233·2
1954	126	149	230·4	239·2
1955	131	160	240·1	257·3
1956	137	167	251·4	268·7
1957	141	171	260·8	275·8

Sources: Market prices of Consumers' Expenditure: 1957 and 1958 NIE.
Retail prices: R. G. D. Allen: On the Decline in the Value of Money (Stamp Memorial Lecture 1957), University of London, 1957. Table II; and March 1959 MDS.   .. =not available.

see what the difference is. The second two columns of Table 3.4 show indexes of retail prices of all items and of foods calculated by Professor R. G. D. Allen. The index numbers from 1948 to 1955 are based on the Ministry of Labour's Interim Indexes described above in section 5(a); the link between 1938 and 1948 is Professor Allen's own estimate; the 1956 and 1957 numbers are obtained by linking the present Retail Price Index to Professor Allen's index by the method described above. We find that according to these indexes the price level of all items between 1938 and 1957 increased by about 161 per cent and of food by about 176 per cent.

The difference between the two sets of estimates is not very great— the percentage difference between the increases is, for all items, about 9 per cent, $\left(\dfrac{176-161}{176}\right)\cdot 100=8\cdot 5$, and for food about 7 per cent, $\left(\dfrac{190-176}{190}\right)\cdot 100=7\cdot 4$. Differences of these sizes, in results referring to changes over a period of twenty years, can not be considered as significant. We are justified in thinking that our results are reliable although rough indicators of the change in retail prices, and we can state the conclusion: on the average retail prices increased by about 170 per cent (with a margin of error of about ten percentage points either way). Note that this increase is much less than the average rise in commodity prices estimated above in section 3.

7. RATIO CHARTS

Suppose the price of a pound of butter was 1s 0d in 1938, 2s 0d in 1948 and 3s 6d in 1958. Let us plot these prices on a graph as in Chart 3.2. Inspection of the chart shows that the price of butter has increased; it also gives the impression that the price of butter increased more rapidly after 1948 than before. This is not so. Between 1938 and 1948 the price of butter doubled; between 1948 and 1958 the increase was only 75 per cent. Actually the rate of increase (the percentage change per decade, or average percentage change per annum) declined, yet the graph leaves a different impression. The reason is that equal distances on the vertical scale of the chart represent equal absolute amounts, i.e. the change from 1s 0d to 2s 0d is represented by a length the same as that from 2s 0d to 3s 0d. Hence such a chart is not well-suited to represent relative changes which are what we are concerned with when we examine rates of increase (or decrease).

What is required is a chart which represents equal percentage changes by equal vertical distances. Such a chart is called a ratio chart, and is obtained by plotting the *logarithms* of the amounts on the vertical scale. For example, the logarithms of 10, 100 and 1,000 are 1·00, 2·00 and 3·00 respectively. 100 is ten times 10 and this relative change is represented on the logarithmic scale by the difference 2·00−1·00=1·00. Similarly 1,000 is ten times 100, represented logarithmically by 3·00−2·00=1·00 also. Thus the relative change

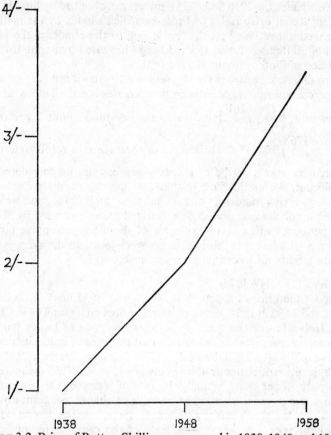

CHART 3.2. Price of Butter. Shillings per pound in 1938, 1948 and 1958. Source: hypothetical data.

from 10 to 100, and the relative change from 100 to 1,000 would both be represented on a ratio scale by a vertical distance equal to 1·00.

The procedure of drawing a ratio chart is as follows: (i) obtain from a book of logarithmic tables the logarithms of the values to be plotted on the vertical axis; (ii) treat the logarithms as ordinary numbers and plot them in the ordinary way as a graph; (iii) when the graph is completed mark off the vertical scale in the original values (instead of leaving it marked in logarithms). We illustrate these rules by plotting the price of butter on a ratio scale. The logarithms of the prices are:

Price of butter in shillings	Logarithm
1·0	0·000
2·0	0·301
3·5	0·544

We prepare our graph in the usual way:

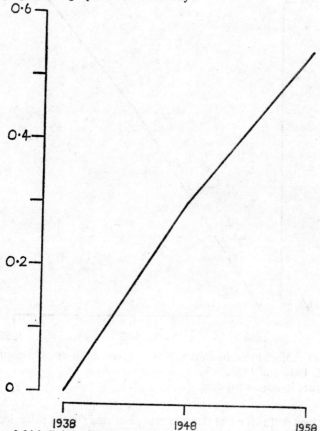

CHART 3.3(a). Price of Butter. RATIO SCALE. Logarithm of shillings per pound in 1938, 1948 and 1958.
Source: hypothetical data.

Finally, we erase the logarithms and substitute the original values
—1s 0d, 2s 0d, 3s 0d and 4s 0d—at the points on the vertical axis
corresponding to their logarithms:

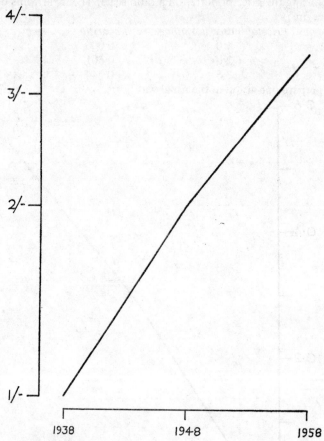

CHART 3.3(b). Price of Butter. RATIO SCALE. Shillings per pound in
1938, 1948 and 1958.
Source: hypothetical data.

In Chart 3.3(b) the fact that the rate of increase in the price declined
after 1948 can now be seen clearly.

In the actual preparation of ratio charts it is common to use
specially ruled *logarithmic paper* with equal absolute distances on the

vertical axis representing equal proportionate changes or equal proportions. This allows the original figures to be plotted straight on to the chart without the necessity for the intermediate step of looking up the logarithms.

We shall use a ratio chart to examine the changes in retail prices between 1938 and 1957. In Chart 3.4 the Market Price Index of total consumers' expenditure (from Table 3.4) is plotted on a ratio scale for the years 1938 and 1946-57. The dashed line joining the points for 1938 and 1946 is a conventional way of showing that the points for the intervening years have been omitted (or that the statistics are not available).

The slope (gradient) of the graph measures the rate of change of the price index: an increase in the slope means that the percentage change per annum has increased; a decrease means that the percentage change per annum has declined. If the graph had the appearance of a straight line over the entire period we would conclude that prices had increased at a constant rate over the entire period. The dashed straight line joining the 1938 and 1946 points needs special mention: its slope measures the *average* rate of change of prices between 1938 and 1946—because we do not have the data for the intervening years we can not say that there was a *constant* rate of change during these years.

Between 1946 and 1948 the rate of increase of prices was more than the average rate of increase during the war years; between 1948 and 1950 the rate of increase declined. The Korean war of 1950-2 was associated with a rise in the rate of increase which between 1952 and 1954 gradually declined. The years 1954-7 witnessed a slight but marked increase in the rate of price change—but this rate of change was still less than the rates of change between 1946 and 1948 and between 1950 and 1952. The history of retail price changes since the end of the war is thus one of a gradually declining rate of increase, with alternating periods of rapid and less than rapid rises.

Further examples of the use of ratio charts are given in Chapters 8 and 12, and in several exercises in many of the chapters.

8. EXERCISES

(1) Derive a quarterly market price index from 1955 to 1958 for total consumers' expenditures, and state the periods when prices rose most rapidly. [HINT: Obtain the implicit price index from the estimates of consumers' expenditure in the MDS. E.g. Table 4, September 1959, gives total expenditure in the 4th quarter of 1958 as £4,030 millions (current prices) and £3,527 millions (average 1954 prices). The index

F

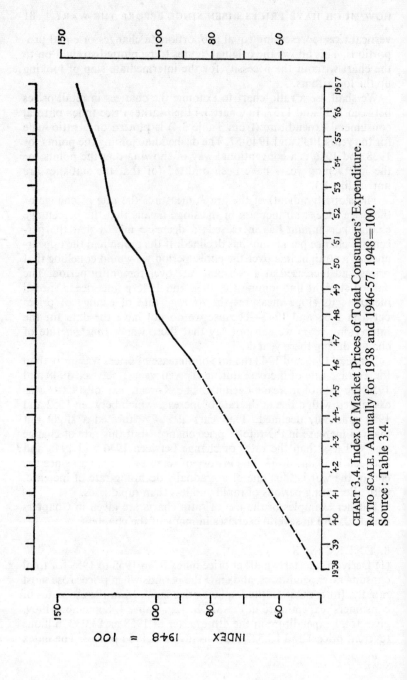

CHART 3.4. Index of Market Prices of Total Consumers' Expenditure.
RATIO SCALE. Annually for 1938 and 1946-57. 1948=100.
Source: Table 3.4.

INDEX   1948 = 100

number for the 4th quarter of 1958 (1954=100) is $\frac{4030}{3527}\cdot100=114\cdot2$.

Plot the series of index numbers so obtained for the sixteen quarters on a ratio chart. (Another index can be obtained by averaging the monthly all-items retail price index given in the MDS, linking the interim index based on January 1952 to the current index based on January 1956.)]

(2) What classes of consumers' goods and services showed the greatest price increases between 1938 and 1946, and between 1948 and 1957? [HINT: use the consumer market price indexes in the 1956 and 1957 NIE to estimate the price changes of the two periods for the main classes of goods—food, alcoholic drink, tobacco, etc. E.g. Table 21 of 1957 NIE gives the fuel and light index as 62 in 1938 and 91 in 1946 (1948=100). Thus fuel and light prices increased by $\frac{91-62}{62}\cdot100=46\cdot7$ per cent.]

(3) Illustrate graphically the decline in the value of the Pound Sterling between 1952 and 1958. [HINT: the value of money is what money can be used to buy (or what money is exchanged for). Rather than compare the quantity of a single good that £1 can buy, we compare the size of a representative bundle of goods and services over the years. We do this by comparing the reciprocals of a retail price index (if the price of 1 lb. of butter rose from 4s 0d to 5s 0d between years 1 and 2, then £1 would buy 5 lb. in year 1 and 4 lb. in year 2, i.e. the value of money in terms of butter declined by 20 per cent). Plot the reciprocals of a retail price index from 1952 to 1958 on a ratio chart.]

(4) From either the AAS or the MDS you will find that there has been a large and nearly continuous fall in beer consumption in the United Kingdom since the war years. Is it likely that this decline is due to changes in the relative price of beer (price of beer in terms of other goods)? HINT: calculate an index of the relative price of beer by dividing the index of beer prices by the index of market prices of all consumers' expenditure for each year since 1946. Both indexes, based on 1948=100, are in the 1957 NIE.] What other explanation of the fall in beer consumption can you offer? [HINT: compare the wartime with the pre-war level of consumption.]

CHAPTER FOUR

Changes in Incomes

1. INCOME, OUTPUT AND EXPENDITURE

Income has at least three meanings. It can refer to the satisfactions obtained from consuming, or enjoying the use of, material goods and services—this is *psychic income* and can not be measured directly. Secondly, income means the goods and services themselves which we consume or use. This is called *real income*, and is measureable. Finally, as most of us work for a money wage or salary which we use to buy the goods and services we want, we are familiar with the idea of *money income*—the payments made to us for the services we render to others, and the payments we receive in the form of grants such as pensions and allowances. Real income and money income are the ideas which interest the economist.

The economist aims at understanding the workings of the economic system and its effects upon people's lives. This system, whether it is organized on collective or individualistic lines, embraces thousands of industries, millions of types of goods and services and a variety of methods of organization. To understand it inevitably means to simplify it to get a bird's eye view of its main features. After we have understood the main features we can then fill in the details as is necessary. It is the purpose of the estimates of national income, expenditure and output to give a bird's eye view of some of the more important features of the economy—the size, composition, origin and use of the income produced in the economy.

The *national income* is the flow of goods and services produced in the economy in a given period of time, expressed in money terms, after allowance has been made for the value of goods and services used up in the process of production. Note first that a number of arbitrary or conventional decisions have to be made about the extent of the economy (the geographical area covered: in this chapter we are concerned with political unit known as the United Kingdom), and the period of time during which we measure the value of the goods and services produced (for statistical reasons this is one year or one quarter). The word flow is used in the definition to distinguish the idea of national income from the related idea of capital and natural resources which is a stock of wealth. In economics we usually speak of the stock of capital and natural resources (including the abilities of the human population) producing a flow of real income. Note also that we deduct the value of the goods and services used up in the process of production. If a tanner, for example, produced £100 worth of leather and sold it to a bootmaker who out of it made boots which he sold for £300, it would be wrong to calculate the national income as £100+£300=£400, for the £300 worth of boots produced includes the £100 worth of leather—the activities of the tanner and bootmaker combined contribute £300, not £400, to the national income. An alternative way of deriving the correct figure is to say that the *net output* of the bootmaker is £300−£100=£200 (the value of the boots *less* the value of the leather); the net output of the tanner is £100 (assuming he has used up no materials); and the sum of the net outputs is the national income, i.e. £200+£100=£300.

The production of goods and services involves paying money incomes which are spent in buying the goods and services. Thus there are three ways of measuring national income—from the output (or production) side, from the money income side, and from the expenditure side. These are three aspects of the same thing, but each approach may have its own particular uses. Measurement from the output side consists of adding up the net outputs of all firms, farms and productive enterprises. The money income method consists of adding the incomes earned by the owners of productive services—the services being those of the four factors of production: labour, capital, land and enterprise; and the money incomes being wages and salaries, interest and profits, and rent. The expenditure method consists of adding the value of expenditures on all goods and services intended either for current consumption (such as household purchases of food and clothes) or for adding to the stock of wealth (such as new factories and houses, new vehicles, and new plant and machinery). We can summarize these relationships as follows:

the production of goods and services by these industries:	creates these incomes:	which is spent on the goods and services for these purposes:
—agriculture	—wages	—household consumption
—manufacturing	—salaries	—Government consumption
—transport	—rents	
—distribution	—dividends	—adding to wealth
—public administration etc.	etc.	

The idea of flows of goods and services, of money incomes and of expenditures is fundamental in the presentation of the national income statistics, and also to their understanding. We shall briefly discuss some of these flows here, reserving a more detailed discussion for the following chapter. The student will remember that we are simplifying to some extent: trying to get a bird's eye view of the important features of the economy. The first set of flows consists of the flow of productive services from their owners to businesses—firms, farms and productive enterprises. In exchange there is a flow of money income from the businesses to the owners of productive services. The second set of flows consists of the flow of goods and services from businesses (which produced them) to the final consumers who are the owners of productive services, in exchange for the flow of money payments (expenditures) from the final consumers to businesses. These two sets of flows constitute the hard core of the economic transactions of a modern economy.[1]

As well as the main flows described above, there are the flows caused by the existence of Government, by the activity of investment (adding to wealth) and by the relationships of our economy with other economies. We shall not describe these in detail here, but shall illustrate them by describing some typical flows. Government provides services for individuals and groups in the economy, some of which are not sold or bought, such as police services, and some of which are sold and bought, such as postal services. To enable the Government to buy the productive services (such as labour) and the goods (such as paper) needed to produce its services, the Government raises money by taxation. So in the case of Government we have the set of flows consisting of the flow of Government-produced goods and services going to business and to final consumers, the flow of productive services from their owners to Government, the flow of money incomes from Government to the owners of the productive services, and the flow of tax payments from businesses and the owners of productive services.

Not all the goods and services produced in the economy are purchased for consumption. Part are purchased by businesses in order to add to wealth or replace wealth which had been used up in production. The goods are called investment goods and the activity is called investment or capital formation. The complementary activity is saving: refraining from using money income to buy consumption goods (on the part of the owners of productive services) and 'plough-

[1] We say modern to exclude economies which do not make extensive use of a medium of exchange like money.

ing back' profits, i.e. not distributing profits in the form of dividends (on the part of businesses). The representation of these flows is complicated by the fact that financial intermediaries such as banks and insurance companies channel the flows of savings to businesses who require them to finance their investment. We can however envisage the essence of these activities as a flow of investment goods from the industries which produce them to the businesses which are adding to or replacing their capital, a flow of savings from the owners of productive services to the businesses (via the financial intermediaries), and a flow of payments from the businesses to the industries producing investment goods.

Finally, our economy does not stand isolated in the world. Not all of the goods and services produced are bought at home—part is exported. Also, goods are imported from abroad to be used as raw materials in our industries or to be purchased directly by final consumers. The set of flows of these overseas transactions (of which those mentioned are the most important but not the only ones) can be represented by a flow of goods and services overseas, a flow of payments in return, a flow of goods and services from overseas, and another flow of payments in return (this time abroad).[1]

What we have been talking about in this section is a framework for arranging statistical information. We now turn to the statistics themselves and their arrangement.

2. THE ESTIMATES OF NATIONAL INCOME, EXPENDITURE AND OUTPUT OF THE UNITED KINGDOM

The main source of the estimates is NIE. Quarterly statistics are presented in MDS and ET, and a summary of the annual statistics is given in AAS. The official reference book on methods of estimation has already been referred to in Chapter 2.[2] The first part of NIE—in what follows we shall be referring to the 1959 edition unless the contrary is stated—contains summary tables, followed by parts dealing with the personal sector (households), companies, Government, etc., as well as special subjects such as output and expenditure at constant prices.

We shall first consider the three approaches to national income.

---

[1] Any difference in the payments flow has to be financed. This financing is connected with the savings flows and the financial intermediaries and is discussed in Chapter 5 below.

[2] Central Statistical Office: *National Income Statistics. Sources and Methods* (HMSO, 1956).

TABLE 4.1

United Kingdom National Income, 1957

All figures in £ million

Output approach: Gross national product by industry

	£ million
Agriculture, forestry and fishing	847
Mining and quarrying	703
Manufacturing	6,872
Building and contracting	1,115
Gas, electricity and water	483
Transport and communication	1,625
Distributive trades	2,387
Insurance, banking and finance (including real estate)	564
Other services	1,940
Total production and trade	16,536
Public administration and defence	1,164
Public health and educational services	679
Ownership of dwellings	618
Domestic services to households	97
Services to private non-profit-making bodies	88
Residual error	57
less Stock appreciation	−100
Gross domestic product at factor cost	19,139
Net income from abroad	231
Gross national product at factor cost	19,370
less Capital consumption	−1,778
National income	17,592

Income approach: Shares in the gross national product (factor incomes)

	£ million
Income from employment	12,919
Income from self-employment	1,786
Gross trading profits of companies	3,151
Gross trading surpluses of public corporations	322
Gross profits of other public enterprises	129
Rent	875
Residual error	57
Total domestic income	19,239
less Stock appreciation	−100
Gross domestic product at factor cost	19,139
Net income from abroad	231
Gross national product at factor cost	19,370
less Capital consumption	−1,778
National income	17,592

Expenditure approach: Gross national product by category of expenditure at factor cost

	£ million
Consumers' expenditure	12,107
Public authorities' current expenditure on goods and services	3,489
Gross fixed capital formation at home	3,536
Value of physical increase in stocks and work in progress	
Exports of goods and services	4,440
Total final expenditure	23,572
less Imports of goods and services	−4,433
Gross domestic product at factor cost	19,139
Net income from abroad	231
Gross national product at factor cost	19,370
less Capital consumption	−1,778
National income	17,592

Table 1—lower half: 'Shares in the gross national product (factor incomes)'—shows the estimate obtained by adding incomes. Table 10—'Gross national product by industry'—is the estimate derived from adding the net outputs of industries. Table 11—lower half: 'Gross national product by category of expenditure at factor cost'— is the estimate obtained by adding different types of expenditure. These three estimates are shown together for comparison in Table 4.1.

In the output column of Table 4.1 are the values of the net outputs of the industrial groups (based on the Standard Industrial Classification: see section 11, Chapter 1). They are net in the sense that they exclude (i) all purchases by one industry from another, and (ii) imports. They are thus free of duplication and represent the value of output created by productive services in the United Kingdom. Note that the service industries are treated similarly to the industries producing goods: net output of transport and distribution, for example, is the value of the services rendered by those industries, i.e. it is their wage and salary bills plus their profits. In a similar way the net output of public administration and defence is the value of services rendered—the wages and salaries paid by the various Government authorities. The sum of the net outputs is called 'Gross domestic product at factor cost', or GDP(fc) for short. We shall explain the items 'Residual error' and 'Stock appreciation' below. To GDP(fc) is added 'Net income from abroad'—rent, interest, profits and dividends received by United Kingdom residents from overseas *less* similar items paid abroad—to obtain 'Gross national product at factor cost', or GNP(fc) for short. Finally, as the production of goods and services has used up some of the wealth of the country, i.e. buildings, plant and machinery and vehicles have been worn out or used up, an allowance for 'Capital consumption' is deducted to obtain 'National income'.[1]

This calculation provides us with more than just the size of the national income. It allows us to examine the industrial composition of output, e.g. it is useful to know that Manufacturing in 1957 produced 35 per cent of GNP(fc), that the next largest industry was Distribution (producing 12 per cent), and that only 1·3 per cent of the national income was derived from net income from abroad. Clearly this sort of information is of the greatest importance for an understanding of the structure of the economy and the importance of the various parts. To quote just one other figure, it is frequently a source

---

[1] National income is sometimes called 'Net national product at factor cost', the net in this case referring to the fact that allowance has been made for capital consumption.

of astonishment that the service industries (all the industries coming after Gas, electricity and water in the list) produce about 50 per cent of GNP(fc).

The definition of national income and the other totals of necessity involves some conventions. These conventions depend in the last resort upon available information. For example, farmers usually themselves consume part of the produce of the farms. An estimate can be made of the value of this and it is correctly included in the net output figure of Agriculture. But the net output of food from domestic poultry keeping and vegetable growing in gardens and allotments is not included because of the statistical difficulties of making an accurate estimate. In the case of Domestic services to households, the value of the services of domestic servants are included, but those of housewives are not. The reason is not that servants are paid and housewives are not, but that to estimate the value of housewives' services would be an entirely arbitrary matter.[1] In the case of the services of the Ownership of dwellings, enough information is available to enable both the value of the services of rented houses to be included and the value of the services of houses occupied by their owners. Note that some of the instances mentioned in this paragraph involve estimating the value of output which is not sold (not exchanged for money). There is a flow of real income which is not matched by a corresponding flow of money income. In order that the estimates of national income from the income and expenditure sides (which we are about to describe) will equal the estimate from the output side it is necessary to include an equivalent item on the income side (called *imputed* income) to match the net output which is not sold, and a similar item on the expenditure side.

On the income side (middle column in Table 4.1) is a classification of the receipts of the owners of productive services. 'Income from employment' includes wages and salaries, pay in cash and in kind of the armed forces, and employers' contributions to various insurance and superannuation schemes of their employees. 'Income from self-employment' includes the incomes of professional persons, farmers (both money receipts and the imputed income of farm produce consumed on the farms) and the trading profits of other non-corporate business such as sole traders and partnerships. 'Gross trading profits of companies' are trading profits before the deduction of tax, dividend and interest payments. 'Gross trading surpluses of public corporations' are the surpluses of the nationalized industries providing

[1] The effect of this statistical treatment of housewives is that when a man marries his housekeeper he reduces the national income.

coal, electricity, gas, transport, etc., also before payment of taxes and interest. 'Gross profits of other public enterprises' are the profits of such enterprises as the Post Office, and local authority undertakings providing water, passenger transport, harbours, docks, etc., again before payment of tax and interest. 'Rent' includes receipts for the ownership of land and buildings together with an estimate of the imputed rent of owner-occupied dwelling houses and farms.[1] Thus the sum of these items (together with the residual error) is 'Total domestic income', which after adjustment has been made for stock appreciation is GDP(fc). This figure can be adjusted for net income from abroad and capital consumption to give, as did the output method, national income.

Finally, we consider the expenditure side. 'Consumers' expenditures' includes expenditures on consumers' goods and services by households together with the value of income in kind and imputed income included in the output and income estimates (such as pay in kind of the armed forces, and the imputed rents of owner-occupied dwellings). 'Public authorities current expenditure on goods and services' is current (i.e. non-capital) purchases by the central and local Governments of goods and services, and Governmental wages and salaries. It excludes grants, subsidies, Government interest payments and all other transfer payments, as well as excluding loans and loan-payments. 'Gross fixed capital formation at home' is expenditure on fixed capital assets (buildings, vehicles, plant and machinery, etc.) either for replacing or adding to the stock of fixed assets. It includes both private and public capital expenditures. 'The value of physical increase in stocks and work in progress' is the change in the quantity of stocks and work in progress held by private and public businesses. Note that this is intended to be the change in the *quantity* held during the year. It is derived from the change in the value of stocks by deducting an estimate of that part of the change in value which is due to a change in prices alone during the year—this latter part of the change in the value is called 'Stock appreciation'. Because it has been deducted from the expenditure side it must also be deducted from the output and income sides. As stocks may increase or decrease, both the value of physical increase in stocks and stock appreciation may be either positive or negative. The item which is officially called the value of physical increase in stocks and work in progress is frequently called stock (or inventory) investment, to dis-

[1] No attempt is made to isolate the imputed rent of land and buildings both owned and occupied by a business: this is contained in gross trading profits and surpluses.

tinguish it from fixed investment (gross fixed capital formation). Note that in Table 11 of the 1959 NIE which we use as the source of the figures in our Table 4.1 these two types of investment are not distinguished.

The items already listed on the expenditure side do not add up to the value of GDP(fc) because not all the United Kingdom output is sold at home. Nor are all the goods purchased at home produced at home—some of the expenditures we have listed have been made to purchase imported goods. We add 'Exports of goods and services' to obtain 'Total final expenditure' and then subtract 'Imports of goods and services' to get GDP(fc). The final adjustments for net income from abroad and capital consumption to get national income are the same as before.

The existence of three methods of estimating national income is significant for two reasons. First, each method allows a certain type of information to be classified and the importance of the components to be judged. Second, each method gives an independent estimate of national income, and so allows the accuracy of the calculations to be checked. There are small discrepancies between on one hand the income and output estimates (which are based on the same procedures) and on the other hand the expenditure estimate. This discrepancy is the 'Residual error', which by convention is entered in the income and output columns. It can of course be either positive or negative.

The student will have noticed that the estimates of gross domestic product discussed above are described 'at factor cost'. This shows that output and expenditures are valued at prices which make them equal to the sum of incomes earned by the owners of productive services (factor incomes). However, many goods are sold at prices which are greater than factor cost by the amount of indirect or sales tax levied on them. These taxes are called 'Taxes on expenditure'. Also, some goods are sold at prices which are less than factor cost by the amount of the subsidy given to the producers. Thus if we added up the purchases of goods and services at the prices actually paid for them—'at market prices'—we obtain an estimate of national income from the expenditure side which differs from the estimate given in the lower half of Table 11 in NIE and used in Table 4.1. The market price estimate is shown in the upper half of Table 11 in NIE. If from this estimate we subtract taxes on expenditure and add subsidies we obtain our original GNP(fc). These calculations are done in the upper half of Table 1 in NIE. The point to remember about these complications is that the value of output equals the sum of incomes of the owners of productive services. Expenditure taxes and subsidies upset this equality, and if we estimate national income by adding expenditures at market prices we must make the adjustments of subtracting expenditure taxes and adding subsidies. The student should note that it is usual to present the expenditure statistics at market prices. The detailed statistics of expenditures given in other parts of NIE are all at market prices, viz.

consumers' expenditures: Tables 18-19
public authorities' current expenditure: Tables 41-42
gross fixed capital formation: Tables 47-53
value of physical increase in stocks: Tables 58-60.

The official statisticians do not round off their estimates beyond the nearest £ million, and in the tables in NIE component items add up to the totals given. This does not imply that all the figures presented are without large possible errors. Many items, given to the nearest £ million, may in fact be correct only to the nearest £5 million, and the statisticians say that some of the larger items may be correct only to the nearest £50 million. Items to be regarded as especially unreliable (with errors of more than 10 per cent either way) are net income from abroad and stock investment. Note, however, that the main totals such as GDP(fc) are more reliable than some of their component items because the main totals are estimated in three ways and are thus subject to a double cross-checking.

3. DIFFERENT MEASURES OF INCOME

The measure of income used in the previous section—the value of the annual flow of goods and services produced in the economy—is the basic economic idea. There are, however, other useful measures of income. No one of them is the correct measure: each is appropriate in certain circumstances. It will be clear to the student that national income is not the same thing as the income of households. This latter idea is called 'Personal income' (see upper half of Table 2 of NIE) and is obtained by adding to the incomes from employment and self-employment (i) the part of gross trading profits of companies and gross trading surpluses of public corporations which is distributed to households as dividends and interest (this allocation is shown in the bottom half of Table 3 of NIE), (ii) rent paid to households, and (iii) *transfer payments* from public authorities, i.e. national insurance benefits, family allowances, scholarships and grants to universities, the cost of providing school meals and milk, etc. (details are shown in Table 41 in NIE). These transfer payments, like subsidies, because they represent a redistribution of income between sectors of the economy by the medium of Government, and are not generated by the production of output, do not appear in estimates of the national income. They must however be included in the incomes of those people who receive them.

TABLE 4.2

United Kingdom Personal, Private and National Income, 1957

	£ million	
Wages	7,650	
Salaries	4,090	
Pay in cash and kind of the Forces	392	
Employers' contributions	787	
Income from Employment		12,919
Professional persons	280	
Farmers	435	
Other sole traders and partnerships	1,071	
Income from Self-employment		1,786
Rent, dividends and interest		1,954
National insurance benefits and other current grants from Public Authorities		1,252
Personal Income		17,911
Undistributed profits of Companies and Public Corporations		2,933
Private Income		20,844
Gross profits of other public enterprises		129
less rent, dividends and interest paid by Public Authorities		−343
less current grants to persons by Public Authorities		−1,252
Additions to dividend and tax reserves		35
Residual error		57
less Stock appreciation		−100
Gross National Product at factor cost		19,370
less Capital consumption		−1,778
National Income		17,592

Source: 1959 NIE, Tables 2 and 8.

Personal income is clearly a useful measure when we are interested in the fortunes and habits of individuals and households. Personal income after income tax payments and national insurance and health

contributions is called 'Disposable personal income', and its allocation between expenditure and saving is shown in the lower half of
Table 2 in NIE.

If to personal income we add the undistributed profits and surpluses of companies and public corporations, we obtain 'Private
income'. If to private income we add the income which the Government derives from its property, and *subtract* the Government's transfer and interest payments to households, we have estimated GNP(fc)
by an alternative route. (Note that this route has included net income
from abroad in the separate incomes of households, companies,
public corporations and Government.) The relationship between
these various measures of income in 1957 is shown in Table 4.2 which
is based directly upon Tables 2 and 8 of NIE.

Quite apart from its other uses, Table 4.2 throws considerable
light upon the structure of the economy. Income from employment
in 1957 made up 73 per cent of national income; undistributed profits
and surpluses of companies and public corporations made up another
20 per cent. In personal income, only 7 per cent is contributed by
national insurance benefits and other current grants from public
authorities (although this by no means measures the importance of
Government activities in the economy) and 11 per cent by rent,
dividends and interest.

4. OUTPUT AND EXPENDITURE AT CONSTANT PRICES

From Table 1 of NIE we can calculate that GDP(fc) increased by
£8,882 millions or about 86·6 per cent between 1948 and 1957. As we
know that prices rose during this period this figure must overstate the
increase in real income—the physical increase in the flow of goods
and services. A change in the *value* of output reflects changes in prices
as well as changes in volume. To isolate the changes in volume, the
value of output in different years is calculated at the unchanging
prices of one of these years. A difference in the constant price estimates of any two years will then indicate a difference in volume alone.
(This procedure has been illustrated in the case of consumers' expenditure in section 2, Chapter 2, above.)

Constant price estimates are shown in Tables 13 and 14 of NIE.
The upper half of Table 13 estimates GDP using expenditures at
market prices and revaluing them at 1954 market prices. The resulting
figure is also shown as a *volume index* (1954=100) to allow percentage
changes since 1954 to be easily read off. The lower half of the table
uses expenditures at factor cost and revalues at 1954 factor cost

GDP, GNP and national income (net national product). All three estimates are shown as indexes (1954=100) also.

The estimates of Table 13 have been based on the expenditure method. Table 14 arrives at GDP at 1954 factor cost by the output method: the net outputs of the industrial sectors are revalued at 1954 prices.[1] This information is presented in the form of volume indexes. Because the two sets of figures of GDP at 1954 factor cost—from the expenditure side and from the output side—are based on different types of information and each involves a certain amount of guess-work, the results differ slightly. It is very reassuring, however, that they are surprisingly close.

We can now see that the 87 per cent increase in GDP(fc) between 1948 and 1957 calculated above contains a large element of price change. GDP at 1954 factor cost increased by 28·4 per cent (according to Table 13) and at 1954 market prices the increase was 25·6 per cent An increase of 28·4 per cent over the nine years is an average compounded rate of increase of 2·8 per cent per year, i.e. on the average real income increased by 2·8 per cent every year between 1948 and 1957. We consider the increase in real income *per head of population* in section 7 below.

When the official statisticians began to provide constant price estimates of national income, expenditure and output they chose 1948 as the base, i.e. expenditures and output were valued at 1948 prices. Editions of NIE up to and including the 1958 edition show the constant price estimates at 1948 prices. Beginning with the 1959 edition a new base is used—1954 prices, and the expenditures previously given at 1948 prices have been revalued at 1954 prices. (Actually the 1958 edition of NIE reflects the transition to 1954 prices: the main tables of GDP at constant prices use 1948 prices, but there are also estimates given of consumers' expenditure and gross fixed capital formation at 1954 prices.)

Such a rebasing of constant price estimates of national income is necessary from time to time for the same reasons that indexes of prices

---

[1] This simple statement hides a host of statistical difficulties. The correct procedure for estimating net output at 1954 prices is to subtract the value of raw materials, fuel, etc., at 1954 prices from the value of gross output at 1954 prices. In fact this procedure is only followed in the case of agricultural net output: because of lack of information a less direct method is followed in the case of other industries. The service industries, particularly those like public administration whose output has no easily recognizable 'price', present special problems. The methods used are discussed in Central Statistical Office: *National Income Statistics. Sources and Methods* (HMSO, 1956).

must be rebased periodically. For the student who uses these statistics this presents no special difficulties, providing he is aware of differences of calculation and presentation in successive editions of NIE. These differences are indicated in the notes contained in NIE which should always be consulted.

5. INDEXES OF PRODUCTION

In the previous section the indexes of GDP at 1954 prices were described as volume indexes, i.e. they measure changes in the volume (or quantity) of goods and services, as distinct from their value. We can consider them from a different point of view. Suppose we have figures of the quantity of output of various industries for 1954 and 1957. From these figures we can calculate *volume* (*or quantity*) *ratios*—the ratio of the 1957 output to the 1954 output—as we do for price ratios. These quantity ratios allow us to say what is the percentage change in output between the two dates. Normally the volume ratios for different products will differ indicating that the outputs of different products have changed differently. We ask the same question as we did in the case of price ratios : what is the average or typical change in output? In calculating the average change in the level of output we weight each volume ratio by its contribution to total output, i.e. by its net output in some base period. This weighted average of the volume ratios is a volume index which in fact is the same thing as the volume indexes shown in NIE. Thus the index of GDP at 1954 factor cost in Table 14 of NIE is a fixed weight volume index (1954=100) whose weights are the net outputs of the goods and services in 1954.

In Table 14 there are separate indexes for the major industrial groups—Agriculture, forestry and fishing; Mining and quarrying; Manufacturing; etc. These indexes show the changes in the volume of output of different industries, e.g. the volume of mining and quarrying output increased by 8·9 per cent between 1948 and 1957, while that of manufacturing increased by 39 per cent. Obviously such information is valuable for the study of the changing structure of the economy, and the fortunes of industries.

Volume indexes are even more useful when they are presented in sufficient detail to enable the changes in the output of the various manufacturing industries to be distinguished. In Chapter 1 we considered the problem of getting an indicator of changes in the output of the cotton industry. We in fact selected representative products as indicators, but where an industry produces a wide range of different products—as, for example, does the engineering industry—this method is not always possible or useful. Instead it is better to use a

G

volume index of the output of the industry, i.e. it is better to use a measure of changes in the average level of output.[1]

Volume indexes of the output of the main manufacturing industries (based on the Standard Industrial Classification) are published in AAS and MDS, with 1954=100·0. They are called *Indexes of Industrial Production*. The September 1959 MDS, Table 40, shows indexes for eighteen manufacturing industries as well as indexes for some of these industries in combination. There are also indexes for 'Mining and quarrying', 'Construction', 'Gas, electricity and water', and 'Total manufacturing' (which are the same as the indexes in NIE) and an index called 'Total all industries' for all the industrial groups mentioned in combination. The MDS gives annual figures from 1955 to 1958 and monthly figures for a period of about two years (September 1959 MDS gives monthly figures from January 1957 to July 1959).[2]

For short period changes in the volume of industrial output—from month to month, from quarter to quarter—the MDS is the basic source. The student of an industry will normally first consult the appropriate index of production to obtain a general idea—or a bird's-eye view—of what has happened in the industry. Furthermore, the monthly index for All Industries is a reliable indicator of the changes in national income occurring during the course of a year between the dates when the annual output statistics are published in NIE.

As well as the indexes mentioned above, MDS gives two additional calculations: the indexes for All Industries and for Total Manufacturing Industries are shown 'seasonally adjusted'. This means that the industries are adjusted for holidays and other causes of seasonal variation, i.e. the effects of holidays and other seasonal factors upon the level of output are as far as possible removed from the index. This permits us to study month to month changes with the assurance that the changes are not just due, for instance, to the incidence of public holidays. All the monthly indexes, whether described as seasonally adjusted or not, have had the effects of variations in the lengths of calendar months removed, i.e. they all refer to a standard month.

There is inevitably delay in obtaining information upon which the official statisticians can estimate the index number for the most recent months. Index numbers for the most recent months—especially for the latest month shown in the MDS—are always based on incom-

---

[1] There will be occasions, of course, when we will be interested in the individual products of an industry and their different changes—as when we compare the changes in output of cotton and artificial fibre goods in the textile industry. The volume index gives a broad picture, disregarding details.

[2] The Construction index is calculated only quarterly.

plete information, and must always be regarded as provisional and liable to be revised. The main revision will normally be shown in the succeeding issue of the MDS, although occasionally further revisions will be made at later dates. The student who is collecting a series of monthly figures over a lengthy period from different issues of MDS must take care that provisional figures from old issues are not used.

The present index of production replaced an index based on 1948 with 1948 weights. The 1948 based index was begun by the official statisticians in 1952, and monthly figures were calculated back to 1950 and annual figures to 1946. The index was continued up to the middle of 1958. It can be found in editions of AAS up to and including the 1958 edition, and in the MDS up to and including the September 1958 issue.

The new, 1954-based index was begun in the MDS of October 1958. It has been calculated monthly from January 1957 and annual figures have been calculated back to 1946 (see ET, June 1959, Table A). For most purposes, therefore, it is not necessary to use the 1948-based index at all. For monthly output figures before 1957, however, the student would use the old index shown in early issues of MDS.

The most obvious difference between the old and new indexes is the difference in weights. The importance of different products (and of industries in the combined indexes) is measured by their contribution to the net output. As the composition of output changes over the years so the importance of products and industries change; thus weights based on 1954 net outputs are to be expected to give results differing from those of old weights based on 1948 net outputs. Actually, as far as the indexes for all industries and total manufacturing industries are concerned the effect of the changed weights is small (although in the cases of the indexes for individual industries the effects are substantial in one or two instances). The other important difference between the old and new indexes arises from the introduction of new products and the use of better methods of measuring quantities in the new index. Unlike the difference in weights, this does make a considerable difference to the indexes of individual industries (although not to the totals where the differences appear to offset one another). The most striking example is Vehicles, where the percentage increase between 1954 and January-June 1958 according to the old index was 11·2 per cent, and according to the new index was 24·4 per cent.[1]

[1] These differences are discussed in an article in ET, November 1958, where the new index is described.

We have mentioned these differences between the two indexes, even though the student will have little occasion to use the old index, for two reasons. First, it is valuable to know that differences in the weighting patterns even when the weights refer to the composition of outputs six years apart do not give greatly differing results. Second, the calculations of the new index back to 1946 are derived partly from a linking of the output estimates used in the old index to the output estimates in the new index (1954 weights being used throughout, of course). We have explained the difficulties inherent in such a linking process in the case of index numbers of retail prices (sections 5 and 6, Chapter 3, above). The same difficulties are present here, and the results of using the index to measure changes in the level of output over a ten year period—or longer—must be regarded as giving no more than a rough indication of changes in levels of output.

6. QUARTERLY INCOME AND EXPENDITURE STATISTICS

The annual income and expenditure statistics are published first in Government White Papers in the April following the year to which they refer and provide an important part of the information upon which the United Kingdom Government bases its economic policy for the succeeding year. However, reliance upon annual data often means that information is provided too infrequently for Government policy to be changed rapidly enough to meet changing circumstances. At the end of the previous section we mentioned the usefulness of the index of production in providing monthly information about the state of a large part of the economy. In recent years in the United Kingdom there has also been published quarterly national income and expenditure statistics, containing not as much detail as can be found in the annual statistics, but sufficient to enable frequent studies to be made of the changing economic climate. These quarterly estimates are not as reliable as the annual statistics and involve much more guesswork in their compilation.

The quarterly estimates are published in MDS and ET. Table 1 of the September 1959 MDS gives estimates of GDP(fc) from the expenditure side both at current and 1954 prices (note that the individual items of expenditure are at market prices). Table 2 shows GDP(fc) calculated from the income side. Table 3 gives details of personal income and expenditure. Tables 4 to 8 present detailed estimates of consumers' and Government expenditure, gross fixed capital formation and changes in the *value* of stocks. In ET, January

1960, official seasonally adjusted national income and expenditure estimates were presented for the first time. These estimates are now published regularly in MDS.[1]

7. THE CHANGE IN REAL INCOME PER HEAD BETWEEN 1948 AND 1957

In section 4 above we estimated the increase in GDP at 1954 factor cost between 1948 and 1957 to be 28·4 per cent, or on the average 2·8 per cent per year. But if we are interested in the flow of real income to households or people, or if we wish to compare increases at different times or between different countries, it is the change in annual income per household or per person which is the more useful and interesting figure. We can not say that real income per person increased by 28·4 per cent because the population of the United Kingdom increased during the period.

There are two conceptual difficulties in estimating real income per person. First, there is the question of deciding whether all people should be treated equally. In particular, do we treat children as equivalent to adults? As consumers, they could be treated as, say, half an adult because they may consume only one half of what an adult does. If the proportion of children in the population does not change markedly over time, then this problem is unimportant. Second, there is the question of what we consider as real income flowing to persons. Real income per person could simply mean the share of national income which each person would get if it was all divided out equally. This idea is sometimes considered uninteresting because it means that everyone is getting not only a share of consumption goods and services but also a share of the additions to wealth such as blast furnaces which are not real income themselves but stores of real income. Thus another idea is to treat as real income only consumers' expenditure and public authorities' current expenditure. But this time it is argued that while some Government expenditure, such as that on education and health, may be real income, other parts, such as military expenditure, are not.[2] The difficulty with this line of reasoning is that it is difficult to know where to draw a generally

[1] The methods of the seasonal adjustments which we have mentioned in this chapter are explained below in Chapter 9.

[2] It is sometimes argued that all or most of Government expenditure is a cost incurred in producing income, to be deducted from gross output as are purchases of raw materials and fuel. Governmental wages and salaries, according to this view, would be treated as transfer payments. No official statisticians recognize this view officially.

acceptable line. Here we shall adopt the view that we aim no more than to provide an indicator of changes in real income, and to this end we treat all persons alike and take real income to comprise GDP(fc). This approach is sometimes justified by saying that it is a 'productive capacity' view of real income, i.e. assuming the economic system is fully employed, national income is a measure of the capacity of the system to produce goods and services—what actually is the composition of the goods and services, is irrelevent in these circumstances.

Our procedure is as follows: (i) From Table 13 of the 1959 NIE we obtain the index numbers of GDP at 1954 factor cost: the figure for 1948 is 83·1; the figure for 1957 is 106·7. (ii) Population statistics are given in the AAS. Table 6 of the 1958 AAS gives the total population of the United Kingdom in mid-1957 as 51,657 thousand persons. An earlier edition of the AAS gives the mid-1948 total population as 50,065 thousand persons. (iii) To find the increase in real income per person we take the ratio of the population figures $\left(\dfrac{51,657}{50,065}=1\cdot0317\right)$ and divide this into the ratio of the GDP indexes $\left(\dfrac{106\cdot7}{83\cdot1}=1\cdot2839\right)$ i.e. $\dfrac{1\cdot2839}{1\cdot0317}=1\cdot2444.$

Thus real income per head increased by 24·4 per cent between 1948 and 1957. This represents an average compounded rate of increase of 2·5 per cent per year.[1]

Note on Population Statistics

In estimating real income per head above, we used the figure of *total population* which includes the United Kingdom military forces serving overseas and excludes allied forces stationed in the United Kingdom. An alternative measure is *de facto* or *home population* which includes all military forces in the United Kingdom and the mercantile marine in home waters, and excludes United Kingdom forces serving overseas. Estimates of home population are not available for the years 1940-50: for this reason in our exercise we used total population.

The AAS and MDS both give statistics of home population for recent years, classified regionally, by age and by sex. For further

[1] With the possible error due to rounding in the original population and GDP figures taken into account, the true annual percentage increase lies between 2·4 per cent and 2·6 per cent.

information on population statistics the student should refer to a pamphlet published by the General Register Office: *Matters of Life and Death* (HMSO, 3rd ed., 1956).

8. EXERCISES

(1) Did real income per person increase as rapidly after 1955 as it had in the four years before? [HINT: calculate annual real income per person by dividing GDP at 1954 factor cost by the mid-year home population—the result will be so many £ per head each year. Plot these estimates on a ratio chart.]

(2) Has the rise in average annual wages and salaries in manufacturing industries since 1948 kept pace with the rise in the cost of living? [HINT: use Table 17 of NIE to calculate average annual wage per wage-earner and annual average salary per salary-earner from 1948 to 1958. Plot these estimates on a ratio chart and compare with the index of market prices of all consumers' expenditure.]

(3) Compare the changes in the share of income from employment with the share of income from self-employment since 1948. [HINT: use Table 1 of NIE.] Has the rise in incomes from self-employment since 1948 kept pace with the rise in prices? [HINT: Plot on a ratio chart the three types of incomes from self-employment—Table 2 of NIE—and compare with the index of market prices of all consumers' expenditure.]

(4) It is generally recognized that after 1955 the rate of growth of United Kingdom output showed a marked decline. What is the evidence for this? Can you find any evidence that any of the major categories of expenditure (consumers' expenditure, gross fixed capital formation at home, etc.) declined or ceased rising about 1955? [HINT: to get a broad picture of the situation, for the years 1950 to 1958 plot (preferably on a ratio chart) GDP and the items of final expenditure at 1954 prices on a graph. The value of physical increase in stocks can be added to gross fixed capital formation at home to get a single figure of capital formation. The graph should be inspected to see in what periods the different types of expenditure rose or fell, and what the contribution of their changes was to the total changes in GDP.]

(5) The indexes of production in the MDS show that production in the ferrous metal manufacturing (iron and steel) industry fell in 1958. When did production start to rise again? [HINT: use the monthly indexes of production for this industry. Plot on a chart the index numbers from January 1957 up to the most recent month (alternatively, calculate the average index for each quarter, and plot the quarterly series). Inspect the graph to determine the seasonal pattern.]

As an aid in establishing the date at which production began to rise, compare each month's index with the index one year earlier. You will find that until early 1959 each month's index was below that of a year earlier. When the indexes of a succession of two or three months are unmistakably higher than the indexes of a year earlier, you have evidence that production started to rise in those months.]

CHAPTER FIVE

The Social Accounts

1. SECTORS, ACTIVITIES AND ACCOUNTS

In Chapter 4 we explained the idea of national income and the three ways of estimating it. National income refers to the economy as a whole, although in estimating it we considered the incomes, expenditures and output of different parts of the economy. In particular, we discussed personal income—the sum of the incomes of individuals and households. The usefulness of the national income statistics is greatly increased if we have estimates of income, expenditure and output of the parts of the economy, and if we know the relationship between the parts. The purpose of the *social accounts* is to present estimates of the income, output and expenditure of the parts of the economy in an organized way, in order to show the relationships between the parts and the totals.

The parts into which the United Kingdom economy is divided for this purpose are called *sectors*. They are:

Persons
Corporate enterprises—
    companies
    public corporations
Public authorities—
    Central Government
    local authorities
The rest of the world.

Economic activities are classified into three functions: production, consumption and adding to capital. For each function there is an account which records the economic activities: for *production* there is the production (or operating, or trading) account; for *consumption* there is the current (or income/expenditure, or revenue, or appropriation) account; for *adding to capital* there is the capital (or savings/investment, or sources and uses of funds) account.[1] A *production*

---

[1] We give the alternative names of the accounts because neither in business accounting nor amongst official statisticians is there any standard form. In this chapter we shall use the terms production, current and capital accounts only.

account records the expenditure incurred in producing output, and the receipts from sales or disposals of the output. The difference between total expenditure and total receipts is trading profit or income. Production accounts are drawn up only for business enterprises, e.g. for companies and public corporations. A *current account* records the ways in which trading profit or income is used. A business enterprise uses its trading profit to pay taxes and dividends and to save (undistributed profits). Households use their incomes to pay taxes, to buy goods and services and to save. A *capital account* records the increases in assets (fixed capital, cash, securities, etc.) and the sources of finance to purchase these assets (savings, borrowings, etc.).

This chapter is devoted to expounding the principles of these accounts and for the most part we make use of the hypothetical transactions of an imaginary economy. In the final section we describe where to find the social accounts of the United Kingdom in NIE.

2. THE ACCOUNTS OF FIRMS

We shall describe sector accounts and the relationships between them by means of a simplified, imaginary economy. Our economy contains only three firms—A and B, who are manufacturers, and C who is a retailer—who together form the company sector. There is also a Central Government, and a number of households who form the personal sector. We also assume there is a bank in our economy, and that the method of making payments is the transfer of bank deposits by cheque. (A bank would normally produce a net output—the value of its banking services—which would contribute to national income, but we shall neglect this.)[1] The rest of the assumptions about the activities of the economy will be introduced as we deal with the accounts of the various sectors.

A's production activities are summarized in its production account (see Table 5.1). £10 million are spent on the wages and salaries of its labour force and management; £5 million on materials from firm B; and another £5 million on imported materials. With these materials and labour—and with the assistance of what fixed capital the firm posesses—goods to the value of £25 million are produced, of which £5 million are sold to B; £15 million to retailer C; and £5 million are exported. The surplus of receipts over expenditures is the trading

---

[1] Without complicating our example, but to make it more realistic, the reader could assume that the bank is a free Government service, staffed by civil servants whose wages are paid by the Government and whose contribution to national income is included under the net output of the public administration industry.

profit of £5 million. The current account shows how the £5 million trading profit is allocated: £1 million is paid as company income tax to the Central Government; £1 million is paid as dividends to the owners of the firm (householders); £1 million is set aside to cover the year's depreciation of the fixed capital; leaving £2 million undistributed profit which is set aside as a reserve.

The changes in the firm's assets during year 1 can be found by

TABLE 5.1
Accounts and Balance Sheet of Firm A

Production Account				Current Account			
Expenditure	*£m.*	*Receipts*	*£m.*	*Expenditure*	*£m.*	*Receipts*	*£m.*
Wages and salaries	10	Sales to B	5	Income Tax	1	Trading profit	5
Materials from B	5	Sales to C	15	Dividends	1		
Imported materials	5	Exports	5	Depreciation	1		
Trading profit	5			Undistributed profit	2		
	25		25		5		5

BALANCE SHEETS

end year 0				end year 1			
Liabilities	*£m.*	*Assets*	*£m.*	*Liabilities*	*£m.*	*Assets*	*£m.*
Accumulated depreciation	15	Fixed capital	49	Accumulated depreciation	16	Fixed capital	53
Bank overdraft	3	Trade credit	4	Bank overdraft	7	Trade credit	7
Share capital	30	Government securities	2	Share capital	30	Government securities	2
Reserves	7			Reserves	9		
	55		55		62		62

Capital Account

Expenditure	*£m.*	*Receipts*	*£m.*
Fixed capital formation	4	Depreciation	1
Increase in trade credit	3	Undistributed profit	2
		Increase in bank overdraft	4
	7		7

comparing the firm's balance sheet at the end of year 0 with that at the end of year 1. The balance sheet lists both the assets owned by the firm and its liabilities (debts) to its shareholders and others.[1] At the end of year 0, firm A's assets comprise fixed capital valued at its original purchase price of £49 million; trade credit of £4 million (the value of goods bought by B and C from A and not yet paid for); and £2 million of financial assets in the form of holdings of Government

---

[1] Note that a company like our firm is treated both in book-keeping and in English law as an entity distinct from its shareholders—the firm itself owns property and incurs debts.

securities.[1] These assets are balanced by A's liabilities: those it owes to its shareholders—accumulated depreciation funds of £15 million, share capital of £36 million, and reserves of £7 million; and those it owes to others—a bank overdraft of £3 million. (In some firms' balance sheets the figure for fixed capital is entered net of depreciation, i.e. £49 million — £15 million = £34 million. In this case the figure for depreciation disappears from the liabilities side.) The firm's posi-

TABLE 5.2

Accounts and Balance Sheet of Firm B

Production Account				Current Account			
Expenditure	*£m.*	*Receipts*	*£m.*	*Expenditure*	*£m.*	*Receipts*	*£m.*
Wages and salaries	15	Sales to A	5	Income tax	3	Trading profit	10
Materials from A	5	Sales to C	5	Dividends	2		
Imported materials	15	Sales of		Depreciation	2		
Trading profit	10	capital		Undistributed			
		equipment		profit	3		
		at home	10				
		Exports	25				
	45		45		10		10

BALANCE SHEETS

end year 0				end year 1			
Liabilities	*£m.*	*Assets*	*£m.*	*Liabilities*	*£m.*	*Assets*	*£m.*
Accumulated		Fixed capital	60	Accumulated		Fixed capital	66
depreciation	17	Trade credit	6	depreciation	19	Trade credit	6
Bank overdraft	3			Bank overdraft	1		
Share capital	36			Share capital	39		
Reserves	10			Reserves	13		
	66		66		72		72

Capital Account			
Expenditure	*£m.*	*Receipts*	*£m.*
Fixed capital formation	6	Depreciation	2
Reduction in bank		Undistributed profit	3
overdraft	2	Issue of shares	3
	8		8

tion at the end of year 1 is shown in the end-year 1 balance sheet. It has increased its fixed capital and trade credit, it has increased its accumulated depreciation fund and its reserves (compare with its current account), while its bank overdraft has gone up.

These *changes* in A's assets and liabilities during year 1 are shown in the capital account, where the expenditures are the changes in

[1] Normally if a firm did hold Government securities it would receive interest from the Government which would be entered in the receipts side of its current account as *non-trading income*.

assets between end-year 0 and end-year 1, and the receipts are the changes in liabilities between end-year 0 and end-year 1. It is obvious why the receipts of the capital account are sometimes called *sources of funds*, and expenditures *uses of funds*. We see that the funds available for increasing assets (or for investment) in year 1 consist of the year's depreciation allowance and the year's undistributed profit (which together are called gross company savings); plus £4 million

TABLE 5.3

Accounts and Balance Sheet of Firm C

Production Account				Current Account			
Expenditure	£m.	*Receipts*	£m.	*Expenditure*	£m.	*Receipts*	£m.
Wages and salaries	3	Sales	38	Income tax	1	Trading profit	3
Goods from A	15	Stocks of A's		Depreciation	1		
Goods from B	5	goods at		Dividend	1		
Imported goods	6	end of year					
Sales tax	7	1	1				
Stocks of A's goods		Stocks of im-					
at end of year 0	3	ported					
Stocks of imported		goods at					
goods at end of		end of year					
year 0	1	1	4				
Trading profit	3						
	43		43		3		3

BALANCE SHEETS

end year 0				end year 1			
Liabilities	£m.	*Assets*	£m.	*Liabilities*	£m.	*Assets*	£m.
Accumulated		Fixed capital	7	Accumulated		Fixed capital	7
depreciation	2	Stocks	4	depreciation	3	Stocks	5
Bank overdraft	4			Bank overdraft	1		
Trade credit	1			Trade credit	4		
Share capital	2			Share capital	2		
Reserves	2			Reserves	2		
	11		11		12		12

Capital Account			
Expenditure	£m.	*Receipts*	£m.
Change in stocks	1	Depreciation	1
Reduction in bank overdraft	3	Trade credit	3
	4		4

borrowed from the bank (increase in bank overdraft). The total of £7 million was used partly to purchase £4 million of fixed capital and partly to extend £3 million trade credit to other firms.

The activities of firm B, summarized in its accounts and balance sheets, introduce no new principles. The new activities we have shown in B's accounts are (i) in the production account along with the sales of goods to A and C, is the value of fixed capital equipment which B produces and sells to other firms in the economy (part of this is bought by A as we saw from A's capital account); (ii) from the balance sheets and capital account we see that B raises £3 million by selling new shares, and uses part of its funds to reduce its bank overdraft; and (iii) B increases its fixed capital by £6 million—this is where the remaining £6 million of the £10 million of capital equipment which itself produced went to.

Firm C is a retailer who buys goods from A and B as well as importing goods, and sells them to households and to the Government. We assume that it holds stocks of goods so as to meet unforseen changes in sales and deliveries. In year 1 it spent £3 million on wages and salaries, bought goods worth £20 million from A and B, and also imported £6 million of goods from abroad. At the end of year 0 it held stocks of £3 million of goods A had produced, and £1 million of imported goods (these stocks are valued at the prices which C paid for them—wholesale prices). We introduce an additional complication here: the Government levies a sales tax of $33\frac{1}{3}$ per cent on the retail value of household purchases of goods produced by A. We suppose that the value of C's sales is made up as follows:

	wholesale value £ million		retailer's margin £ million		sales tax £ million		market value £ million
sales of A's goods to households	17	+	4	+	7	=	28
sales of B's goods to Government	5	+	1			=	6
sales of imported goods to households	3	+	1			=	4

C's receipts are £38 million from total sales. £7 million of this collected on behalf of the Government to whom it is payed (see expenditure side of production account).

What happens to C's stocks? £3 million of A's goods were held at the end of year 0; £15 million were bought from A during the year; £17 million were sold. Thus C's stocks of A's goods at end of year 1 are £1 million. (Note that all these values are at the prices paid by C —wholesale prices; there are various methods used by firms in valuing their stocks, and this method of valuation at cost is one of the commonest.) Also, £1 million of imported goods were held at end of year 0; £6 million were bought during the year; and £3 million were sold. Thus £4 million remained in stock at the end of year 1. In C's production account stocks held at end of year 0 are entered in the expenditure side and stocks held at end of year 1 in the receipts side.[1] Note that most firms will hold stocks of materials and goods, and their production accounts will show their transactions in stocks. We have excluded stock changes from the accounts of A and B so as not to introduce too many complications at once.

The remainder of C's accounts fall into the standard pattern except for the treatment of stocks. Stocks are shown as an asset in the balance sheets, and the change in stocks is an expenditure in the capital account, i.e. funds have been used to finance investment in stocks. Note also that during the course of the year C's bank overdraft was reduced, and the trade credit received increased by £3 million—this is the trade credit granted by A: £3 million of the goods C bought from A had not been paid for at the end of year 1.

3. THE ACCOUNTS OF THE PERSONAL SECTOR AND OF GOVERNMENT

The Personal sector comprises the households. We shall not bother about separate accounts for each household, but shall draw up the consolidated accounts instead. A production account is not drawn up for households.[2] The current account of our households is shown in Table 5.4. On the receipts side is shown the income of households: wages and salaries from A, B and C (which are recorded in the firms' production accounts), salaries of £8 million from the Government, current grants (pensions) of £8 million from the Government, dividends of £4 million from A and B, and £2 million interest payments from the Government (we assume the households hold Government securities). The expenditure side of the account shows how this income is disposed of. Consumers' purchases of goods from C are £32 million, income tax payments are £12 million, £1 million is sent

---

[1] This accounting convention is based on the fiction that at the beginning of a year a firm in its capacity as producer or trader buys stocks from itself in its capacity as a stockholder, selling back at the end of the year what remains. Thus an increase in stocks resulting from the year's transactions is matched by a corresponding trading profit. How the investment in stocks is financed is shown in the capital account. We are not concerned here with the additional complication of the effect of price changes upon the value of stocks—the problem of stock appreciation.

[2] Of necessity the transactions of a personal sector will include the affairs of small business. In this respect a production account could be drawn up (see below, section 8).

abroad to relations, and the balance of £5 million is saved. The capital account shows how the £5 million savings are used: £3 million of B's securities—new issue of share capital—are bought, £1 million of new Government securities are bought, and bank deposits increase

TABLE 5.4

Accounts of Personal Sector

Current Account

Expenditure	£m.	Receipts		£m.
Consumers' expenditure	32	Wages and salaries		
Remittances abroad	1	from A	10	
Income tax	12	from B	15	
Saving	5	from C	3	
		from Government	8	
		Total	36	
		Current grants (pensions)		8
		Dividends		4
		Interest from Government		2
	50			50

Capital Account

Expenditure	£m.	Receipts	£m.
Purchase of firm's securities	3	Savings	5
Purchase of Government securities	1		
Increase in bank deposits	1		
	5		5

by £1 million. Note that these accounts are a summary of the Personal sector's transactions with other sectors—any sales and purchases of, for example, securities between households will cancel out in the consolidated households' account.

Governments, in their general administrative capacity, produce output in the form of the services of the police, the armed forces, etc. A production account for these services could be drawn up but it would be an arbitrary matter because such Government services are not sold in the market in civilized countries. In other capacities, such as managing the Post Office, Governments do produce saleable services and in these cases it would be appropriate to construct production accounts. However in our imaginary economy we shall assume that the Government provides only general administrative services and shall not draw up a production account. The Government's current account (see Table 5.5) shows that the Government receives

£12 million income tax from households, and £5 million from firms, £7 million sales tax from firm C and £3 million interest from Government investments overseas (i.e. interest from loans to foreigners). Its expenditures consist of £8 million wages and salaries, £6 million

TABLE 5.5

Accounts of Government

Current Account

Expenditure	£m.	Receipts	£m.
Wages and salaries	8	Income tax	
Goods from C	6	from firms	5
Pensions	8	from households	12
Interest	2	Sales tax	7
Current surplus	3	Interest from abroad	3
	—		—
	27		27

Capital Account

Expenditure	£m.	Receipts	£m.
Loan abroad	4	Current surplus	3
Increase in bank deposit	1	Issue of securities	2
	—		—
	5		5

purchases of goods from C, £8 million pension payments, and £2 million interest payments paid to households who hold some of its securities (National Debt). This leaves a current surplus of £3 million.

The Government's capital account shows its funds available for investment comprise the £3 million current surplus and £2 million new borrowing (from £1 million securities bought by households and £1 million bought by the bank). These funds are used to make a £4 million loan abroad (to an overseas Government) and to increase the Government's bank deposits by £1 million.

We have not shown balance sheets for Government or the Personal sector, but they could be constructed on the lines of those of firms.

4. OVERSEAS TRANSACTIONS

The rest of the world is considered as one sector and its accounts record the transactions between the other sectors (the domestic sectors) and the rest of the world—broadly speaking, the transactions of international trade and its finance. These transactions are summarized in a current account and a capital account. We already have contained in the domestic sectors' accounts the information we need for

H

this current account. By convention we treat the expenditures and receipts from the point of view of residents of our economy, i.e. of the

TABLE 5.6

Accounts of the Rest of the World

Current Account

Expenditure	£m.	Receipts	£m.
Imports	26	Exports	30
Remittance abroad	1	Government income from	
Surplus	6	abroad	3
	33		33

Capital Account

Expenditure	£m.	Receipts	£m.
Government loan abroad	4	Current surplus	6
Increase in foreigners'			
bank borrowing	2		
	6		6

domestic sectors. On the expenditure side are the transactions which result in domestic sectors owing payment to the rest of the world: imports by firms A, B and C of £26 million, and households' remittances abroad of £1 million. On the receipts side are transactions which result in the rest of the world owing payment to the domestic sectors: exports to the rest of the world of £30 million, and Government interest from abroad of £3 million. The surplus of what the domestic sectors are owed over what they owe, £6 million, is the *current surplus on the balance of payments*. This is what the rest of the world owes the residents of our economy after the year's transactions have been set off against each other—it is the rest of the world's current deficit with our economy.

The rest of the world's capital account summarizes the methods by which this surplus (or deficit) was financed. The rest of the world received a loan of £4 million from our Government, and was permitted by the bank to increase its overdraft by £2 million: giving a total of £6 million equalling the surplus. Our economy's current surplus *less* any capital grants abroad is called *net investment abroad* (or net overseas investment). In our example there are no capital grants (examples of which would be United States aid to Europe under the post-war European Recovery Programmes) and so our economy's net investment abroad is £6 million.

Net investment abroad is the increase in overseas assets owned by residents of our economy *less* the increase in assets in our economy owned by foreigners. We have shown examples of increases in two types of overseas assets—Government loans to foreigners, and bank loans to foreigners (increase in foreigners' overdraft with our bank). Other types which we have not dealt with are purchases of foreign securities, the acquisition of fixed assets abroad (e.g. by buying a factory or building a factory in an overseas country), and accumulating the currency or money of overseas countries (e.g. by residents of our economy increasing their deposits in the banks in overseas countries or by our Government increasing its holdings of gold and foreign currency). The overseas capital account in reality would summarize all these transactions—some of which of course are not directly concerned with international trade but which represent movements of liquid capital between countries, for purely financial reasons.

5. SECTOR AND NATIONAL ACCOUNTS

In our presentation of household accounts we treated them as those of one Personal sector without going through the preliminary process of building them up from the separate accounts of the individual households. In the case of firms, however, so far we have only presented the accounts of each firm. To show what is involved in the process of consolidation of accounts we shall now present the combined firms' accounts, calling them the accounts of the Company sector.

The accounts record the firms' transactions with other sectors. Transactions between the firms offset each other and are omitted. In the combined production account, for instance, the expenditure side is obtained by listing all expenditures by all firms and the receipts side by listing all receipts of all firms. Inter-firm transactions appear on both sides and are cancelled out, e.g. on the expenditure side is recorded A's purchase of £5 million materials from B; on the receipts side this recorded as a receipt of B—the two entries cancel each other out. The remaining transactions are those outside the Company sector and are shown in Table 5.7 (as well as the transactions in the production account, the trade credit transactions in the capital account cancel out and the change in bank deposits is a net figure).

For our economy we now have a complete set of accounts for the four sectors: Personal, Government, Companies and the Rest of the World. The next step is to derive the estimate of national income from these sector accounts. We shall do this first from the output side, i.e. by adding the net outputs of all productive enterprises. This is not done on a sector basis but on an industrial basis. The industries in our economy are :[1]

Manufacturing (firms A and B)
Distribution (firm C)
Public Administration (Government)

TABLE 5.7

Accounts of Company Sector (combined firms)

Production Account

Expenditure	£m.	Receipts	£m.
Wages and salaries	28	Sales to Government and	
Imports	26	households	38
Stock at end year 0	4	Exports	30
Sales tax	7	Sales of capital equipment	10
Trading profit	18	Stocks at end year 1	5
	—		—
	83		83

Current Account

Expenditure	£m.	Receipts	£m.
Income tax	5	Trading profits	18
Dividends	4		
Depreciation	4		
Undistributed profit	5		
	—		—
	18		18

Capital Account

Expenditure	£m.	Receipts	£m.
Fixed capital formation	10	Depreciation	4
Change in stocks	1	Undistributed profits	5
Net reduction in bank over-		Issue of shares	3
drafts	1		
	—		—
	12		12

The net output of an industry is the value of its gross output *less* the costs of purchased materials. This is identically equal to the incomes of the owners of productive services (factor incomes) generated by production. In the case of service industries such as Distribution and Public Administration net output is normally measured directly as the sum of the factor incomes generated in those industries. The net outputs of the three industries are:

[1] The reader will remember that we assume that the bank produces no net output (or if it does it is included in the net output of Government).

£ million

Manufacturing:

Gross output	70	(total sales of A and B)
less materials	−30	(purchases from A and B and imported materials)
Net output	40	(equal to wages and salaries—£25 million—and trading profits—£15 million)

Distribution:

wages and salaries	3
trading profit	3
Net output	6

Public Administration:

wages and salaries	8
Net output	8

Gross domestic product at factor cost	54

If to GDP(fc) we add net income from abroad (represented in our economy by Government interest receipts from abroad of £3 million) we obtain GNP(fc) of £57 million.

TABLE 5.8

National Income and Expenditure

Expenditure generating gross national product

At market prices	£ million	
Consumers' expenditure	32	Household current account
Public authorities' current expenditure on goods and services	14	Government current account (wages +salaries +goods)
Gross fixed capital formation	10	Company capital account
Value of increase in stocks	1	Company capital account
Total domestic expenditure at market prices	57	
Exports and income from abroad	33	Rest of world current account
less Imports	−26	Rest of world current account
less Taxes on expenditure	− 7	Government current account
Gross national expenditure at factor cost	57	

Shares in the gross national product (factor incomes)

Income from employment	36	Household current account
Gross trading profits of companies	18	Company current account
Gross domestic product at factor cost	54	
Net income from abroad	3	Rest of world current account
Gross national product	57	

The estimates of national income from the expenditure and income sides are shown in Table 5.8. They are arranged in the way they are set out for the United Kingdom in Table 1 of NIE with the corresponding titles. The sector accounts from which the figures are drawn are indicated.

6. COMBINED CAPITAL ACCOUNT

We have shown in section 2 how the capital accounts of firms can be derived from their balance sheets and are to be regarded as showing the changes in firms' assets and liabilities. We did not show this derivation for the Personal sector and Government but the principle is the same for their capital accounts. We now present an analysis of the changes in the assets and liabilities of the whole economy based on the capital accounts. The analysis is shown in Table 5.9.

TABLE 5.9

Changes in Assets and Liabilities

£ million

	Companies		Personal	Govern- ment	Bank	Net Change
	Manufac- turing	Dist'n				
Current Account						
(Saving)	8	1	5	3	0	17
Capital Account						
(a) *Domestic Financial Assets*						
Trade credit	3	−3	0	0	0	0
Domestic Bank Deposits	−2	3	1	1	−3	0
Government securities	0	0	1	−2	1	0
Firms' securities	−3	0	3	0	0	0
Total	−2	0	5	−1	−2	0
(b) *Domestic Capital Formation*						
Fixed Capital Formation	10	0	0	0	0	10
Change in stocks	0	1	0	0	0	1
Total	10	1	0	0	0	11
(c) *Overseas Assets*						
Non-residents' bank deposits	0	0	0	0	2	2
Loan abroad	0	0	0	4	0	4
Total	0	0	0	4	2	6
Net change	8	1	5	3	0	17

[− means a decrease in the assets of a sector].

In the table there is a column for the changes in the assets of each domestic sector—we have distinguished Manufacturing from Distribution to show the changes in more detail. We also include a column for the bank which hitherto we have not explicitly considered. In the first row are listed the savings of each sector. These are the sums carried over from their current accounts into their capital accounts. In the case of firms they include undistributed profits and depreciation allowances. The bank which produces, we assume, no net output has no savings. In the lower half of the table the changes in the assets of each sector are recorded, each different type of asset being separately listed. Manufacturing increases its assets by granting £3 million trade credit, reduces its assets by increasing its overdraft by £2 million, and reduces its assets by issuing £3 million of securities. Thus as far as financial assets are concerned it has increased its liabilities by £2 million. Manufacturing however increases its fixed assets by £10 million, thus the net increase in its assets as a whole is £8 million: which equals its savings. The changes for Distribution, the Personal sector and Government are set out in the same way.

This leaves the column for the bank. Deposits in the bank are a liability of the bank; a bank advance (an overdraft granted to some sector) is a bank asset. Net change in domestic bank deposits is obtained by summing the row for domestic bank deposits: deposits rise (overdrafts fall) by £3 million, thus bank liabilities rise by £3 million. Bank assets rise by the £1 million securities the bank buys from Government, thus the net fall in the bank's domestic assets is £2 million. This is matched by the bank's loan overseas of £2 million (the rest of the world's overdraft at the bank is an asset of the bank). Note that although the bank is only a financial intermediary, the record of its transactions in the table is necessary to give a complete account of the financial and real capital transactions of the economy.

The net change over the whole economy is shown in the final column. Total savings are £17 million. The net change in domestic financial assets is zero because such transactions are merely transfers of assets between the domestic sectors. Investment in fixed capital and stocks is £11 million, and the increase in our economy's ownership of overseas assets (net investment abroad) is £6 million. The net increase in assets equals total saving.

The information shown in the table can be summarized in a combined capital account. This can be derived either by adding the individual sectors' capital accounts (cancelling inter-sector transactions) or by using the top row and final column of Table 5.9. The combined capital account is shown in Table 5.10.

TABLE 5.10

Combined Capital Account

Expenditure	£m.	Receipts	£m.
Fixed capital formation	10	Savings	
Change in stocks	1	of households	5
Net investment abroad	6	of companies	9
		of Government	3
	17		17

7. INPUT-OUTPUT TABLE

The accounts explained in the previous sections comprise the social accounts of our imaginary economy. Together they provide a summary of the transactions of each sector and its relationships with other sectors. They are an organized method of presenting information about the structure of the economy by means of the double classification by sector and economic function. They coincide with the concepts of both business accounting and modern economic theory, and they are more and more becoming the standard form of presenting a large part of the mass of statistical information available nowadays in modern economies.

As well as the accounting form of presentation there is a special tabular form, called an *input-output table*, which we shall now describe. An input-output table records the transactions between industries and sectors, showing who produces goods and services and who uses them. The input-output table for our imaginary economy is shown in Table 5.11.

There is both a column and a row for each industry (we have distinguished our three firms for purposes of illustration), and purchases—inputs—are entered in columns, and sales—outputs—in rows. Thus in column 1, row 2, the entry £5 million means that firm A purchased £5 million of goods from firm B. To total inputs of goods and services (row 6) are added wages and salaries (row 7), trading profits (row 8) and the expenditure taxes levied on an industry's output (row 9) to obtain total inputs.[1]

The rows for the manufacturing industries show, first, to what manufacturing industries a particular manufacturer's goods are sold —the total of these sales is called *intermediate output* (column 5). Secondly, the rows show to what final buyers the remainder of a manufacturer's output is ultimately sold (the distributor is not taken into account here). Thus in row 1 we see that of the output of firm A

---

[1] Note that expenditure taxes are treated as an input of the industry on whose goods they are levied. Subsidies would be treated as a negative input.

TABLE 5.11
Inter-industry Relations
£ million

	Manufacturer A (1)	Manufacturer B (2)	Distribution (3)	Public Administration (4)	Total intermediate output (5)	Households (6)	Government (7)	Fixed capital formation (8)	Change in stocks (9)	Exports (10)	Total final output (11)	Total output (12)
1 Manufacturer A	—	5	0	0	5	24	0	0	−2	5	27	32
2 Manufacturer B	5	—	0	0	5	0	5	10	0	25	40	45
3 Distribution	0	0	—	0	0	5	1	0	0	0	6	6
4 Public Administration	0	0	0	—	0	0	8	0	0	0	8	8
5 Imports	5	15	0	0	20	3	0	0	3	0	6	26
6 Total goods and services	10	20	0	0	30	32	14	10	1	30	87	117
7 Income from employment	10	15	3	8	36	0	0	0	0	0	0	36
8 Gross profits	5	10	3	0	18	0	0	0	0	0	0	18
9 Taxes on expenditure	7	0	0	0	7	0	0	0	0	0	0	7
10 Total input	32	45	6	8	91	32	14	10	1	30	87	178

FINAL BUYERS (columns 6–10)

£24 million goes to households (column 6), £5 million to exports (column 10) and the −£2 million in column 9 represents the reduction in the stocks of A's goods by whoever held them (we know in fact they were held by firm C). Column 11 records total final output, i.e. total purchases by final buyers; and column 12 records total output (sum of columns 5 and 11). The output entries are measured at market prices, hence the value of total output equals the value of total input.

This treatment of manufacturers' output applies to all industries except distribution and transport (represented in our economy by firm C). Such industries which transport and distribute the goods of other industries are treated as if their output is transporting and distributive services, and their inputs are the goods and services required to produce these services—measured in the case of distribution by the retailer's gross markup. Thus the inputs of firm C (column 3) are income from employment and trading profit,[1] and the firm's output (row 3) is its gross markup allocated to final buyers in proportion to their purchases (we have allocated it in accordance with the assumptions made in section 2 above). Note that this treatment of distribution's output fits naturally the definition of its net output given in section 5 above.

The only other point to note about the table is that the output of Public Administration (row 4) is all sold to Government.

Like all accounting methods the input-output table is based on conventions. Provided these are appreciated it gives a very useful picture of the flows of goods and services within an economy, and the types of inter-dependence between industries (which are much greater than is suggested by the example of our imaginary economy). An important use of the table is in calculating the amount of a certain type of input required to produce a certain type of output. This problem is discussed below in Chapter 11.

8. THE SOCIAL ACCOUNTS OF THE UNITED KINGDOM

For the United Kingdom much of the statistical information which we assumed was available in our imaginary economy is either not available or not presented.[2] In this section we explain what social

---

[1] In reality a retailer would have inputs of goods as well, e.g. pencils and paper, bought from other industries.

[2] It is to be expected that more information will become available in the future, and that future editions of NIE will present this information.

accounts for the sectors of the United Kingdom economy are available in NIE.

First, the definition of sectors is inevitably a difficult matter. Ideally, the Personal sector's accounts should include only those transactions of households acting as consumers. In practice, this is impossible because of the impossibility of separating the personal accounts from the business accounts of professional people, farmers and some types of unincorporated business. Thus income of the Personal sector includes *all* the incomes of professional people, farmers and individual traders and partnerships, and this sector's savings include savings that would be better regarded as undistributed profits. For lack of information the Personal sector also includes private non-profit-making bodies such as churches, charities and universities, and the funds of life insurance companies.

The current account of the Personal sector is in Table 2, 1959 NIE, 'personal income and expenditure'. Details of consumers' expenditure are shown in Table 18. The capital account of the Personal sector is in Table 24.[1] Note that it includes amongst the increases in assets the gross fixed capital formation and the increase of stocks of unincorporated business.

For the business sectors of the economy a production account is given only for Public Corporations (Table 30: 'combined operating account').[2] Current accounts ('appropriation accounts') are shown both for Companies in Table 25, with details of company trading profits in Table 29, and for Public Corporations in Tables 31 and 33. There is a capital account for Public Corporations in Tables 32 and 34, and one for Companies (excluding insurance, banking and finance) in Table 27 and for all Companies in Table 46.

The Public Authorities' accounts in NIE are very detailed:

Central Government
  current account: Table 35: 'Revenue account' (with a summary in Table 4 and separate details of National Insurance Funds in Table 37).
  capital account: Table 36.
Local authorities
  current account: Table 38 (with summary in Table 5).
  capital account: Table 39.

---

[1] Discussed in detail in Chapter 6 below.

[2] In this account the *increase* in the value of stocks and work in progress is entered as a *negative* item in the payments column: this is merely a rearrangement of the method of recording stocks adopted in the production account of firm C in Table 5.3 above.

Combined public authorities
current and capital accounts: Tables 40 to 45 (especially Table 41 :
'Analysis of expenditure').

For the Rest of the World only a summary current account is given
in Table 7: 'Transactions with the Rest of the World'.[1]

A summary combined capital account for the whole United Kingdom economy is given in Table 6 (the figures for 1957 are reproduced
in Table 6.1 in the following chapter).[2] Some items are included in the
receipts side which we have not dealt with in our imaginary economy:
'Taxes on capital' (estate duties paid by households to the Central
Government) are deducted from Government saving. They represent
a transfer of assets between domestic sectors—an alternative treatment is to deduct them from personal savings as is done in Table 46.
'Transfers to capital accounts' are certain payments (war damage and
town and country planning compensation) from Government current
accounts into the capital accounts of the sectors which receive them.
'Additions to dividend, interest and tax reserves' are earmarked
personal and business funds which temporarily are available for
investment. 'Capital grants from overseas Government (net)' contains mainly the United Kingdom receipts of aid under the European
Recovery Programme and stops after 1951. 'Stock appreciation' is
subtracted from the receipts side because stock investment on the
expenditure side is recorded as the value of the *physical* increase in
stocks. Note also that savings are 'gross', i.e. they include depreciation allowances, and consequently fixed investment is also recorded
as gross, i.e. it includes all fixed investment whether for replacing or
adding to capital.

In Table 46 summary details of the capital accounts of all sectors
are shown in such a way that 'net acquisition of financial assets *plus*
net overseas investment' is distinguished for each sector. But note
that separate figures for the acquisition of financial assets alone are
not given (this is likely to be one of the ways in which the United
Kingdom social accounts will be improved in future editions of
NIE). Details of gross and net fixed investment and capital consumption are shown in Tables 47 to 57, and investment in stocks in Tables
58 to 60.

In our summary of the capital transactions between sectors in our
imaginary economy (Table 5.9) we introduced separate accounts for

---

[1] The main source of statistics of overseas transactions is not NIE but the
separate balance of payments publications. See Chapter 7 below.

[2] p. 126.

the bank. The bank represented what are usually known as the 'financial intermediaries'—insurance companies, banks, building societies, pension funds, etc.—which in some respects may be regarded as channelling the savings of other sectors into investment. The financial intermediaries will, of course, normally earn income from their services and will save themselves. A complete statement of the capital transactions of an economy should show the loans to or deposits made with the financial intermediaries by the other sectors, and the uses of these funds by the intermediaries. This detailed information is not yet available in the United Kingdom social accounts. The Company sector in both Table 6 and Table 46 includes the financial intermediaries. Table 27, however, gives a summary capital account of companies excluding insurance, banking and finance.

A United Kingdom input-output table for 1954 is shown in Table 18 of the 1958 NIE. (In editions of NIE from 1953 to 1956 a table for 1950 was shown.) The table is constructed on the lines discussed in section 7 above where the special treatment of transport and distribution (and also financial services), of expenditure taxes and subsidies and of stocks was explained. The industries are divided into eleven groups (manufacturing into five). The mixed group 'other industries' (public administration and defence, public health and educational services, ownership of dwellings, etc.) is assumed to sell all its output to either Persons or Public authorities. Row 13 'sales by final buyers' is a small mixed bag including sales by industry of second-hand fixed capital, and various fees paid by Persons to Public authorities for goods and services (National Health prescriptions; public baths; etc.). The use of the table and the supplementary Tables 19 to 24 is discussed below in Chapter 11.[1]

This section has been intended to be a sketch map of the landscape. The student should now browse through NIE, studying each table—particularly those mentioned in this section—and relating it to the system described in this chapter. Practical uses of the information in the social accounts are discussed in several of the following chapters—particularly Chapters 6, 8, 11 and 12.

[1] Note that the 1959 NIE contains no input-output table. Future editions of NIE are likely to contain input-output tables referring to years after 1954.

CHAPTER SIX

Who Saves and Invests?

1. THE SOURCES OF SAVINGS

In this chapter we use the social accounts to answer some questions about saving and investment in the United Kingdom economy. First we examine the contributions to savings made by the sectors. The combined capital account for 1957 from Table 6 of the 1959 NIE is reproduced in Table 6.1. Company savings were the largest source of

TABLE 6.1

Combined Capital Account of the United Kingdom, 1957

RECEIPTS	£ million	PAYMENTS	£ million
Saving:		Gross fixed capital forma-	
Persons	1,359	tion at home	3,400
Companies	1,764	Value of physical increase in	
Public corporations	175	stocks and work in pro-	
Central Government:		gress	360
Surplus on revenue account	611	Net investment abroad	263
less Taxes on capital	−176		
Transfers to capital accounts	82		
Local authorities	163		
Additions to dividend and in-			
terest reserves	35		
Additions to tax reserves	49		
Total national saving, before pro-			
viding for depreciation and			
stock appreciation	4,062		
less Stock appreciation	−100		
Capital transfers from abroad:			
Capital grant from overseas			
Government (net)	—		
Other Central Government re-			
ceipts	4		
Residual error	57		
Total	4,023	Total investment	4,023

Source: 1959 NIE, Table 6.

funds available for investment in 1957, and NIE shows that this has been the case in all years for which figures are available. Personal

savings—which include the savings of unincorporated business—
were nearly as large, but it is only since 1952 that these savings have
been an important proportion of total savings. Between 1948 and
1951 personal savings were between one fifth and one sixth of company savings—the large rise in personal savings after 1951 is one of
the most interesting (and important) changes in economic behaviour
since the war.

The savings of local authorities and public corporations are seen
to be relatively small. Much more important are the savings of the
Central Government although these have declined in proportion
since 1948. Taken together these savings of the public sectors—public
authorities and public corporations—were in 1957 about one quarter
of total savings.

The lower half of Table 6 (right hand side of Table 6.1 above) shows
the uses of these funds. The bulk of them financed gross fixed capital
formation at home, with smaller amounts for investment in stocks
and net investment abroad. The table, of course, is a summary table,
and leaves out the transactions—borrowing and lending—between
sectors. Investment in fixed capital was made by the business sectors
and it is clear that they must, on balance, have borrowed from the
other sectors. To see how each sector disposed of its savings we refer
to Table 46 of NIE.

Table 46 sets out the saving and investment transactions of the
sectors so as to separate the acquisition of financial assets from the
acquisition of physical assets. The borrowing and lending between
domestic sectors should of course add to zero. Unfortunately this can
not be shown as in the present state of the construction of the social
accounts it is impossible to separate the acquisition of domestic
financial assets from net overseas investment (both physical and
financial). However it is possible to see which sectors in the economy
were on balance lending to other sectors and so providing the funds
for the borrowing sectors' investment. In 1957 the sectors which had
a negative entry for 'net acquisition of financial assets *plus* net overseas investment' i.e. which were net borrowers, were public corporations and local authorities. Persons, companies and Central Government were all net lenders. Note also that this situation is typical of
the period since 1951.

The Central Government has obligations to assist the financing of
the investment of public corporations and local authorities—this
partly explains why the Central Government appears as a lender and
the other two sectors as borrowers in the table. (The fact that these
three sectors' finances are inter-related and in the last resort con-

trolled by the Central Government is the reason why in some statistical accounts the three sectors are grouped together as the public sector.) What might be surprising are the facts that in recent years the Personal sector has become such a large acquirer of financial assets, and that Companies—after making a large part of the fixed investment in the economy—are able to acquire on balance financial assets also.[1] Because domestic financial assets are included with net overseas investment in these statistics it is not clear to what extent Companies are lending to other United Kingdom sectors (e.g. by the purchase of Government securities), as distinct from lending abroad. In the following two sections we shall consider the capital accounts of Companies and the Personal sector in more detail.

2. THE PERSONAL SECTOR

We have explained that the accounts of the Personal sector include some of the business transactions of unincorporated business. This is particularly evident in the Personal sector's capital account. This account is given in Table 24 of NIE—the information in the table is not that of a complete account, but is to be regarded as what is known about the Personal sector's capital transactions at the present time. The upper part of the table ('Net increase in assets') shows the sources of funds available for investment, of which the main part is personal savings—the savings of households, or self-employed persons and of the private non-profit-making bodies. The lower half of the table shows what is known about how these funds were invested.

It is important to note that personal savings are estimated as a residual or 'balancing' item—personal income *less* consumers' expenditures. Any item estimated residually will probably contain a greater possible error than an item estimated directly: for this reason it is desirable to make a direct estimation. The statistical value of the accounting system explained in the last chapter is that all totals in the social accounts can be estimated in more than one way. Thus although personal savings are estimated residually, it is theoretically possible to estimate the uses of personal savings directly and hence check the accuracy of the estimate of personal savings. This can not be done at present as we shall see below, but it may be noted that there are other checks on the reliability of the estimate of personal savings. In particular, personal savings are included in the receipts side of the United

[1] Table 46 of course includes the financial intermediaries with companies (see section 8, Chapter 5). The most interesting information is in Table 27 which shows that the non-financial companies have acquired financial assets (and invested abroad) also.

Kingdom combined capital account, and total receipts equal total investment all items of which are estimated directly. Any discrepancy between total receipts and total investment will be partly due to errors in the estimate of personal savings.[1] Table 6 of NIE shows that this discrepancy—the residual error—has been very small in relation to the estimate of personal savings in 1955 to 1957, although it was larger—in the region of 20 per cent—from 1951 to 1954.

We return to the Personal sector's accounts. Table 24 of NIE is summarized and rearranged slightly in Table 6.2. (Another summary form is given in the first column of Table 46 of NIE.) One feature of this presentation is to show in row 5 under 'Use of funds' the size of the change in unidentified items—the difference between the sum of rows 1, 2, 3 and 4, and the total funds available. The unidentified items include: holdings of securities; sales or purchases of second hand fixed assets; bank deposits and trade credits of unincorporated business; currency holdings; and hire purchase credit before 1955. According to the figures in the table, holdings of these unidentified assets were reduced each year from 1948 to 1957. One possible explanation of this is that personal savings which are the main part of total funds available for investment may be consistently underestimated. This is possible, of course, but the large number of items which to date have not been identified, and the size of the residual error in Table 6 of NIE, suggest that consistent underestimation would not account for all the supposed decrease in unidentified assets. Another explanation, which does not rely on statistical deficiencies, is that after the war households were exceptionally liquid—they held large amounts of financial assets which could be easily sold—and since 1948 they have been selling these assets to finance the purchase of other things (such as household durable goods). This explanation would also explain why households did not save much out of current income shortly after the war.

The student should refer to Table 24 of NIE for descriptions and details of the items included under the headings of Table 6.2. Here we shall briefly indicate the main items included under 'Use of funds'. Row 1 includes both employers' and employees' contributions to pension schemes, individual insurance premiums and property income (rent, dividends and interest) of the life assurance funds and superannuation schemes, *less* pensions paid and administrative costs. Row 2 includes the gross investment of unincorporated businesses, together with capital formation in new dwellings. The most important

---

[1] Although all items will have some amount of likely error, personal savings in this account will have the most.

I

TABLE 6.2

Summary Capital Account of the Personal Sector, United Kingdom 1948-57

	1948	1949	1950	1951	1952	1953	1954	1955	1956	1957
Funds available for investment:										
Gross saving	85	204	197	229	663	732	582	856	1,215	1,359
Other items	−133	−234	−233	−261	−125	−116	−134	−130	−116	−157
Total	−48	30	36	32	538	616	448	726	1,099	1,202
Use of funds:										
1 Net increase in funds of life assurance, superannuation schemes, etc.	218	238	270	314	351	386	428	467	505	573
2 Net increase in identified non-financial assets (fixed capital formation and stock investment)	268	282	304	351	301	416	521	595	612	661
3 Net increase in identified financial assets (other than life assurance, etc. funds)	162	126	82	65	101	197	385	313	334	404
4 less Increase in identified debt	−106	−121	−119	−119	−130	−158	−213	−259	−111	−256
5 plus Decrease in unidentified items*	−590	−495	−501	−579	−85	−225	−673	−390	−241	−180
Total (net increase in assets)	−48	30	36	32	538	616	448	726	1,099	1,202

* Residual or balancing item (includes errors and omissions).

Source: 1959 NIE, Table 24.

items in row 3 are changes in personal bank deposits and deposits with building societies, and changes in savings bank deposits. Row 4 includes hire purchase debt (since 1955) and loans from insurance companies, local authorities and building societies.

In view of the incomplete nature of Table 24 of NIE a thorough analysis of the savings and changes in assets of the Personal sector can not be made at present. The table does however draw attention to some important feature of the behaviour of households as a group. For example, from 1955-7 about half of personal savings was used to pay insurance premiums and contribute to pension schemes and the like (although this is not conclusive evidence of savings *habits* because a large part of the contributions to pensions funds are made by employers—these contributions are included in personal savings). Also, if we regard the £323 million invested in 1957 by unincorporated business in fixed capital (NIE, Table 24) as showing the approximate size of unincorporated business's savings, and deduct this as well as employers' contributions to pension schemes (NIE, Table 24) from personal savings, the resulting figure of about £500 million for the rest of the savings of ordinary households and the non-profit-making bodies does not appear impressively large—about £10 for each man, woman and child in 1957.

At the end of the last section we remarked on the fact that the Personal sector had, on balance, acquired financial assets on a relatively large scale during the last few years. Our information is still incomplete, but it is clear that the assets are mainly life assurance and pension funds, and (of lesser importance) deposits with building societies and banks.

3. THE COMPANY SECTOR

The information given in the 1958 NIE about the savings and investment position of companies is the capital account (excluding insurance, banking and finance) in the lower half of Table 27 and the account for all companies in Table 46. These are presented in summary form with little detail. Their main interest is that they show that for the non-financial[1] companies as a group undistributed profits and reserve funds have been amply sufficient in recent years to finance investment in fixed capital at home and stocks. In fact, in each year between 1948 and 1957 companies have had a surplus, over and above the funds needed for investment at home, to acquire financial assets and invest abroad. This conclusion does not mean that acquiring

[1] Excluding insurance, banking and finance.

financial assets and investing abroad are what a company does with 'surplus' funds—these actions may be positive actions in the forefront of a company's plans. Nor does the conclusion mean that all or even most companies had sufficient ploughed-back profits to finance investment—we only know the over-all picture from the summary statistics.

We have not got separate figures of company investment abroad. If we compare the figures of net investment abroad by *all* United Kingdom sectors given in the current balance of payments (Table 7 in NIE) with the net acquisition of financial assets *plus* net investment abroad of non-financial companies in Table 27, we see that from 1951 to 1955 the latter figure is greater than the first, indicating that at least in these years companies were almost certainly acquiring financial assets over and above their investment abroad.[1]

It has been suggested that these statistics are evidence that companies are 'highly liquid'—they have surplus funds which they keep as cash or bank deposits, or use to purchase securities. It is further argued that this liquidity is excessive: showing either that prices and profits are too high, or that fixed investment is too low; and rendering a tight money policy ineffective because of the company sector's independence of the money markets.

The truth of this important matter is not at all clear. As we have seen, the position of investment abroad is uncertain. It is not known to what class of companies the accusation should be made. Nor is there any clear criterion for judging excess liquidity—large holdings of liquid funds may reflect anything from unnatural caution to a sensible provision for seasonal demands on finance.

There are other sources of information besides the NIE statistics. The balance sheets of individual companies provide details of financial activities, and the National Institute of Economic and Social Research, followed by the Board of Trade, now present analyses of the finance of public companies whose shares are quoted on the Stock Exchanges.[2] The profits of these companies are about 60 per cent of all company profits, and their output is about 53 per cent of total manufacturing output. They are, of course, the larger companies. The statistics are published in ET, Nos. 52 (February 1958) and

[1] We only say 'almost certainly' because as the foreign investment is net there is the possibility that foreign investment in the United Kingdom may have offset company investment abroad.

[2] Public in this context refers of course to registered limited liability companies whose shares are open to the public, i.e. anybody's, subscription. It does not refer to public corporations, i.e. the nationalized industries.

64 (February 1959). An appropriation (current) account, a summary of the balance sheet, and a capital account (called 'Sources and Uses of Capital Funds') are shown, with separate details for those companies engaged in manufacturing.

From these accounts it emerges that in most years between 1949 and 1956 (the years for which figures are available) quoted companies have been *net borrowers*, i.e. their savings have been insufficient to finance their own investment (see Table C, ET No. 64, p. iv). From this it follows that it is the unquoted companies, including the private companies and the smaller companies, which have been the net lenders—although there is nothing to suggest that they have lent to the quoted companies directly.

TABLE 6.3

Liquidity Ratios of Quoted Companies, 1948-56

Ratios	1948	1949	1950	1951	1952	1953	1954	1955	1956
Current assets to current liabilities	2·13	2·17	2·21	2·13	2·23	2·33	2·33	2·28	2·20
Liquid assets[1] to current liabilities	1·15	1·17	1·18	1·05	1·13	1·23	1·23	1·18	1·10
Liquid assets[2] to current liabilities	0·56	0·55	0·53	0·42	0·45	0·53	0·51	0·44	0·37

[1] Including trade and other debtors.
[2] Excluding trade and other debtors.

Note: *Current assets:* stocks and work in progress, trade and other debtors, marketable securities, tax reserve certificates, cash.
     Liquid assets: Current assets *less* stocks and work in progress.
     Current liabilities: bank overdrafts and loans, trade and other creditors, dividends and interest due, current taxation, provisions.

Sources: ET, Nos. 52 and 64; *Company Income and Finance*, 1949-53 (*NIESR* 1957).

The liquidity position of the quoted companies can be analysed from their balance sheets. In Table 6.3 information about liquidity is presented as the ratio of current (and liquid) assets to current liabilities. The liquid asset ratios are the more relevent: they represent the proportion of current claims on the companies covered by cash or easily realizable assets. Consider the first two ratios in the table. In 1955 and 1956 these ratios were about the same as those of 1948 to 1950. In 1951 and 1952 they were lower; in 1953 and 1954 they were markedly higher. There is no evidence that quoted companies became progressively more liquid over the entire eight year period. The higher liquidity of 1953-4 is not necessarily significant: 1952 was a year of depressed business in many parts of the economy, and it is to be expected that companies would make efforts to increase their liquidity; these efforts may have needed time to be effective, by which time business had recovered in 1954 and—because of the time lags— liquidity was accidentally high.

If trade and other debtors are excluded from liquid assets—while trade credit is a current asset (or liability) it is not necessarily highly liquid (firms as well as households do not always pay their bills)—it is seen in the third ratio in the table that only half the value of current liabilities are covered by the remaining liquid assets. Without knowledge of the payment habits of firms it is very difficult to interpret the significance of such information, but it does not seem on this count that the companies are excessively liquid—in fact, the second liquid asset ratio has tended to decline over time.

The statistics of the finances of quoted companies contain valuable information about a wide range of matters. Here we draw the attention of the student to the importance of trade credit in business finance. Of the total current assets (£7,928 million) of the quoted companies at the end of 1956, £2,609 million was represented by trade debtors (unpaid accounts owed to the companies). Of total current liabilities of £3,604 million, trade creditors (unpaid accounts owed by the companies) were £2,050 million. Bank overdrafts and loans (lent to the companies) were small in relation to these sums— £444 million. One interesting feature of these statistics is that the quoted companies gave more trade credit than they received—they gave net trade credit of £559 million to other parts of the economy (slightly more than their outstanding bank overdrafts and loans). It is clear that trade credit is an important source of finance, and that the quoted (larger) companies are an important provider of short-term finance to other parts of the economy. All the statistics quoted in this paragraph are from Table 1.B, ET No. 64, February 1959, p. viii.

4. FIXED INVESTMENT AND CAPITAL CONSUMPTION

Gross fixed capital formation at home absorbed slightly more than 16 per cent of GNP in 1957 (see Table 11 of NIE). This total includes the fixed investment of public authorities, public corporations, companies, the unincorporated businesses included in the Personal sector and new private dwellings. The student should note the definition of fixed investment in the Personal sector's capital account. Generally, it means the increase in productive physical assets such as houses, factories, machinery and equipment, vehicles and roads. It does not include the purchase of durable household equipment (such as cookers and washing machines) and furniture, nor does it include cars bought by households. The ordinary householder may think of such purchases as investments, but in the national income accounts they are regarded as current consumers' expenditures. For those economists who think it is misleading to treat the purchase of a new house as fixed investment but the purchase of furniture to go in it as not, enough information is available in NIE to allow them to rearrange the accounts to suit their own tastes. The difficulty is to know where to draw the line between what is to be called fixed investment and what is to be called a current expenditure. Is clothing capital equipment?[1]

There is another problem of definition arising from the measurement of fixed investment. The distinction between a stock of capital and the flow of income which it produces in co-operation with labour and other services, is familiar to economists. Also, as we pointed out in Chapter 4, it is accepted that income should be measured after allowance has been made for any capital used up in the production of the income, i.e. true or net income is gross income *less* capital consumption. The same reasoning shows that total fixed investment, or total expenditures on productive physical assets during any period, can not be regarded as the addition to the stock of capital, for part of the fixed investment is used to replace the capital consumed during the period. The addition to the stock of capital, or *net investment*, is gross fixed capital formation *less* capital consumption.

To estimate both national income and net capital formation it is necessary to measure capital consumption. There is no simple way of doing this, and the statisticians adopt a conventional procedure which is based upon business depreciation accounting practices. It is assumed that a new fixed asset will have a certain productive life. Each year during this lifetime the value of the asset declines by a certain amount due to wear and tear and loss of efficiency, and the amount of the annual fall in value is regarded as the capital consumption. The estimate is first made in the prices of the year in which the asset was bought or installed, and then the figure of capital consumption is revalued at the prices of similar assets in the year the capital is consumed. The estimate is thus one of the current cost of replacing fixed capital currently used up in production. (Business depreciation practices for tax purposes are based on historical cost.)

---

[1] In the measurement of the concepts of economic theory these questions of classification are important. For example, the size and variation over time of the marginal propensity to consume (the proportion of an increment of income spent on consumption goods) depends upon whether durable consumers' goods are treated as consumption or investment.

These estimates are more controversial than any others in the national income framework. The issues are over both their reliability and their meaning. In the matter of reliability, it can be argued that the assumed annual reduction in the value of an asset does not—by the methods adopted—satisfactorily reflect the reduction in the efficiency of the asset. Until more methods have been tried this matter can not be settled. As far as meaning is concerned, it can be doubted whether there is any use in knowing the present cost of replacing a certain type of asset when that asset may not be replaced by a similar asset at all. We shall not go further into these matters beyond pointing out that many economists prefer to avoid using the estimates of national income and net capital formation and instead use GNP and gross capital formation.

Figures of net fixed capital formation, by type of asset and sector, in both current and 1954 prices, are shown in Tables 54 and 55 of NIE. Tables 56 and 57 give the corresponding estimates of capital consumption. These estimates show that more than half of the gross fixed capital formation in 1957 replaced currently consumed capital. If we grant that the replacing assets were more efficient than the replaced assets (allowing for differences in age) because of technical improvements, then the proportion of *productive capacity* replaced to productive capacity installed could be much less than one half.

Figures for the statutory depreciation allowances for tax purposes are given in a table on p. 76 of NIE. Note that firms may in fact set aside more or less than these statutory allowances, and may invest more or less than them in fixed capital in the years to which they refer.

5. A WARNING ABOUT REVISED ESTIMATES

The fact that the main aggregates such as GDP and national income are estimated in three different ways reduces the possibility of large error in the social accounts. However, the estimation of individual items in the main aggregates is likely to involve some error which in some cases may be very large. This is particularly true of the preliminary estimates of a year which appear in the following April.[1] Subsequently, revisions are made as more and better information becomes available. The process of revision may continue over some years and successive editions of NIE will show the changes. These revisions seldom alter the original estimate of the main aggregates by more

[1] The preliminary estimates are published in a White Paper entitled 'Preliminary Estimates of National Income and Expenditure' and also in the annual 'Economic Survey'.

than 1 per cent; they do however considerably alter the original estimates of component items, especially of expenditures. The student is warned that if provisional estimates for any year show small differences (of less than about 2 per cent) from the estimates of the previous year, conclusions based on these small differences must not be considered as important or significant. It is also sensible to adopt the habit of comparing successive editions of NIE to see what major revisions have been made.

The provisional expenditure estimates which are most likely to be revised are those of investment in stocks. As an illustration we shall consider the worst example on record—the successive revisions to the figures of the value of physical increase in stocks and work in progress in 1954. The estimates are shown in Table 6.4. The first estimate,

TABLE 6.4

Estimates of Investment in Stocks, 1954

£ million

Source	Value of physical increase in stocks and work in progress		
	1954	1953	Change between 1953 and 1954
1 Economic Survey, March 1955 (based on a quarterly inquiry into stocks)	175	125	+50
2 NIE, August 1955 (based on provisional results of 1954 Census of Production)	225	125	+100
3 Economic Survey, March 1956	125	125	0
4 NIE, August 1956	75	125	−50
5 NIE, August 1957	50	125	−75

based upon a Board of Trade quarterly inquiry into the stocks held by a sample of manufacturers and some other sectors, showed that stock investment in 1954 was £175 million, or £50 million more than stock investment in 1953. The second estimate some months later (in the 1955 NIE) was based on the first returns of the 1954 Census of Production: this estimate was greater than the previous one. But after that, as more complete information from the Census became available, the estimate was reduced, until the 1957 NIE gave a figure for stock investment in 1954 of only £50 million, indicating a *reduction* between 1953 and 1954 of £75 million. Subsequently the figures have not been revised.

We have two observations to make here. First, stock investment is calculated from the difference in the value of stocks at two dates. It is estimated that the total value of stocks held at the end of 1953 was

£7,500 million. The range of the estimates of stock investment in 1954 shown in Table 6.4 is £225 million—£50 million=£175 million. This range is only 2 per cent of the total value held at the end of 1953. Considering it is derived from the differences of independent estimates—and thus combines any errors in those independent estimates—it can be argued that it is hard to be more accurate.

Second, we have remarked above in Chapter 4 that the national income estimates are used in the framing of Government economic policy. It is likely that the information given to the Chancellor of the Exchequer in early 1955—showing that it was likely that stock investment in 1954 had been high, and that industry had sufficient reserves of raw materials, etc.—influenced the decisions not to adopt a deflationary policy in the April 1955 budget. In fact, stocks were low and industry was in the process of increasing its imports of raw materials which eventually strained the United Kingdom balance of payments (see section 2, Chapter 7, below). This example is not used here to suggest that erroneous estimates of stock investment caused the 1955 crisis—that was an extremely difficult situation to analyse, and erroneous stock investment estimates were only one of a number of difficulties that faced economists and statesmen. However we do use the example to show that preliminary estimates based on incomplete information contain a large error whose nature is unknown, and that students of the economic situation must bear this in mind. The deficiencies of these official statistics which became apparent in 1955 and 1956 resulted in decisions to collect more and better information about stocks and investment in stocks which is now being incorporated in the official estimates.

6. EXERCISES

(1) According to Table 53 in 1959 NIE, fixed investment in many manufacturing industries stopped rising (and in some cases fell) in 1952 and 1953. Is there any evidence of a fall in company profits at that time which may have checked investment? [HINT: use the statistics of company trading profits by industry, Table 29 in NIE.]

(2) What part did the Central Government play in financing investment during the years 1948 to 1957? [HINT: use Tables 6 and 36 of NIE. Distinguish between the Government's own fixed investment and its grants and loans to other sectors. Note the changes in policy evident in the figures from time to time, e.g. the reduced current surplus after 1952 and the increased lending to public corporations after 1953.]

(3) What proportion of the national income was devoted to net

fixed capital formation in each of the years 1938 and 1948-57? [HINT:
use the constant price estimates (for 1938 use the 1957 NIE). Note
that it was not until 1953 that the 1938 level of net fixed investment
was exceeded—largely due to the relatively low level of investment
in dwellings.]

(4) What proportion of company fixed investment is financed by
the issue of share and loan capital? [HINT: this can not be answered
from NIE, but for quoted companies it can be answered from the
NIESR and Board of Trade statistics in ET, No. 64, February 1959,
Table 1C, p. ix: 'Sources and uses of capital funds'. Use figures of
receipts from issue of loan and share capital, and expenditure on
tangible fixed assets.]

CHAPTER SEVEN

United Kingdom Transactions with the Rest of the World

1. THE BALANCE OF PAYMENTS

In the social accounting system (described in Chapter 5) the rest of the world is treated as a sector alongside the domestic sectors. In NIE an account of the rest of the world's current transactions with the domestic sectors is presented (Table 7); this is usually described as the United Kingdom balance of payments on current account.[1] The balance of payments is reproduced in a slightly rearranged form

TABLE 7.1

United Kingdom Balance of Payments on Current Account, 1957

£ *millions*

UNITED KINGDOM DEBITS		UNITED KINGDOM CREDITS	
Imports of merchandise	3,573	Exports and re-exports of merchandise	3,515
Other imports of goods and services	860	Other exports of goods and services	1,033
Property income paid abroad	458	Property income received from abroad	689
Imports and income paid abroad	4,891		
Current transfers:		Exports and income received from abroad	5,237
To persons (net)	50		
To overseas governments and international organizations	58	Current transfers from overseas governments	21
Investment and financing:		Other central government receipts	4
Net investment abroad	263		
less Capital grants from overseas governments (net)	—		
Total investment and financing (surplus on current account)	263		
Total	5,262	Total	5,262

Source: Table 7, 1959 NIE.

[1] The expressions *external* or *overseas* balance of payments are sometimes used to show that the payments are between the United Kingdom and overseas countries.

in Table 7.1. On the left of the table (United Kingdom debits) are entered all current transactions which involve the United Kingdom in making a payment (or incurring a debt) to the rest of the world; on the right hand side (United Kingdom credits) are those transactions which involve the rest of the world making a payment (or incurring a debt) to the United Kingdom. The difference between total receipts (credits) and total payments (debits) is the *surplus on current account*. This surplus *plus* net capital grants from abroad such as aid received under the European Recovery Programmes) is called *net investment abroad*. Note that there have been no net capital grants since 1951.

The items in the current account fall into three groups. The first contains those concerned with ordinary trade: merchandise imports and exports; and 'other imports and exports of goods and services'— payments for shipping, travel and Government current expenditures abroad. The balance of the items in this first group is sometimes called the *balance of trade*. The second group is the current transfers (e.g. personal remittances abroad). The third is property income— rent, interest, profits and dividends paid to and received from overseas: the United Kingdom receives a net income from abroad.[1] The situation shown in Table 7.1 is one where the debits and credits in the first and second groups almost balance (i.e. trade and current transfers balance), and net income from abroad is about the same size as net investment abroad—in terms of real income, the United Kingdom reinvested abroad her net income from abroad.[2]

If the United Kingdom has a surplus on current account in any year foreigners through the ordinary processes of trade and transfer have on balance incurred debts with the United Kingdom. Thus the United Kingdom has on balance invested abroad. In Chapter 5 we explained that this investment can take various forms, and that it is one of the items in the United Kingdom combined capital account. Table 7 of NIE does not give details of net investment abroad, nor does it show how the investment was financed (except in the accounting sense that it equals the current surplus). For the details it is necessary

---

[1] In other sources (including the Treasury balance of payment statistics discussed below) merchandise imports and exports are called *visible* items, and the rest of the items in the three groups *invisibles*. For the national income estimates income from abroad has to be distinguished from the other invisibles in order that GDP can be estimated from the expenditure side and GNP from the income and output sides (see Chapter 4).

[2] The interested student may note that this situation appears to be the same as in the century before 1914. The magnitude of the items, and the ratio of net investment to exports, was different in 1957 from earlier years.

to refer to the Balance of Payments statistics prepared by the United Kingdom Treasury. These statistics are published in several sources:

Balance of Payments White Paper (half-yearly, giving annual figures since 1946 and half-yearly figures for recent years).

HM Treasury: *United Kingdom Balance of Payments, 1946-57* (HMSO, 1959) (full statistics for the years 1946-57, with definitions and notes on basic sources).

AAS (summary of the White Paper statistics).

MDS (a small selection of the White Paper statistics).

ET (summary of White Paper statistics, and—beginning in No. 69 of July 1959—quarterly statistics as from the 1st quarter of 1958).

The most recent figures in all these publications must always be regarded as provisional and liable to be revised.

The Treasury Balance of Payment statistics are arranged under six headings (see Table 1, *United Kingdom Balance of Payments, 1946-57*, pp. 16-17):

A. *Current account:* visible trade (imports and exports of merchandise); invisibles (services and current transfers). This account is similar to that shown in Table 7.1 above, and the balance is the current surplus.

B. *Special grants:* these are the capital grants, such as American aid, shown in Table 7.1 above.

C. *Long-term capital account:* inter-Governmental loans to and by the United Kingdom; United Kingdom subscriptions to international organizations; 'other long-term capital (net)', i.e. net long-term investment (both public and private) by the United Kingdom in the rest of the world.

D. *Monetary movements:* changes in the holdings of sterling by overseas countries and international organizations (these holdings include United Kingdom bank deposits and securities); the United Kingdom balance with the European Payments Union; changes in the gold and dollar reserves; and 'miscellaneous capital (net)', i.e. identified capital transactions, not included elsewhere, mainly of a short-term, monetary nature such as changes in foreign currency balances held by banks and oil companies.

E. *Inter-area transfers:* these are not included in the general balance of payments but in tables for the United Kingdom balance with areas of the world allowance has to be made for transactions which affect the regional disposition of the United Kingdoms' assets and liabilities, e.g. South African sales of gold (for sterling) to the United Kingdom.

Items B, C, D and E are to be regarded as showing the ways in which the current surplus is financed, together with other monetary transactions which may not be directly connected with trading transactions as such (e.g. a change in overseas holdings of sterling may be due to the desire of foreigners to sell sterling to buy Swiss francs because they think it safer to hold francs).

F. *Balancing item:* the difference between the current surplus (A) and the identified sources of its finance and other monetary movements (B+C+D+E). It is the net total of errors and omissions from the other items, and includes both current and capital items.

The balance of payments for 1957 according to this arrangement is set out in Table 7.2. The student should note the convention about signs which can be confusing: the rule is that all the items in the table should sum to zero. To achieve this, under headings A and B a receipt of the United Kingdom (or payment owed to the United Kingdom) has a positive sign; in C, D and F an increase in United Kingdom assets (e.g. United Kingdom lending abroad) or a decrease in United Kingdom liabilities (e.g. a reduction of foreigners' holdings of sterling) is shown with a negative sign. The over-all picture can best be seen when the items are arranged in the form of a capital account (sources and uses of funds). This we have done in summary form at the end of Table 7.2. In 1957 the funds available to the United Kingdom consisted of (*a*) the current balance, (*b*) net miscellaneous investment by foreigners in the United Kingdom (item 12: it is positive indicating that the United Kingdom is borrowing), (*c*) credit granted to the United Kingdom through the medium of the European Payments Union (item 14: positive sign showing United Kingdom borrowing), and (*d*) the balancing item which as it was positive in 1957 is to be considered as an increase in United Kingdom liabilities (United Kingdom borrowing). The ways in which these funds were used were (i) net long-term investment abroad by the United Kingdom (sum of items 9 and 11: negative indicating United Kingdom lending), (ii) a reduction in foreigners' holdings of sterling—foreigners sold sterling in exchange for gold or foreign currencies (item 13: negative showing a reduction in United Kingdom liabilities), and (iii) increase in the United Kingdom's holdings or foreign currency and gold (items 15 and 16).

Thus in 1957 the United Kingdom used her current surplus together with foreigners' loans to her (these loans being mainly of a short-term nature) for three purposes: to make long-term investments abroad, to reduce her short-term liabilities represented by

TABLE 7.2

United Kingdom Balance of Payments, 1957

GENERAL BALANCE OF PAYMENTS

				£ million
A.		Current Account		
		Visible trade		
	1	(a) Imports (f.o.b.)	3,573	
		(b) Exports and re-exports (f.o.b.)	3,517	
		TOTAL		−56
		Invisibles		
	2	Government (a) debits	−248	
		(b) credits	+105	
	3	Shipping (a) debits	−444	
		(b) credits	+554	
	4	Interest, profits and dividends (a) debits	−251	
		(b) credits	+361	
	5	Travel (a) debits	−146	
		(b) credits	+129	
	6	Migrants' funds, legacies and private gifts (net)	− 33	
	7	Other (net)	+301	
		TOTAL		+328
		CURRENT BALANCE		+272
B.	8	Special Grants		—
C.		Long-Term Capital Account		
	9	(a) Inter-governmental loans by United Kingdom (net)	+ 13	
		(b) Inter-governmental loans to United Kingdom (net)	+ 59	
	11	Other long-term capital (net)	−280	
		BALANCE OF LONG-TERM CAPITAL		−208
		BALANCE OF CURRENT AND LONG-TERM CAPITAL TRANSACTIONS		+64
D.		Monetary Movements		
	12	Miscellaneous capital (net)	+ 10	
	13	Overseas sterling holdings of:		
		(a) countries	−151	
		(b) IMF	+ 2	
		(c) other non-territorial organizations	− 26	
	14	United Kingdom balance in EPU	+ 11	
	15	United Kingdom official holdings of non-dollar currencies	− 22	
	16	Gold and dollar reserves	− 13	
		TOTAL		−189
F.	19	Balancing item		+125
				−64

Summary of General Balance of Payments:

UNITED KINGDOM CAPITAL ACCOUNT WITH REST OF WORLD

Sources of Funds (Increase in Liabilities)	£ million	Uses of Funds (Increase in Assets)	£ million
Current balance	272	Net long-term investment	208
Net miscellaneous investment	10	Reduction in overseas sterling	
Balance in EPU	11	holdings	175
Errors and omissions (balancing item)	125	Increase in currency and gold	35
	418		418

Source: Table 1, *United Kingdom Balance of Payments*, 1946-57 (HMSO, 1959)

Note: The numbers of the items are those used in the source. The summary capital account is not in the source, but is obtained by rearranging the balance of payments figures.

overseas holdings of sterling, and to increase by a modest amount her gold and foreign currency reserves. Note that the large size of the balancing item in relation to the other items makes a precise statement about the changes in short-term lending and borrowing impossible.

2. THE UNITED KINGDOM CURRENT ACCOUNT SINCE 1946

Table 7.3 shows the United Kingdom balance on current account with each of the regions into which countries are grouped in the official statistics. The names of the regions are self-explanatory, but the student should refer to one of the official publications listed above for the definitions.

There was an improvement in the current surplus up to 1950, since when the annual surplus has been about £200 million except in the years 1951 and 1955. This surplus of about £200 million is about the same size as net long-term capital investment abroad in recent years (see Table 7.4). (Before 1952 the official statistics do not distinguish long-term investment from monetary movements.) Thus after 1950 the United Kingdom was earning a current surplus which she was investing abroad. The regional pattern shows that in most years there was a large surplus with the rest of the sterling area which had to be offset against other regional deficits—especially with the dollar area. However since 1952 the dollar deficit has declined markedly (except in 1955).

Table 7.4 records the capital and monetary movements which accompanied these current transactions from 1952 to 1957. In 1952 foreigners reduced their holdings of sterling and consequently the

K

TABLE 7.3
United Kingdom Balance on Current Account by Regions, 1946-57

£ million (credit +; debit −)

	1946	1947	1948	1949	1950	1951	1952	1953	1954	1955	1956	1957
Rest of sterling area	− 26	+128	+256	+299	+283	+320	+348	+152	+267	+214	+306	+360
Dollar area	−299	−506	−241	−291	− 79	−427	−166	+ 8	− 60	−184	− 2	− 89
Other western hemisphere countries	− 24	− 65	− 38	+ 62	+ 26	+ 5	+ 93	− 24	+ 8	+ 2	+ 5	+ 25
OEEC countries	+ 78	+ 1	+ 79	− 22	+104	−209	− 42	+ 72	+ 26	− 54	− 62	− 25
Other non-sterling countries	− 16	+ 12	− 40	− 6	− 32	− 99	—	− 15	− 21	− 45	+ 18	+ 3
Non-territorial organizations	− 8	− 12	− 9	− 4	− 5	− 9	− 6	− 14	− 9	− 6	− 7	− 2
TOTAL	−295	−442	+ 7	+ 38	+297	−419	+227	+179	+211	− 73	+258	+272

Source: *United Kingdom Balance of Payments, 1946-57*, Table 9.

TABLE 7.4

Long-term Capital and Monetary Movements, 1952-7

£ million (increase in United Kingdom liabilities +; increase in United Kingdom assets —)

	1952	1953	1954	1955	1956	1957
C. Long-term Capital Account						
9 Net inter-governmental loans	—	— 31	— 20	— 53	— 51	+ 72
11 Other long-term capital (net)	—180	—210	—220	—130	—190	—280
BALANCE OF LONG-TERM CAPITAL	—180	—241	—240	—183	—241	—208
Balance of current and long-term capital transactions	+ 47	— 62	— 29	—256	+ 17	+ 64
D. Monetary Movements						
12 Miscellaneous capital (net)	+ 60	+ 30	+ 10	+ 60	— 70	+ 10
13 Overseas sterling holdings of:						
(a) countries	—358	+274	+210	—127	—155	—151
(b) IMF	—	— 56	— 40	—	+202	+ 2
(c) other non-territorial organizations	+ 1	—	+ 5	—	+ 2	+ 26
14 United Kingdom balance in EPU	+ 53	— 21	— 78	+ 1	+ 4	+ 11
15 United Kingdom official holdings of non-dollar currencies	— 26	+ 30	— 3	—	— 1	— 22
16 Gold and dollar reserves (increase —; decrease +)	+175	—240	— 87	+229	— 42	— 13
TOTAL	— 95	+ 17	+ 17	+156	— 64	—189
F. 19 Balancing Item	+ 48	+ 45	+ 12	+100	+ 47	+125

Source: *United Kingdom Balance of Payments*, 1946-57, Table 1.

United Kingdom gold and dollar reserves declined. In 1953 and 1954 the reverse movement occurred and foreign currencies flowed back to the United Kingdom. Note that these movements were much greater than the movement required to balance the small surplus or deficit remaining after long-term investment is set against the current surplus ('balance of current and long-term capital transactions')—indicating that these movements were concerned with the safety of holding sterling.

In 1955 there was a current deficit, and although long-term investment declined, a large reduction in the reserves ensued. Foreigners sold sterling in 1955 and again in 1956 and 1957. The threat to the gold and dollar reserves that these sales implied was reduced by the improvement in the current balance in 1956 and the purchase in 1956 of dollars from the International Monetary Fund (shown in Table 7.4 as an increase in the IMF's holding of sterling). This brief description of the United Kingdom balance of payments position in recent years is intended to show the sort of analysis that can be made from these figures. It should however be supplemented and confirmed by other evidence of the history of these years, e.g. reports in the financial journals and newspapers of the nature and circumstances of the transactions with the IMF in 1956.

Even the above brief survey allows us to speculate upon a matter that exercises many economists and statesmen these days: the size of Britain's gold and dollar reserves. It is frequently argued that the size of these reserves—the most liquid international assets—is not large enough for Britain to escape the consequences of periodic deficits on current account and sales of sterling holdings that are inevitable in her position as a large international trader and banker. The guidance of economic policy—it is argued—would be so much easier if only the reserves were larger. This is quite true, but it is doubtful if Britain alone can do anything about it. As our brief analysis shows, the normal current surplus of recent years is used to finance long-term investment abroad—on balance there has been hardly anything which could be used to add to the reserves. Now, we may take it as obvious that the reason why overseas countries accept British investment is because they can not pay in cash or in kind for the British goods they require—this is to say that it is more than likely that the size of the United Kingdom current surplus in normal years depends upon the amount of British long-term investment. As the one is the financial counterpart of the other statistically, so it is in reality. This situation appears to have been typical of the period beginning with the early 1950's, and we may expect that the structure of the economy is adjusted to it—by structure we mean the proportion of resources used by the exporting industries and the proportion of resources imported from abroad. Consequently to increase the size of the current surplus would require large structural changes—a substitution of imports by home produced goods (which unfortunately would reduce the ability of foreigners to pay us for our exports) or the creation of a situation where we could encroach upon the markets of our competitors (which may result in retaliation). None of the ways we can increase our reserves single-handed is easy, nor would it be without cost and risk, nor could it take place in a short period of time. Without doubt, international measures—such as short-term lending by the IMF—are more practicable.

The student will observe that the argument of the preceding paragraph depends at several points on facts—some of which we have verified, some of which we have not. It illustrates the importance both of reliable information and its sensible interpretation in the ability to appreciate economic problems and form policy. In particular it shows how important it is to have knowledge of the forms of overseas investment—unfortunately this is one sphere where the official statistics are deficient.

3. EXERCISES

(1) Why did the United Kingdom balance on current account become a deficit in 1955? [HINT: use Table 1, *United Kingdom Balance of Payments, 1946-57*, (or a recent White Paper). The current balance fell by £284 million between 1954 and 1955. The most important item causing this fall was the rise in merchandise imports of £412 million. For details of imports (and exports) use the Trade and Navigation Accounts (December 1955). *Note:* the import and export statistics in the balance of payments tables differ from those in the Trade Accounts. The latter value imports to include insurance and freight charges—in the former insurance and freight charges are included separately as invisible trade. Also, the trade statistics record *shipments;* the balance of payments records payments which may be made before or after shipment: thus discrepancies between the sources must be expected. Such discrepancies, however, do not prevent the joint use of the different sources in this exercise.]

(2) Why did the United Kingdom current balance improve in 1956? [HINT: consider the regional pattern of exports.]

(3) To what areas of the world has British long-term investment been directed since 1946? [HINT: use Tables 2 to 9 in *United Kingdom Balance of Payments, 1946-57* (or a recent White Paper).]

(4) There was a series of crises of confidence in sterling from 1955 to 1957. What effect did these crises have upon overseas sterling holdings and what holders were influenced by them? [HINT: as well as the half-yearly figures of sterling holdings in the White Papers, there are statistics (for the end of each quarter) in ET and MDS. See September 1959 MDS, Tables 156 and 157; and May 1958 ET for a description of the statistics.] What effect did the crises have upon the gold and dollar reserves? [HINT: the White Papers and the AAS contain reserves statistics for the end of each quarter (expressed in both sterling and dollars); the MDS gives end of month figures (in sterling).]

CHAPTER EIGHT

International Comparisons of
Income and Output

1. INTERNATIONAL STATISTICS

Most Governments nowadays maintain statistical services which publish information similar to the United Kingdom data we have discussed in earlier chapters. The reliability and comparability of these statistics varies considerably, and certain international institutions try to present them in standard, comparable forms. We give here a short list of the most reliable sources which the student will find in most large libraries:

Europe:
1. Organization for European Economic Co-operation: *OEEC Statistical Bulletin, General Statistics* (OEEC, Paris). Monthly.
2. United Nations Economic Commission for Europe: *Economic Survey of Europe* (ECE, Geneva). Annually.

The World (including Europe):
3. United Nations: *Monthly Bulletin of Statistics* (UN, New York). Monthly.
4. United Nations: *Yearbook of National Accounts Statistics* (UN, New York). Annually.
5. International Monetary Fund: *International Financial Statistics* (IMF, Washington). Monthly.

United States statistics are included in the sources listed above, but because of their importance we discuss them in more detail in Chapter 12, p. 209.

2. CHANGES IN OUTPUT PER HEAD

In this chapter we are concerned with two problems. Countries differ both in the absolute size of their levels of output or income, and in the change in these levels over time. The first difference raises the problem of a comparison of levels of output which we consider in section 3. The second difference is concerned with comparative rates of growth: we discuss this in this section.

We start with the question: of the three countries—France, Italy and Western Germany—in which one has industrial output grown most rapidly since 1938? Note that we have selected only three countries for the comparison of growth of industrial output since 1938. What countries, what type of outputs, and what period we choose depends both upon the purpose of the inquiry and the available statistics. The OEEC in one of its special bulletins *Industrial Statistics, 1900-57* (OEEC, Paris, 1958) gives indexes of total industrial production for most West European countries (and for Canada and the USA). The indexes are based on 1938 and are calculated for each year from 1947 to 1957 (and for some countries back to 1900). Industrial production in these statistics means manufacturing and mining output (it excludes agricultural output and the public utilities). These statistics are some of the most reliable we have and will be used in our example. Note that index numbers for the war years—1939-46—are not given.

TABLE 8.1

Industrial Production per Head of Population, 1938-57

1938=100

Year	France	West Germany	Italy
1938	100	100	100
1947	93	30	87
1948	108	45	95
1949	118	63	101
1950	119	78	116
1951	131	92	132
1952	135	98	136
1953	130	105	149
1954	141	116	164
1955	152	134	178
1956	167	143	199
1957	180	151	202

Source: *Industrial Statistics*, 1900-57 (OEEC, Paris, 1958), Table a and 2.
Note: Post-war boundaries in all cases.

A country may experience an increase in output simply because its population or its labour force is increasing. The most appropriate measure of output for comparative purposes is then production per head of the labour force or of population. The OEEC bulletin we are using gives numbers of total population for 1938 and 1947-57: we shall use these population figures and choose an index of industrial production per head of population as our measure.[1] We calculate this

[1] The student is warned that industrial production per person employed would be more difficult to estimate: each country's own sources would have to be used for employment statistics, and differences in coverage allowed for.

by converting the population figures into indexes for each country (1938 = 100) and divide the production indexes by the population indexes to get the indexes of production per head. These indexes are shown in Table 8.1.

It is clear that the answer to our question about differences in growth depends whether we compare growths since 1938 or since 1947. Since 1938 Italian industrial output has grown most rapidly; but since 1947 the growth of West German output has been the greatest. The trends in growth can be seen most clearly if the indexes are plotted on a ratio chart where similar vertical distances represent similar relative changes (or rates of growth). This is done in Chart 8.1 which draws attention to some interesting features. From 1947 to

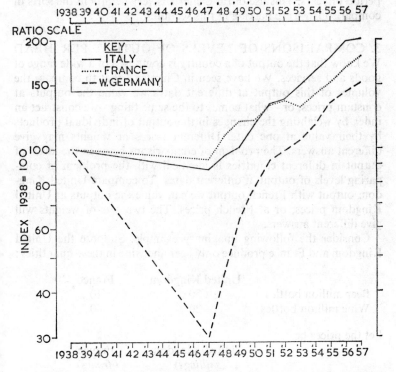

CHART 8.1. Indexes of Industrial Production per Head of Population of Italy, France and Western Germany. RATIO SCALE. Annually for 1938 and 1947-57. 1938 = 100.
Source: Table 8.1.

1951 German growth was very rapid; subsequently it slowed down and since 1951 the average rates of growth of all three countries have been remarkably similar. Notice also the almost constant Italian rate of growth since 1947 which is contrasted with the variations in the French rate of growth.

We have used the expression 'average rate of growth' above. The rate of growth per annum is of course the percentage increase in an index between two years, and on the ratio chart is measured by the gradient (or slope) of the line. If we imagine a straight line ruled through one of the plotted lines in the chart, representing the trend or general direction of the line during a period of years, then the gradient of this straight line is the average rate of growth during that period of years. This use of ratio charts is very helpful in the sorts of comparisons we are making in this section.[1]

3. COMPARISONS OF LEVELS OF OUTPUT PER HEAD

We know that the output of a country is composed of a wide range of goods and services. We have seen in Chapter 4 that to compare the volumes of this output at different dates we value the outputs at constant prices, or—what comes to the same thing—we construct an index by weighting the changes in the output of individual products by their value at one date. Different prices or weights may give different answers. The problem of comparisons between the levels of output in different countries is identical with the problem of comparing levels of output at different dates. To compare United Kingdom output with French output we can value the outputs at United Kingdom prices, or at French prices. The two sets of weights will give different answers.

Consider the following imaginary example. Suppose the United Kingdom and France produce only beer and wine in these quantities:

	United Kingdom	France
Beer million bottles	50	10
Wine million bottles	20	60

Let the prices be

	United Kingdom (*shillings*)	France (*francs*)
Beer 1 bottle	2	150
Wine 1 bottle	5	500

[1] The idea of 'trend' and its measurement is discussed in more detail below in Chapter 9.

First we compare the value of the outputs using United Kingdom prices: the value of United Kingdom output at United Kingdom prices is 200 shillings; the value of the French output at United Kingdom prices is 320 shillings. The French output is thus 60 per cent greater. But if we value the output at French prices we find: value of United Kingdom output at French prices is 17,500 francs; value of French output at French prices is 31,500 francs. The French output is by this method 80 per cent greater. These estimates of the differences in levels of output must be regarded as the answers to two different questions. One question asks what is the difference in outputs when the weights are United Kingdom prices; the other asks what is the difference when the weights are French prices.

Calculations of this sort encounter a number of practical difficulties—some products may not be bought in one country and there may not be quoted prices for them; qualities of supposedly similar products may differ almost to the extent of making them different products. Again, if the calculations are interpreted to measure differences in the standards of living in the two countries, deficiencies in the data available may lead to biases, e.g. statistics of output do not include estimates of the value of housewives; services which in some countries may be more important and better than in others.

When the weights or prices do not differ very much between countries,[1] so that the resulting comparisons of levels of output produce approximately similar results, it is customary to average the results (usually by taking the geometric mean) to obtain a single estimate of differences in levels of output. But when the sets of weights differ considerably as they would in the case of—say—the United States and India, such an average has no useful meaning. In such cases it is better to quote separately the results of using both sets of weights. The usefulness of comparisons of countries' levels of output or standards of living is disputable; what is certain is that the more similar in composition are the baskets of goods produced and consumed in different countries, and the closer are the peoples' attitudes to material goods, the more sensible and useful are these comparisons.

Comparisons of levels of output and real income per head between different countries have been made by several private investigators, one of the pioneers being Colin Clark.[2] Recently the statisticians of

[1] As in the case of volume indexes measuring output at different dates, we think of the difference in weights as being the difference in the proportions of the value of products in the value of total output.

[2] See his *Conditions of Economic Progress* (3rd ed., London, 1957).

OEEC made a detailed study of some Western European countries and the United States.[1] Table 8.2 gives a summary of their calculations. Output per head in eight European countries and the United

TABLE 8.2

Indexes of Gross National Product per Head of Population of
Eight European Countries, 1955

United States = 100

Country	US price weights	Average European price weights
Denmark	56	46
United Kingdom	64	51
Norway	61	50
Belgium	58	49
France	56	43
Netherlands	53	42
Germany	58	44
Italy	35	24

Source: Gilbert: *Comparative National Products and Price Levels* (OEEC, Paris, 1958) Table 4, p. 28.

States in 1955 is compared in two ways. First, outputs are valued at 1955 United States prices. This shows that the European outputs per head are considerably lower than the United States figure. For comparisons between these European countries, however, European price weights are more appropriate. The OEEC statisticians have not presented a comparison with weights based on each European country's prices (i.e. eight comparisons each embracing eight countries). Instead they have selected average European weights for a single comparison. This shows that there are three 'high output' countries—the United Kingdom, Norway and Belgium; a group of 'medium output' countries with outputs per head about 10 per cent lower than the first group; and a 'low output' country—Italy—well below the others.

No importance can be attached to small differences between the outputs per head of different countries, e.g. between that of the United Kingdom and Norway. However, the fact that both sets of weights reveal large differences between, say, the United States and Italy, suggests that these results are reliable. What do they mean in terms of comparative poverty or wealth? Almost certainly the difference between the Italian and the United Kingdom figures means that the average Italian family receives fewer goods and services, i.e. has a lower real income, than the average United Kingdom family. If this

[1] M. Gilbert and associates: *Comparative National Products and Price Levels* (OEEC, Paris, 1958).

is supported by evidence of more malnutrition, more illiteracy, etc., amongst Italians than amongst Britons then we conclude that Italians are poorer in the material sense. But where the differences are smaller than that between Italy and the United Kingdom we must recognize that differences in tastes and needs resulting in differences in the composition of the basket of goods and services consumed may account for part or all of the gaps disclosed by the figures. Finally, we note that estimates of output per head take no account of the evenness with which income is distributed amongst the people of a country. For this reason we used the expression 'average family' above without any precise definition.[1]

4. EXERCISES

(1) Compare the growth in industrial output per head since 1938 in the United Kingdom and the United States with Italy, France and Western Germany. [HINT: use *Industrial Statistics, 1900-57* (OEEC, Paris, 1958), Tables *a* (population) and 2 (index of industrial production).]

(2) In section 3 of this chapter we compared GNP per head in European countries and in the United States. Do comparisons of the major components of national expenditure—personal consumption, investment, Government purchases—show similar differences between countries? [HINT: see Table 7, p. 36, of Gilbert: *Comparative National Products and Price Levels* (OEEC, Paris, 1958).]

(3) What proportions of GNP are derived from (*a*) manufacturing, mining and public utilities, and (*b*) agriculture, forestry and fishing, in the European countries? [HINT: the most convenient source of national income statistics of European countries is the *OEEC Statistical Bulletin: General Statistics* (OEEC, Paris). See for example the July 1959 issue: p. 99 (Belgium), p. 101 (France), p. 102 (West Germany), etc. Make your calculations from an average of the last five years.]

(4) What proportions of GNP are used by the European countries for (*a*) defence, and (*b*) gross fixed capital formation? [HINT: source as in exercise (3) above.]

---

[1] The description of an average Italian family is further complicated by the different ways of life of northerners and southerners.

CHAPTER NINE

Trend and Seasonal Movements in Fruit and Vegetable Prices

1. THE TIME SERIES OF FRUIT AND VEGETABLE PRICES

A time series is a sequence of measurements at successive dates or periods of time. Most of the statistics we have described and used in the previous chapters have been time series, e.g. monthly and annual indexes of production; quarterly and annual estimates of national income. The measurements can refer to any interval of time (e.g. daily stock market quotations of share prices; ten-yearly Census of Population estimates), and the measurements can be made at any point or period of time (e.g. the daily stock market quotations can be the prices when the market closes, or the daily average of hourly prices; the Census of Population estimates refer to the day on which the Census is taken; monthly indexes of retail prices usually refer to a day in the middle of the month; monthly production indexes refer to production during the month).

The time series which we use in this chapter is a quarterly index of retail prices of fruit and vegetables. Fruit and vegetable prices are of interest to the general economist for a number of reasons—according to the 1959 NIE, Table 18, in 1958 about 18 per cent of total household food expenditures went on fruit and vegetables. Furthermore, official studies of household food budgets show that one of the main features which distinguishes the budgets of high income households from those with low incomes is the greater consumption per head of fruit and vegetables in the high income households. Finally, except for the tinned and frozen varieties, fruit and vegetables are sold in conditions where prices are rapidly responsive both to changes in the supplies coming on to the markets and to changes in the consumers' demand; and as fruit and vegetables are the products of agriculture and horticulture we expect that the weather and the seasons will cause large changes—especially in supplies. Thus the level of fruit and vegetable prices besides being an important element in the cost of foodstuffs in general is of particular interest because it is responsive to several influences which are likely to cause fluctuations in the price level. These influences can be briefly summarized as: (1) the changes in the value of money which affect all prices (or are reflected in the changes in all prices); (2) seasonal changes in supply and demand; (3) other changes in supply and demand, e.g. the invention of deep-freezing, or a gradual rise in incomes which causes the demand for luxury fruits to grow. Any of these types of change may be slow or rapid, regular or unique. The most pronounced regularity is likely to be due to the seasonal changes.

TABLE 9.1

Retail Price Index of Fruit and Vegetables, 1952-8

January 15, 1952=100

		(1)	(2) Four quarterly centred moving average
1952	January	100	—
	April	113	—
	July	114	107
	October	100	108
1953	January	103	111
	April	120	111
	July	124	110
	October	93	110
1954	January	104	112
	April	120	115
	July	136	117
	October	104	119
1955	January	110	123
	April	130	128
	July	160	134
	October	123	143
1956	January	132	147
	April	187	143
	July	132	142
	October	119	134
1957	January	128	131
	April	132	138
	July	160	143
	October	141	151
1958	January	150	155
	April	175	153
	July	145	154
	October	144	—
1959	January	154	—

Source: MDS.

Note: Interim Index linked with Current Index on January 17, 1956.

We shall examine the time series of fruit and vegetable prices to see to what extent these various influences can be isolated, measured and analysed. One of our objects is to explain the methods used to seasonally adjust a time series. In Chapter 2 we discussed the difficulties which arise when we use monthly or quarterly statistics containing a large seasonal factor. In Chapter 4 we described the official monthly indexes of production which are presented in a seasonally adjusted form, i.e. with some of the regular seasonal factors removed to make interpretation less difficult. Here we shall discuss the standard procedure by applying it to the index of fruit and vegetable prices.[1]

The index of fruit and vegetable prices shown in column 1 of Table 9.1 is contructed by linking the old Interim Index of Retail Prices (January 1952=100) of the single sub-group of fruit and vegetables to the current Indexes of Retail Prices (January 1956=100) of the two separate sub-groups of fruit and vegetables. (The two sub-groups are weighted with the official weights). The figures were obtained from issues of MDS going back to 1952. The result is a single index for January, April, July and October of each year from 1952 to the beginning of 1959, with January 1952=100. This is a time series, and is shown as a graph in Chart 9.1.

2. ANALYSIS OF THE TIME SERIES

Inspection of Chart 9.1 shows the following features. (1) The price level shows a tendency to rise during the entire period, although this tendency is broken by a peak in early 1956 followed by a fall in late 1956 and early 1957. By late 1957 the rising tendency is again in evidence. Such a tendency is called a *rising trend*. Trends can either rise or fall; on the other hand there need be no evidence of a trend at all. As used here, the term trend is a summary description of a feature of a time series. It describes; it does not explain. It has however economic implications which we shall consider below.

(2) The second feature is the fluctuating character of the price level. As it is a graph of a quarterly series we suspect that part—at least—of the fluctuation is due to seasonal factors. We note that without exception each successive October figure is lower than the preceding July; each successive January figure is higher than the preceding October; each successive April figure is higher than the preceding January; and—excepting in 1956 and 1958—each successive July figure is higher than the preceding April. Also, except for

---

[1] In fact the official indexes of retail prices are not seasonally adjusted.

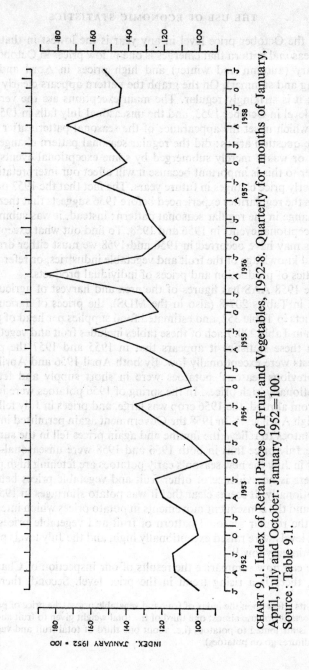

CHART 9.1. Index of Retail Prices of Fruit and Vegetables, 1952-8. Quarterly for months of January, April, July and October. January 1952=100.
Source: Table 9.1.

1952, the October price level in any year is the lowest in that year. The seasonal pattern that emerges is one of low prices in October and January (autumn and winter) and high prices in April and July (spring and summer). On the graph the pattern appears clearly up to 1956: it is strikingly regular. The main exceptions are the very low price level in October 1953, and the unseasonal July falls in 1956 and 1958 which upset the appearance of the seasonal pattern after 1955.

The question arises: did the regular seasonal pattern change after 1955, or was it merely submerged by some exceptional events? The answer to this is important because it will affect our interpretation of quarterly price changes in future years. The fact that the 1957 pattern shows the regularities experienced before 1956 suggests that there was no change in the regular seasonal pattern; instead, it was submerged by exceptional events in 1956 and 1958. To find out what exceptional events may have occurred in 1956 and 1958 we must either draw on special knowledge of the fruit and vegetable industries, or refer to the statistics of production and prices of individual products.

The 1958 AAS has figures of the area and harvest of agricultural crops in Tables 207-8 (also in the MDS), the prices of agricultural products in Table 352, and estimated food supplies per head of population in Table 220. Each of these tables includes fruit and vegetables. From these statistics it appears that in 1955 and 1957 the potato harvests were exceptionally low. By both April 1956 and April 1958 the previous seasons' potatoes were in short supply and fetching exceptionally high prices. In the spring of 1956 potatoes were imported from abroad, the 1956 crop was large, and prices in July fell from the high April level. In 1958 the Government again permitted imports of potatoes to relieve the famine and again prices fell in the summer. These July price falls in both 1956 and 1958 were unseasonal—normally in July the new season's early potatoes are fetching high prices.

There is no evidence of other fruit and vegetable prices behaving exceptionally. It seems clear that it was potato shortages in 1956 and 1958 and the consequent movements in potato prices which interfered with the regular seasonal pattern of fruit and vegetable prices. The April levels were raised exceptionally high, and the July levels pushed exceptionally low.[1]

We can now summarize the results of our inspection of Chart 9.1. First, there is a rising trend in the price level. Second, there is a

[1] In its effect upon the index of fruit and vegetable prices, the price of potatoes is important because almost one third of the total weight given to fruit and vegetables is attributed to potatoes (i.e. about one third of total fruit and vegetable expenditures go on potatoes).

regular seasonal pattern. Third, there are irregular movements of which the most obvious are the consequences of the potato famines of early 1956 and 1958. Most weekly, monthly or quarterly time series show these three features of trend, regular seasonal pattern and irregularities.[1] A time series is usefully considered as composed of trend, seasonal pattern and irregularities, and the analysis of a time series into these constituent factors is called the *decomposition* of the time series.

Each of the components presents certain problems of definition. In the case of the regular seasonal pattern we are supposing that there is a regular cycle of seasonal events—the weather and holidays in particular. But the weather is not always perfectly regular, and holiday times are sometimes altered. What we understand by a regular seasonal pattern is a typical or average seasonal pattern. Deviations from the typical pattern will fall into the class of irregular factors, e.g. the very low price level in October 1953 was partly typical, partly irregular because of a particularly warm autumn. The most difficult problem of seasonal patterns arises when a pattern which previously has been judged typical later changes. Such a change may be in process in fruit and vegetable prices: it may be that poor potato harvests will become common in the future—those of 1955 and 1957 being the first indications. In this case the 1956 and 1958 seasonal patterns of prices will become typical. Or, an even worse complication would be an alternation of good and bad harvests, with an alternation of the two types of seasonal pattern. The student must be on his guard to recognize such difficulties especially in time series extending over lengthy periods of time.

The trend presents a different type of problem. We have emphasized that it is a descriptive term. It need by no means be evidence of the workings of a single economic factor. Fruit and vegetable prices may have tended to rise since 1952 for a number of different reasons. Yet economic events are usually highly interdependent and a trend can often be explained as the outward sign of one or more identifiable and basic economic events. Furthermore such an explanation is useful confirmation that the trend is not just an illusion produced by the fluctuations of a time series.

What could have caused the rising trend in fruit and vegetable prices? First, the general depreciation in the value of money affecting all prices which we noticed in Chapter 3 above. Second, an increased

---

[1] Also, a time series which extends over several decades may show lengthy fluctuations of the type associated with the trade cycle—booms and depressions.

demand for fruits and vegetables arising from increased incomes. In this case supplies might not respond rapidly enough, or might only be forthcoming at an increased cost.[1] If fruit and vegetable prices have increased more than retail prices in general, we have evidence which confirms our second explanation. In Table 9.2 the changes in retail prices of all items and of food are compared with those of fruit and vegetables. The fruit and vegetable price index has increased more

TABLE 9.2

Indexes of Retail Prices, 1952-8

January 1952 = 100

	(1) All items (monthly averages)	(2) Food (monthly averages)	(3) Fruit and vegetables (quarterly averages)	(4) Ratio of fruit and vegetables to all items
1952	102·6	105·4	107	1·04
1953	105·8	111·3	110	1·04
1954	107·7	114·2	116	1·08
1955	112·6	122·8	131	1·16
1956	118·2	128·2	143	1·21
1957	122·5	131·7	140	1·15
1958	126·3	134·4	154	1·21

Source: MDS.
Note: Interim Index linked with Current Index.

than those of all items and of food (which of course include fruit and vegetables amongst their constituents). It is clear that as well as the effect of the fall in the value of money special factors have affected the trend in fruit and vegetable prices.

We obtain some idea of the relative strength of the general and special factors in the following way. We assume that the changes in the all items retail prices index measure the fall in the value of money. We divide the all items index into the fruit and vegetable index (see Table 9.2). The resulting ratio is an index of the change in fruit and vegetable prices after allowance has been made for the fall in the value of money. We see that this adjusted index shows a rising trend: we conclude that between 1952 and 1958 about one half the increase in fruit and vegetable prices was due to the general fall in the value of

[1] These two explanations are not independent of one another, but serve to distinguish factors common to all goods from factors peculiar to fruit and vegetables.

money; and about one half due to special factors peculiar to fruit and vegetables.[1]

The study of the problems of seasonal pattern and trend in the case of fruit and vegetable prices which we have made in this section is intended to show the sort of investigation which must be made before more sophisticated tools are used to decompose a time series. These tools—which we shall discuss in the following sections—are liable to lead to foolish mistakes if they are used unthinkingly and mechanically.

3. MEASUREMENT OF TREND: THE MOVING AVERAGE

If the index number for fruit and vegetable prices in January 1955 is replaced by an average of the index numbers for dates before and after January 1955, the average is called the *trend value* for January 1955. If the index number at every other date is replaced by an average of the index numbers before and after it, the sequence of average values is called a *moving average* which is used as a measure or description of the trend. The moving average is essentially a device for smoothing the time series, i.e. ironing out the seasonal fluctuations and laying bare the trend. The fluctuations we are concerned with in our example are the regular and irregular seasonal fluctuations— other time series may show other types of fluctuations.

The principle of smoothing can be best seen in the case of a series with no trend but containing a regular seasonal pattern. Consider the following sequence of figures:

Year		I				II			
Quarter	1	2	3	4	1	2	3	4	etc.
Value	2	3	6	1	2	3	6	1	

[1] It is sometimes argued that the separation of price changes by this method into the consequences of special and general factors is misleading because the general factor (the fall of the value of money) has different effects upon different goods. However, as these special effects will depend upon such things as elasticities of demand and supply of the goods concerned, it is sensible to separate the effects of a general fall in the value of money into an average effect (felt by all goods) and special effects felt by individual goods. We recognize that these special effects of a fall in the value of money can not be separated by our method from special effects arising from completely different causes (e.g. a gradual reduction in the supply of fruit and vegetables because of a gradual loss of soil fertility)—although it is usually possible to verify special hypotheses by examining the appropriate statistics. We know, for example, that supplies of fruit and vegetables have increased, not decreased, over the period; we know that there were potato famines in early 1956 and 1958; we also know that as income increases the consumption of fruits and vegetables increases more than in proportion.

The average of the values of any four successive quarters is 3, i.e. the average quarterly value calculated over any twelve monthly period is constant, showing no trend either up or down. But the average of a number of successive quarters which is not four (or an integral multiple of four such as eight or twelve) is not constant and would show an irregular trend which would be incorrect and misleading.

The successful smoothing of a time series depends upon two things: (a) the regularity of the pattern of fluctuations, and (b) the choice of the number of values to be averaged. We shall explain the method by a hypothetical example, the details of which are shown in Table 9.3.

TABLE 9.3

Moving Average of Time Series
(hypothetical data)

Year	Month	Tons of coal held by coal merchants on last day of month	Three-quarterly moving average	Four-quarterly moving average Centred
I	March	2		
	June	4	4·67	4·5
	September	8	5·33	5·5 5
	December	4	6	6·5 6
II	March	6	6	7·5 7
	June	8	8·67	8·5 8
	September	12	9·33	9·5 9
	December	8	10	10·5 10
III	March	10	10	11·5 11
	June	12	12·67	12·5 12
	September	16	13·33	
	December	12		

Let us first, *arbitrarily and incorrectly*, take a three-quarterly moving average of the time series of stocks of coal. We average the first three quarters of year I, i.e. $\frac{2+4+8}{3}=4\cdot67$; next, the second, third and fourth quarters, i.e. $\frac{4+8+4}{3}=5\cdot55$; next, the third and fourth quarters of year I and the first of year II, i.e. $\frac{8+4+6}{3}=6\cdot00$; and so on.

We set these trend values against the mid-points of the periods covered by the averages, i.e. the last days of June, September, December, etc. The resulting three-quarterly moving average is by no means smooth, although it does trace an upward trend which is apparent in the original series.

Now let us take a four-quarterly moving average. First, we average the four quarters of year I, i.e. $\dfrac{2+4+8+4}{4}=4\cdot5$. This trend value is set against the mid-point of the interval covered by the averaged values, viz. mid-August. Next we average the second, third and fourth quarters of year I, and the first of year II, i.e. $\dfrac{4+8+4+6}{4}=5\cdot5$, setting this against mid-November; and so on. The resulting moving average increases by one ton from quarter to quarter, and as a graph would appear as a straight line.

The reason for the difference between the two moving averages is that there is a perfectly regular seasonal pattern in the original time series, with a net increase over any four-quarterly period of four tons, or on average one ton per quarter. This is shown correctly in the four-quarterly moving average which increases by one ton per quarter. The three-quarterly moving average does not show this at all—it is in fact misleading because it suggests that the average quarterly increase is irregular, which is not the case. The rule for choosing the number of items to be averaged is : if a cycle of the regular fluctuations spans y months, the number of items averaged should span y months also. This means that to eliminate a regular seasonal pattern in a quarterly time series we take a four-quarterly moving average.

In the case of moving averages of an even number of items, e.g. four quarters or twelve months, an additional step is needed. The average of the four quarters of year I refers to the mid-point of the interval between the last days of March and December, i.e. mid-August. The average of the last three months of year I and the first of year II refers to mid-November. These are not dates to which the values of the original time series refer. To make our trend values refer to the dates of the original series we take a further moving average of successive pairs of trend values. Then, for example, the average of trend values for mid-August and mid-November refers to mid-September. The second moving average is called a *centred* moving average and is the one we would use in subsequent work on the series.

In section 1 above we described the trend as a characteristic of time series. It is a descriptive term with no necessary economic implications. The moving average which precisely measures trend is the result of simple arithmetic—it also has no necessary economic implications. However the idea of trend frequently coincides with other ideas of the workings of economic forces and we frequently make use of the precision given by a moving average to analyse these forces. For this reason we must be aware of peculiarities of moving averages. (i) Exceptionally high or low values in the original time series may raise or lower the moving average over part of its range. The resulting fluctuating moving average with peaks and troughs will misleadingly measure the trend if the exceptionally high or low values are recognized as being due to exceptional economic factors. (ii) A change in the regular seasonal pattern, or an extremely irregular seasonal pattern, may introduce spurious peaks and troughs in a moving average or may locate the real peaks and troughs earlier or later in time than is actually the case.

Because of these peculiarities the first step must be an inspection of the original series as we undertook in section 1. If the seasonal pattern is then seen to be sufficiently regular, the moving average may be calculated to obtain a precise measure of the trend. That being done, the moving average must be inspected for peculiarities before it is used as evidence in economic argument or for the estimation of seasonal adjustments.

4. MOVING AVERAGE OF FRUIT AND VEGETABLE PRICES

The four-quarterly centred moving average of the fruit and vegetable price index is given in Table 9.1 (second column). It is plotted on top of the original time series in Chart 9.2. The moving average describes a trend which rises slowly at first, then more rapidly in 1954 and 1955. (If the moving average is plotted on a ratio scale the annual average, or quarterly, rate of increase in prices is shown to be roughly constant up to early 1956.) The trend has a peak in January 1956 and subsequently declines for a year. After January 1957 the trend again starts to rise, flattening out in early 1958.

Has this moving average any peculiarities? We notice that the peak in January 1956 looks odd. High prices occurred in April 1956, followed by exceptionally low prices in July and October. These low July and October prices have the effect on the arithmetic of the moving average of pulling down the April 1956 trend value. It looks as if the moving average locates the trend peak a little earlier than is actually the case. But note that this possible displacement is not very large and hence not very important.

Another feature of our moving average is important. The purpose of the moving average is to remove regular seasonal fluctuations and smooth remaining irregularities. Thus our moving average probably contains evidence of irregular use, it has been carefully smoothed but the main irregularities were left in. Variation I, were due to the effects of the potato famines of early 1956 and 1957. The question arises, to what extent is the fall in the index figures in 1955 due to this and effects of the famine, which have not been completely smoothed out? In other words, was the 'trend' in fruit and vegetable prices really reversed in 1955, or is this only an effect of the irregular movement? Further it has been argued that we cannot be certain merely from the reversal of the trend that this was not due to ... ments of the irregular. The student will not that the statistical effects of the irregular movements are similar (and are not ...). This should make clear that the movements are irregular, but some aspects of it are treated in another of these articles on the charts.

Our price indices and the moving average of fruit and vegetable prices are ... ... there are no obvious points which except for a small effect due to the 1956 peak, tend to distort the ...of both the price index (dotted line) and the ... with the price figures which we have called irregular variations.

4. SEASONAL ADJUSTMENT

Importers ... an index of retail price levels and we wanted to be able to know whether the general level of prices is going to be able to make allowance for them. We must remember that the changes in the prices which are ... proportionate to fruit and vegetable index ... no measure of the ... recent movements available with certainty. We need to know, roughly, regular seasonal patterns from the irregular fluctuations and patterns ... which are typical of prices on the level. ... ... year prices are (say) 20 per cent below normal. Our next prices in any one year may, of course ... be up to 25 per cent below normal, but we assume ... to be up to 25 per cent below normal is the typical figure.

We regard the ... value ... price series as the general value and the actual index ... due to a variation from the general value is a regular ... which ... others that will ... earlier before our prices ... calculate ... allowance by taking the difference between the ... value and general value of some deviation, or by calculating the index figure due to the ... value relative ... ... what follows ... consider the relative deviation ... ...

The ... ... general values to monthly average values of the ... quantity of the ... ... The general ... level of the fruit and vegetable price index are shown in Table ... section 4. ... the ... ... in Table 9.1 give the index ... average ... ... and the index number ...

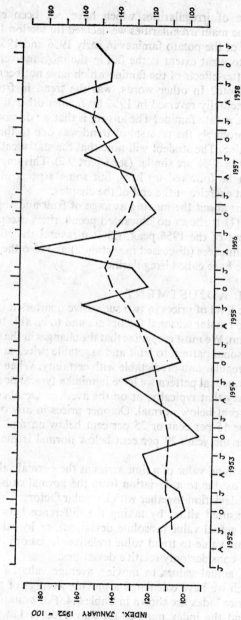

CHART 9.2. Index of Retail Prices of Fruit and Vegetables with Four-Quarterly Centred Moving Average, 1952–8.
Source: Table 9.1.

INDEX, JANUARY 1952 = 100

contains evidence of irregularities which have not been entirely smoothed out. The main irregularities we decided (in section 1) were due to the effects of the potato famines in early 1956 and 1958. The question arises: to what extent is the fall in the moving average in 1956 due to the after-effects of the famine which have not been completely smoothed out? In other words, was the trend in fruit and vegetable prices actually reversed in 1956 by factors other than the after-effects of the potato famine? The answer is that we do not know for certain, but probably the reversal of trend was due to the after-effects of the famine. The student will note that the statistical effects of the same event in 1958 are similar (see Chart 9.2). This interesting problem will not be followed up here, but some aspects of it are treated in the first exercise at the end of the chapter.

Our conclusions about the moving average of fruit and vegetable prices are these. (1) It shows no unwanted peculiarities except for a small displacement of the 1956 peak. (2) It measures the effects of both the trend influences (discussed in section 2) and also the potato famines which we have called irregularities.

5. SEASONAL ADJUSTMENT

In comparing the level of prices in two successive quarters it is useful to know what the regular seasonal factors are and to be able to make allowance for them. We must recognize that the changes in the seasons which give a seasonal pattern to fruit and vegetable prices are by no means perfectly regular and predictable with certainty. When we talk about a regular seasonal pattern we have in mind a typical or average pattern, i.e. we say that typically, or on the average, October prices are (say) 20 per cent below normal. October prices in any one year may of course be 15 per cent or 25 per cent below normal, but we assume that over the years 20 per cent below normal is the typical figure.

We regard the trend value of a time series as the normal value, and the actual value as due to a deviation from the normal caused by a regular seasonal deviation together with irregular factors. The deviation can be measured either by taking the difference between the trend value and actual value (absolute deviation), or by calculating the ratio of actual value to trend value (relative deviation). In what follows we shall consider only relative deviations.

The ratios of actual values to moving average values for each quarter for which we have calculated a moving average of the fruit and vegetable price index are shown in Table 9.4. For example, from Table 9.1 we find the index number for July 1952 is 114 and the

TABLE 9.4

Retail Price Index of Fruit and Vegetables: Ratio of Actual Index to
Moving Average, 1952-1958

	January	April	July	October
1952	—	—	1·07	0·93
1953	0·93	1·08	1·13	0·85
1954	0·93	1·04	1·16	0·87
1955	0·89	1·02	1·19	0·86
1956	0·90	1·31	0·93	0·89
1957	0·98	0·96	1·12	0·93
1958	0·97	1·14	0·94	—

moving average for that quarter is 107. The ratio of these is 1·07—
which means that the actual index is 7 per cent above the normal
value. The ratios in Table 9.4 show clearly the features of the seasonal
pattern. The January prices are always below the trend values, as are
the October prices. The April prices are typically higher—the exception is April 1957. The exceptionally high April prices of 1956 and
1958 are marked by the large ratios of those years. The July prices are
also higher than the trend values, except in 1956 and 1958.

It will be noticed that Table 9.4 conveniently summarizes all the
important features of the seasonal pattern which we have considered
in section 2. The preparation of a table like this is complementary to
the calculation of a moving average and should always be prepared
when a seasonal pattern is being studied. It is a useful check on the
conclusions drawn from inspection of Chart 9.1.

The next step is to estimate the typical ratios for January, April,
July and October. We do this by calculating the arithmetic mean of
each quarter's ratios. For example, the arithmetic mean of the six
January ratios is 0·93; of the six October ratios it is 0·89. This means
that on the average the January price index is 93 per cent of the trend
value (or 7 per cent below the trend value) while the October index is
89 per cent of the trend value.

If we average the April and July ratios in the same way we shall,
however, be allowing factors which we have already decided are
irregular and exceptional (the potato famines) to affect our estimate
of the typical ratio. This would have the effect of making our estimate
of the April ratio unduly high, and the July ratio unduly low. It is
safe and sensible to omit the 1956 and 1958 ratios in the calculation
of the April and July arithmetic means. The omission of ratios can be
justified if a study of the time series has shown that the exceptional
features of the omitted ratios are due to phenomena which were
exceptional over the period of time being considered, and are un-

likely to be regularly repeated in the future. We have already concluded that this is so. Omitting the 1956 and 1958 ratios, the April arithmetic mean is 1·02, and that of July 1·13.

Our four average ratios are thus:

January   0·93
April   1·02
July   1·13
October   0·89

These average ratios are the corrections which we would apply to the actual index numbers to obtain a *seasonally adjusted* time series, i.e. to remove the regular seasonal variation from the time series. Each January index, which on the average is 7 per cent below normal, because of the regular January seasonal factor which pulls the price of fruit and vegetables down, is divided by 0·93—which has the effect of raising it by 7 per cent. Similarly, each April index is divided by 1·02 (to lower it); each July index is divided by 1·13 (to lower it); and each October index is divided by 0·89 (to raise it).[1]

A seasonally adjusted series is most useful in short period comparisons. Consider the index numbers of the actual series for July and October 1958: 145 and 144 respectively. They suggest that the price level was stationary or at most declining only slightly. But seasonally adjusted with our average ratios the index numbers are 128 and 162—the price level with regular seasonal movements removed actually rose sharply. That this was in fact the short period tendency is confirmed by the January 1959 index number.

6. SOME OBSERVATIONS ON SEASONAL ADJUSTMENT

The statisticians who construct the Index of Retail Prices do not adjust the index or any of its sub-indexes for seasonal factors. The official monthly Index of Industrial Production is, however, seasonally adjusted (see Chapter 4). The unadjusted and adjusted series can be found side by side in the MDS. These adjustments are made after continuous and detailed study of the causes and nature of the seasonal pattern and can be regarded as reliable. Every month in ET the adjusted and unadjusted series are presented graphically on a chart.

In 1959 the Board of Trade began publication of seasonally adjusted figures of United Kingdom imports and exports. An article

---

[1] The procedure described in this paragraph may in practice be modified in several respects. Also, before used as corrections the average ratios are adjusted so that *their* average equals unity.

describing the methods used is in BTJ, November 6, 1959, which also contains tables and charts of the adjusted series, quarterly since 1948 and monthly since 1955. The seasonal corrections take into account both the varying lengths of months and the regular seasonal pattern. A special feature of the method is that the seasonal (monthly or quarterly) corrections are allowed to vary over time to accommodate themselves to changes in the regular seasonal pattern. This means that each year a different set of corrections is used.

None of the other important British economic time series are presented in a seasonally adjusted form by the official statisticians.[1] However this service has recently been performed by the National Institute of Economic and Social Research which presents a large number of important statistics in seasonally adjusted form in the *National Institute Economic Review*. Of particular use are the seasonally adjusted quarterly national income and expenditure statistics.[2]

Not all seasonal adjustments can be regarded as reliable, and the student must be prepared to exercise care in using a series of statistics whose seasonal pattern is liable to alteration—especially statistics of expenditures.[3] The importance of care can be appreciated if we refer again to our example of fruit and vegetable prices. In Table 9.4 we note that the April ratios (omitting 1956 and 1958) show a tendency to decline over time. In fact it could be argued that the April price level, which commenced by being a seasonally high price level, by the end of the six year period was a seasonally low one. It looks as if there was some systematic change in the seasonal pattern. Secondly, note that if the exceptional seasonal patterns of 1956 and 1958 herald the emergence of a new type of seasonal pattern—due to regularly recurring potato famines!—the problem of seasonal adjustment becomes much more difficult. It is these possibilities of change in the seasonal pattern, together with large seasonal irregularities which the corrections do not eliminate, which force us to be careful in the use of seasonally adjusted statistics.

But of course this possibility of a changing seasonal pattern is not just a problem of seasonally adjusted series: it is a problem which must be recognized in all time series liable to seasonal influences. In

[1] After this chapter was written official seasonally adjusted quarterly estimates of national income and expenditure were published for the first time. See ET, No 75, January 1960.

[2] In the September 1959 issue of the *Review* the Institute had an article reviewing its adjustment methods, with an account of their probable reliability.

[3] The National Institute discontinued the adjustment of consumers' expenditures on cars in view of the uncertainty of the seasonal pattern.

short period economic analysis and predictions the economist wil[1] be using monthly or quarterly statistics. He must try to understand the seasonal pattern and its changes and irregularities. Usually in short period analysis the economist will study several time series, and will be interested not only in the changes in one series in isolation but also in the pattern of changes in all the series—and the pattern of changes may throw light on seasonal movements even when we may regard seasonally adjusted series as unreliable because of the irregularity of the seasonal pattern.

In this chapter we have emphasized two things. First, the student must try to understand why a time series fluctuates in the way it does. His use of the statistics will depend upon his understanding of their peculiarities: he must be prepared to draw upon supplementary sources of information about causes. Second, he can apply some tools which will organize his knowledge. A moving average, and the ratios of the actual values to the moving average values, are useful tools in themselves to throw light on the irregularities and peculiarities of the seasonal pattern. This is true even if it is concluded that the final step of seasonal adjustment would be unreliable.

7. EXERCISES

(1) According to Table 9.2 above, since 1952 the level of fruit and vegetable prices has risen more than the level of retail prices of all items. This suggests that fruit and vegetable prices have been subjected to special forces as well as those causing the value of money in general to fall. During what periods have the relative changes in fruit and vegetable prices been most marked? [HINT: compare the trend in fruit and vegetable prices with the trend in retail prices of all items. Use the moving average in Table 9.1 to measure the former trend; for the latter construct an index for January, April, July and October of each year since 1952 by linking the interim all items index to the current all items index (from back issues of MDS) and calculate the four-quarterly centred moving average. Plot these two moving averages on a ratio chart. Locate the dates between which the rates of change of the trends in prices were most marked.] Is there any evidence that good or bad agricultural and horticultural seasons caused the relative movements?

(2) What is the seasonal pattern of work in the building industry? [HINT: use the quarterly index of production of the construction industry (MDS). After collecting, plotting and inspecting the series calculate a four-quarterly moving average and the ratios between the original series and the moving average.]

(3) What has been the trend in the numbers of marriages in the United Kingdom since 1950? Is there a seasonal pattern in marriages? [HINT: use the quarterly marriage statistics in the MDS. Beware of the calendar variation of the dates of religious festivals.]

(4) Compare the seasonal patterns of consumers' expenditure on (a) furniture and floor coverings, (b) radio and electrical goods, and (c) cars and motor cycles. Can you explain the differences? [HINT: use quarterly national income statistics at constant prices.]

(*i*) What had been the trend in the numbers of marriages in the
United Kingdom since ... and participation in marriage?
[Hint: use the quarterly marriage statistics in the MDS. Beware of
the seasonal variation of the data of religious festivals.]

(*ii*) ...
(*a*) furniture and floor coverings, (*b*) radio and electrical goods, and
(*c*) cars and motor cycles. Can you explain the differences? [Hint:
use quarterly national income statistics at constant prices.]

CHAPTER TEN

The Productivity of British Industries

1. EFFICIENCY AND PRODUCTIVITY

An important idea in economic discussion is the *efficiency* with which
a certain expenditure of effort produces a result. Efficiency is not a
simple idea: it has several possible meanings. For example, the efficiency of a certain type of petrol in a certain type of motor car could
be defined as the number of miles travelled for each gallon of petrol
consumed. To measure this, we would run the car for a month, and
divide the miles travelled by the gallons of petrol consumed to obtain
the measure of efficiency as 'so many miles per gallon'. But we know
that the efficient use of petrol by the car's engine depends upon the
skill of the driver, the topography of the roads, the state of the tyres,
the average speed of travel, etc. Furthermore, we would know that
petrol consumption can be reduced—within limits—if we are prepared to use more oil. Thus if we were comparing the efficiencies of
petrol in two cars we would attempt to run the cars in identical conditions—on the same roads, using the same amount of oil, etc.—a
state of affairs which can not always be completely achieved.

This everyday example draws attention to two important features
of the idea of efficiency. First, we usually define it as the ratio of an
output (miles travelled) to an input (gallons of petrol consumed) i.e.
so many units of output per unit of input. Second, there are usually
several inputs used in producing the output, and the efficiency of one
of the inputs depends upon the quantity of the other inputs used.

The efficiency of the working population of a country, or of the
labour force of a firm or industry, can be discussed in these terms.
We commonly measure the efficiency of the labour force of an industry as the average annual output per person employed, i.e. we take
the ratio of total annual output to number of people employed. This
measure is called *labour productivity;* it does not depend entirely upon
the willingness to work and the skill and experience of the labour
force, but also upon the kinds of raw materials used, the quantity and
type of machinery, the conditions of work and the way the labour
force is organized and managed. Thus labour productivity in an industry will depend upon what an industry produces and how it produces it.

A distinction must also be made between technically efficient inputs and economical inputs. To return to our motor car example: in similar driving conditions 'Zip' petrol gives thirty miles per gallon, and 'Zoom' gives twenty-five miles per gallon. If the consumption of other inputs is identical, 'Zip' is technically the most efficient petrol. But 'Zip' may be so expensive that nobody buys it. Although technically the least efficient, 'Zoom' is the most economical. Let us apply these considerations to a comparison of labour productivity in the steel industries of two countries, A and B. In A average annual output is 100 tons per worker; in B it is 120. The types of steel produced, the qualities of the raw materials, the willingness to work and the skills of the labour forces are similar; the difference in productivity is due to different machinery and methods of organization chosen to be used in the two countries. The most *economical* machinery and method of production in A may be that which gives a low labour productivity. We can not conclude that low productivity is a sign of economically wasteful methods of production.

In this chapter we are going to compare the changes in labour productivity during the post-war decade in the various United Kingdom manufacturing industries. Change in output is measured by an index of production; to obtain the change in output per head we shall divide the index of production by an index of employment. These calculations are explained in section 2. In the later sections we consider explanations of the differences between the productivity changes of the various industries. We also introduce a graphical technique for measuring economic relationships.

2. CHANGES IN OUTPUT PER PERSON EMPLOYED BETWEEN 1948 AND 1955

We have already explained that in comparing levels of output at different dates it is necessary to value the outputs at constant prices to get a measure of the change in volume of production (Chapter 4). For manufacturing industries this is done for us in the Index of Industrial Production. There is an index of production for each of the fourteen manufacturing industries showing percentage changes in volume of production between different dates. The indexes refer to total output, not to output per person employed; consequently it is necessary to adjust the output indexes by changes in the numbers of persons employed.

Numbers employed (see Chapter 1, section 4) are classified into the fourteen manufacturing industries in the MDS. These figures refer to

M

Great Britain and exclude employers and self-employed. The AAS gives figures of civil employment for June of each year in each of the fourteen industries in Great Britain, i.e. including employers and self-employed. There are arguments supporting both the inclusion and exclusion of employers in measures of productivity—it would probably be best to include 'working proprietors' and exclude all other employers and self-employed (because they represent a separate factor of organization and management). However this refinement is not possible because the statistics do not allow us to make this distinction. Here we shall simply measure productivity as the ratio of output to numbers in civil employment.

As the indexes of production refer to the United Kingdom it would be appropriate to use figures of civil employment in the United Kingdom. This is not possible, however, as civil employment statistics for the separate manufacturing industries are available in the sources only for Great Britain. There are annual estimated numbers of employees for the United Kingdom in the AAS, but as these include the registered unemployed they are not suitable for use in a measure of productivity. In what follows we use the June figures of civil employment in Great Britain.

We want to compare the change in output per head between two dates. Let us choose our dates so that we compare the changes during the decade since the end of the war. Consider first the indexes of production given in Table A of the June 1959 ET: these are the new indexes based on 1954 and recalculated back to 1946. 1948 is a convenient year to measure the change from: it is two years after the end of the war, and we may suppose that most of major post-war industrial dislocation had ended by then; it is a year in the middle of a rising trend extending from 1946 to 1951 in the case of the indexes of all fourteen industries; and was the year selected by the official statisticians to base the old index on. 1948 thus is a convenient base for our comparisons—it is not abnormal in relation to the surrounding years. It is also statistically convenient because we can use the old index of production itself—based on 1948—and reduce the number of our calculations: in what follows we shall use Table 152 of the 1958 AAS which gives the old indexes up to 1957.

What shall be the later date for our comparisons? From 1952 to 1955 the indexes for most industries show a rising trend (the exceptions are textiles and leather with peaks in 1954 and small falls in 1955). After 1955 the output of some industries continued to grow; in others it fell. Total manufacturing production declined in 1956; rose again in 1957; fell again in 1958. This evidence—and there is much more in support—shows that British industrial expansion ceased after 1955. Thus 1955 is the latest year when industrial production all round was growing, i.e. it is the latest year comparable with 1948. We shall compare 1955 with 1948. Note that we could compare the averages of the years, e.g. 1954-6 with 1947-9. This would be a safe method if there was doubt about 1948 and 1955 being normal and comparable, but there seems no strong reason to do this here. If 1956 was compared with 1948 we would be faced with the possibility that output per head in 1956 would appear artificially low due to an underemployment of labour and capital arising from a checked demand for goods and services—this would show the change in the use of the capacity of an industry, but would be misleading as a measure of the change in the productive efficiency of an industry[1].

TABLE 10.1

Change in Output per Head by Industry Between 1948 and 1955

Industry	(1) 1955 index of Production 1948=100·0	(2) 1955 index of civil employment 1948=1·000	(3) Index of output per head 1948=100
Non-metalliferous mining manufactures	128·7	1·098	117
Chemicals and allied trades	178·5	1·177	152
Metal manufacture	133·2	1·075	124
Engineering, shipbuilding and electrical goods	154·7	1·160	133
Vehicles	171·8	1·272	135
Metal goods n.e.i.	124·6	1·021	122
Precision instruments, jewellery, etc.	126·3	1·123	112
Textiles	115·4	1·026	112
Leather, leather goods and fur	96·0	0·927	104
Clothing	118·3	1·040	114
Food, drink and tobacco	117·4	1·201	98
Manufactures of wood and cork	146·6	1·049	140
Paper and printing	168·8	1·189	142
Other manufacturing industries	153·1	1·171	131

Source: 1958 AAS, Tables 131 and 152.

[1] The arguments of the last two paragraphs are not intended to suggest that the choice of the 'correct' dates for comparison will eliminate all ambiguities and difficulties in the measurement of productivity changes—as we explained in the previous section the measurement and interpretation of productivity changes is inherently difficult and ambiguous. We are suggesting that *some* of the more obvious difficulties can be removed by careful choice of dates.

We can thus use the old indexes of production for 1955 to measure changes in output since 1948. These are shown in Table 10.1. To estimate changes in output per head we calculate the proportionate changes in civil employment between June 1948 and June 1955, e.g. for clothing we divide the 1955 number by the 1948 number: $\dfrac{675,000}{649,000}$ =1·040 (a 4 per cent rise). These ratios are entered in column (2) of Table 10.1. The index of clothing production for 1955, 118·3, is adjusted by dividing it by the employment ratio to obtain the index of output per head: $\dfrac{118·3}{1·040}$=114 (a 14 per cent rise between 1948 and 1955). The output per head indexes are shown in column (3) of Table 10.1.

The changes in labour productivity vary considerably. At the top of the list is Chemicals, whose productivity has increased by over 50 per cent, followed by Paper and Printing, Wood Manufactures, Vehicles and Engineering. After a gap these are followed by the metal industries; at the bottom of the list is Food where productivity has fallen.

3. CAUSES OF CHANGES IN PRODUCTIVITY
Why do these industries show such widely differing productivity changes? We shall list some possible explanations of change in productivity:

(1) An increase in the quality and quantity of the machines, tools and power available for use in production—labour is economized by the use of more or better capital equipment. This factor is often separated into two causes: (a) an increase in the amount of a given type of equipment, and (b) the use of improved equipment and better methods of production. In practice it is difficult to disentangle these two causes especially when existing equipment is improved by alteration. It should be noted that this factor can not always be measured by some simple measure of the quantity of capital employed because the use of improved equipment may result in the employment of less capital.

(2) An increase in the demand for the products of the industry may permit output to be increased. If the equipment and the labour force were previously not being fully used, the additional output may be produced with no proportionate increase in the labour force. This is equivalent to the case of the economy of large scale production.

(3) An increase in the willingness and ability of the labour force to

work, e.g. because of longer hours, more co-operation with management, better training, fewer accidents, etc. The efficiency of the management will express itself through this factor as well as through the first factor mentioned above. In fact the operations of these two factors are difficult to disentangle because, for instance, improved organization may reduce accidents which may increase the willingness to perform dangerous tasks.

If the strength of any or all of these factors should be different in different industries we should expect that their productivity changes would be different.

As well as the above classification of productivity changes, there is another approach which for some purposes may be more useful. It is useful to know the circumstances in which productivity changes occur. Do they occur in expanding industries (where demand and total output are tending to increase) or is the expansion or decline of an industry irrelevant? The distinction between expanding and contracting industries is important, because it can be argued that only expanding industries can take advantage of economies of scale and will be prosperous enough to invest in new plant and equipment to raise productivity; declining industries (it can be argued) can not and will not raise their labour productivity.

A study of the causes and circumstances of changes in productivity is valuable both for the understanding of particular industries and for a broader understanding of the growth of the economy as a whole. In the following section we shall examine the relationships between productivity changes and industrial expansion (as measured by the growth of total output). The connection between productivity change and investment in new plant and equipment is considered in an exercise at the end of the chapter.

4. ECONOMIC RELATIONSHIPS

In Chapters 1 and 2 we discussed the procedures to be followed in explaining the changes over time of such activities as the export of cotton goods and home sales of motor cars. We gave a formal statement of the steps to be taken in selecting a plausible explanation of the changes in a sequence of measurements. The method of explaining differences in productivity changes is fundamentally similar: we choose an explanation and inspect the statistics to see whether the explanation is plausible, i.e. to see whether it fits the facts.

'The industries with the greatest proportional increase in production between 1948 and 1955 were also those with the greatest proportional increase in productivity.' This is the hypothesis we wish to test.

The evidence can be examined by comparing the indexes of output with the indexes of productivity in Table 10.1. A useful device is to rank the industries according to the size of their output indexes, and compare this rank with their rank according to the size of their productivity index: this is done in Table 10.2.

TABLE 10.2

Manufacturing Industries Ranked by Change in Production and Change in Output per Head

	Index of production	Index of output per head
Chemicals	1	1
Vehicles	2	4
Paper and printing	3	2
Engineering, shipbuilding and electrical goods	4	5
Other	5	6
Wood and cork	6	3
Metal manufacture	7	7
Non-metalliferous mining	8	9
Precision	9	11 equal
Metal goods, n.e.i.	10	8
Clothing	11	10
Food, drink and tobacco	12	14
Textiles	13	11 equal
Leather	14	13

Source: Text Table 10.1.

This evidence can be interpreted in different ways. The seven industries with the greatest change in output have the greatest change in productivity; the three industries with the smallest change in output have the smallest change in productivity. There is a marked tendency for the output rank of an industry to be the same as its productivity rank. We would sum up this evidence by saying that a large proportional increase in output tends to be associated with a large proportional increase in productivity.

We are considering here an *economic relationship:* the changes in productivity associated with changes in output. We have decided that the evidence supports the view that a relationship of this sort exists. There are two aspects of economic relationships which we must consider: (1) their form, and (2) their reliability. The *form* of the relationship states what change in productivity we expect to find associated with a given (say, 10 per cent) increase in output, in a given situation with all other factors likely to influence productivity remaining unaltered. Obviously other factors hardly ever do remain unchanged—as between industries there will be differences in the ease with which productivity can be altered, and, over time, other factors (such as the flow of inventions) alter and vary between industries. Nevertheless these complications do not disprove the existence of a relationship—they merely make it difficult to isolate it and determine its exact form, and to use it to predict the future.

The *reliability* of the relationship is the extent to which other factors are likely to interfere with the relationship. Suppose our relationship states that a 10 per cent increase in output is associated with a 5 per cent increase in productivity. Suppose further that a certain industry is known to have increased its output by 30 per cent. Is it likely that its productivity will have increased by 15 per cent? Clearly, no. The conditions under which the industry increased its output will be in some respects dissimilar to those assumed in the statement of the relationship, and it is unlikely that other factors will have remained unchanged. We can only say that providing other factors have not changed too much and that the conditions are not too dissimilar, the increase in productivity will be about 15 per cent. Of course, we may know what are the relationships of the other factors to output changes and productivity changes—in that case we would take them into account when predicting what the productivity change is likely to be, and so increase the reliability of our prediction.

In the following section we outline the use of one of the most important tools for investigating an economic relationship. It is an exploratory tool—like an oil drill or a geiger counter. For it to be successful, the user must know the peculiarities of the statistics he is using, and must be able to think of feasible relationships after preliminary inspection of the statistics.

5. SCATTER DIAGRAMS

The purpose of a scatter diagram is to determine the form of a relationship and to illustrate its reliability. Suppose we know that during a certain period, if all other factors remain unchanged, an x per cent increase in output is associated with an $\frac{x}{2}$ per cent increase in productivity in any industry we examine. Suppose also that we examine three industries whose output and productivity changes are:

Industry	Output increase per cent	Productivity increase per cent
A	10	6
B	20	9
C	30	17

A's 6 per cent productivity increase can be divided into two parts: 5 per cent due to the output increase and 1 per cent due to other factors. Similarly, of B's 9 per cent increase, 10 per cent is due to its output increase and −1 per cent (or 1 per cent decrease) is due to other factors; and of C's 17 per cent increase 15 per cent is due to its output increase and 2 per cent to other factors.

We can illustrate this information by preparing a graph with the output change measured on one axis and the productivity change on the other. On this graph we plot for each industry the point represented by its output and productivity increases, i.e. the points (10,6), (20,9) and (30,17): see Chart 10.1.

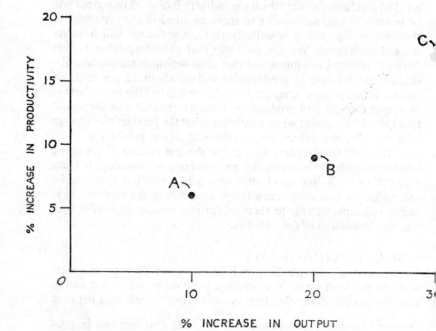

CHART 10.1. Scatter Diagram I: Increase in Output and Increase in Productivity.
Source: hypothetical data.

This is a scatter diagram. (We have indicated the names of each industry for convenience; this is not necessary.) Now we insert the points for each industry represented by its output increase and what its productivity increase would be in the absence of other factors, i.e. we plot the points (10,5), (20,10) and (30,15): see Chart 10.2. The latter points have been joined by a straight line which describes the relationship. The other original points diverge from this because of

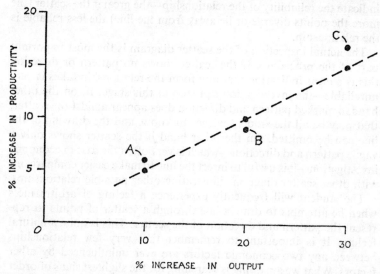

CHART 10.2. Scatter Diagram II: Increase in Output and Increase in Productivity.
Source: hypothetical data.

the existence of other factors. For example, in the case of industry C it can be read off the chart that the 30 per cent increase in output will be associated with a 15 per cent increase in productivity (due to the relationship) together with another 2 per cent increase due to other factors.

In this imaginary example there was no problem because we assumed that we knew what the relationship was before we started. If we suspect that there is a relationship but do not know its form, we have to guess the form. The purpose of the scatter diagram is to assist the guessing. The procedure is: (1) we plot the pair of measurements (output and productivity changes) for each industry so as to form the scatter diagram as in Chart 10.1; (2) we inspect the pattern in the scatter to determine the general form of the relationship. In Chart 10.1 the points are scattered in a north-easterly direction showing that as output increases so does productivity; (3) with a ruler and pencil we draw a straight line which follows the direction of the scatter. (There is no reason why the line should pass through any or all of the points.) The line describes the form of the assumed relationship, and the extent to which the scatter of points clusters around the line will indicate the reliability of the relationship—the greater the scatter (the more the points diverge or lie away from the line) the less reliable is the relationship.

The actual inspection of the scatter diagram is the most important part of the procedure. If the scatter shows no pattern or direction this is a clear indication that any form the relationship takes is very unreliable—the investigation can stop at this stage. If, on the other hand, a marked pattern and direction does appear amidst the scatter, that may be all the student wishes to know, and the drawing of the line can be omitted. On the other hand if the scatter shows only a vague pattern and direction—which is very often the case in economic investigation—it is useful to insert the line to make easier comparisons with other scatter diagrams illustrating other possible relationships.

The student will frequently experience a feeling of arbitrariness when he attempts to draw a line through a scatter of points to represent the pattern and direction of the scatter. This is quite a natural feeling. It is important to remember that very few relationships between any two economic factors are ever uninfluenced by other factors. What we are doing is searching for the slightest signs of order in economic affairs—we shall be lucky if the signs are unmistakable and unambiguous! In drawing the line there are some rules to be observed: (1) plot the point which represents the averages of the two sets of measurements, i.e. the average of the output increase and the average of the productivity increases; (2) draw the line so that it passes through the point of averages. The problem remains of deciding what slope the line should take; (3) whatever slope the line has, there will be points lying above and below it at all parts of it. Try to make these deviations of the points from the line, taken as a whole, as small as possible. This is a matter of trial and error—of rotating a ruler about the point of averages—and is not as difficult as it sounds; (4) if any point lies well outside the pattern formed by the other points, neglect it when the line is being drawn. It probably is influenced by special factors which hide the relationship. (But do not erase it from the scatter diagram—be honest!)

We return now to our British productivity example and its scatter diagram. The points to be plotted are the fourteen pairs of measurements given in Table 10.1—an output index and a productivity index for each industry. These are plotted in Chart 10.3. In this chart the scale of the productivity axis has been chosen to be twice that of the output index. The pattern and direction are unmistakable—as output increases so does productivity. The only point which could be considered as disturbing the pattern is food, drink and tobacco, but

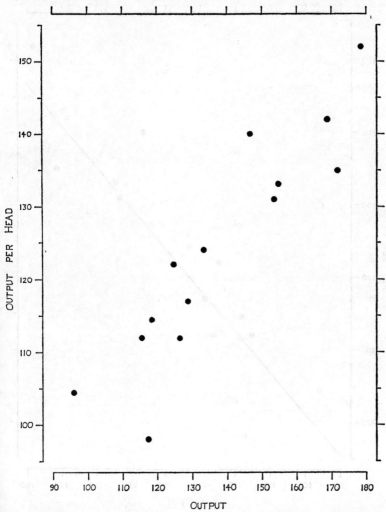

CHART 10.3. Scatter Diagram: 1955 Indexes of Output and Output per Head Employed (1948=100) in Fourteen United Kingdom Manufacturing Industries.
Source: Table 10.1.

that is not too far out of line to be safely neglected. Our conclusions from this inspection are, first, that there is a marked relationship; second, that a straight line will satisfactorily describe it; and third

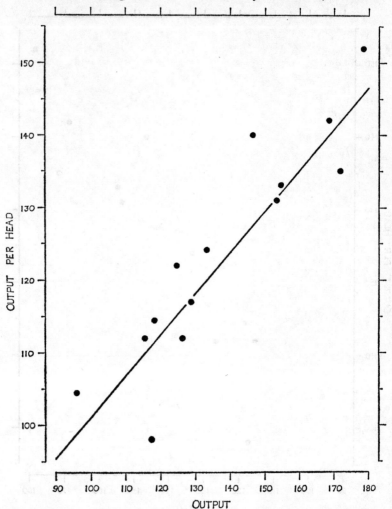

CHART 10.4. Scatter Diagram: 1955 Indexes of Output and Output per Head Employed (1948=100) in Fourteen United Kingdom Manufacturing Industries. With Line Describing Relationship. Source: Table 10.1.

that it appears to be reliable. (Reliability, of course, is a matter of degree, and we shall consider this in more detail below.)

To draw the straight line we first plot the point of averages. The arithmetic mean production index is 138.1; the arithmetic mean output per head index is 124.[1] In Chart 10.4, which is the same scatter diagram as Chart 10.3, a straight line is drawn through it describing the relationship. (We have drawn the line through a new scatter diagram for clarity; the student need normally only plot one and draw the line through that.)

The conclusion about the form of the relationship is that an x per cent increase in output is associated with an $\frac{x}{2}$ per cent increase in productivity, e.g. a 40 per cent increase in output is associated with approximately a 20 per cent increase in productivity. How reliable is this? Consider the scatter of points about the line. If we measure the vertical distances of the points from the line, we find that all except food, drink and tobacco and wood manufactures are within 5 per cent of the increase in output per head given by the relationship. If we measure the horizontal distances of the points from the line we find that again excepting food, drink and tobacco and wood manufactures the points are within 5 per cent of the increase in total output given by the relationship. We state our conclusion about reliability as follows: only 5 per cent of the increase in output per head is *unexplained by* (or unassociated with) the increase in output. If we include the two exceptional industries then approximately 10 per cent is unexplained. This way of stating the conclusion means that if we used the relationship to predict productivity changes in circumstances similar to those we are examining, we could expect to predict correctly on the average to within 5 per cent of the true figure. Note that this need not be a very useful conclusion: the circumstances may be quite different. It would, for instance, be dangerous to use the relationship to predict changes over a seven year period when industries were experiencing a slump—our results refer to boom conditions.

6. SOME WARNINGS AND HINTS
First, some warnings. Relationships may be discovered between economic phenomena which are purely coincidental and useless. (There is the story of the statistician who discovered a strong relationship between the annual change in the number of newly ordained Anglican clergymen and the annual change in the birth rate in India.)

[1] These are unweighted averages.

Situations to be wary of include (i) a relationship between two economic factors which is due to the fact that each of these factors is independently influenced by another, unknown third factor. For instance the familiar relationship between numbers of babies born alive and the numbers of storks observed is probably due to the influence of warm weather on both phenomena. At best this sort of relationship is unreliable; at worst it is positively misleading.

(ii) The second situation to be wary of is a relationship between two time series. If the two time series have strongly marked trends, a scatter diagram of their pairs of values (a point for each year) will always show a marked relationship. This need not be useless, but must be examined with care. (The problem is discussed in the following chapter.) In our productivity example we were not faced with this time series problem, but there is a possibility that some third factor (or set of factors) influences both output and productivity. For this reason we referred to the *association* between output changes and productivity changes. To determine whether one change *causes* another requires further investigation.

So far we have spoken of relationships as if they can all be described by straight lines. While this is true, it is sometimes the case that the best form of relationship is not a straight line, but some other curve. An alternative curve which often appears in scatter diagrams is something resembling a compound interest curve (whose slope increases at a constant rate). If this is the case then a scatter diagram formed from the points plotted from the *logarithms* of the numbers will assume the ordinary straight line pattern.

7. EXERCISES ON THE USE OF SCATTER DIAGRAMS
(a) *Effect of Investment upon Productivity*
In section 3 of this chapter it was suggested that increases in productivity might arise from the use of more and better plant and equipment. It is difficult to measure the quality of plant and equipment, and there are difficulties in even attempting to measure the stock of fixed capital used by an industry. Nevertheless, the connection between investment in fixed assets and changes in productivity is an important one and should be investigated despite difficulties of measurement and interpretation. The exercise is: what is the relationship between investment in fixed assets and changes in productivity?

There are several forms that this relationship could take, and only one of them is suggested here, viz. that an increase in the annual level of investment raises productivity. It is to be expected that increased investment will take some time to affect productivity (major investment projects are often spread over several years: it takes four or five years to build an oil refinery). Consequently, the increase in investment between, say, 1948 and 1955 should be compared with the change in productivity between 1948 and some period after 1955. As we have calculated productivity changes between 1948 and 1955 above, it is sensible to compare these with changes in investment between 1948 and the average of 1952-4. This allows for a delayed effect after an average of two years.

The first part of Table 53 in the 1959 NIE gives figures of investment in fixed assets for the fourteen manufacturing groups. The industrial classification in NIE is not quite the same as that used in AAS (the names of some industries differ) and we give here the list of corresponding groups:

NIE	AAS
Bricks, pottery, glass, etc.	Non-metalliferous mining manufactures
Mineral oil refining	
Other chemicals and allied industries	Chemicals and allied trades
Iron and steel	Metal manufacture
Other metals	
Engineering and electrical	Engineering, shipbuilding and electrical goods
Shipbuilding and marine engineering	
Motor vehicles and cycles	
Aircraft	Vehicles
Other vehicles	

There is no separate investment figure for Precision instruments. The remaining industries are described similarly in both sources, with the exception that Leather is combined with Clothing in the investment statistics. Thus the number of our groups is reduced to twelve.

The procedure for each of the twelve industries is to calculate the annual average investment for the years 1952, 1953 and 1954, and express this as a ratio of the 1948 figure. (The investment figures are in current values, but as we compare the industries over the same period there is no need to construct a volume index—we assume that the price of fixed assets changed the same for all industries.)[1]

The twelve investment ratios are then compared with the twelve productivity ratios from Table 10.1 above. (A combined Leather and

[1] If we were to use our results for predictions in other periods, it would be necessary to adjust for price changes.

Clothing production index is substituted for the two separate ones: a weighted average production index is calculated using the official weights given to the two industries—Table 152, 1958 AAS—the combined index is 110·0. This is divided by the index of civil employment in both industries—102·8—to obtain the combined productivity index of 108.)

Plot the indexes and ratios on a scatter diagram, one axis measuring the investment ratio, the other the productivity index. Note that the resulting pattern is distorted by food, drink and tobacco (which appears to be even more of an exception than it was in the output-productivity relationship; why is this so?). Draw the straight line describing the relationship, omitting food, drink and tobacco from consideration. Estimate the reliability of the relationship.

(b) Effect of Income upon Expenditure

We now turn to a different type of economic relationship: that between personal income and expenditures upon consumption goods. Income is the main factor limiting expenditures, and we expect that households with larger incomes will make larger expenditures. What form does this relationship take? It will probably depend upon the particular goods and services bought.

To estimate the weights used in the official Index of Retail Prices (see Chapter 3, section 5) the Ministry of Labour conducted a survey of household expenditures in 1953-4. The results are summarized in the Ministry's publication *Report of an Inquiry into Household Expenditure in 1953-4* (HMSO, 1957). This is a mine of information about household spending habits, and the information is classified in several useful ways: according to household income, number of people in the household, geographical region, etc. As the starting point of our investigation, we have chosen the average weekly expenditures of households consisting of a man, a woman and one child (Table 21 of the *Report*). For the exercise, we present the expenditures of these households (classified according to the gross income of the household) on total food, all fruit, bread, and total alcoholic drink, in Table 10.3.

The *Report* groups the weekly household incomes into six ranges. This is not convenient for plotting on a graph, so we have given a figure for the average weekly income of the households in each group. This figure has been obtained from the *Report* by adding all expenditures including payments for income tax, mortgages and life insurance, purchases of savings certificates and deposits in savings banks, and net betting expenditures. The resulting average has been

TABLE 10.3

Average Weekly Expenditures of Households Consisting of
Man, Wife and One Child

Weekly income of household		Number of households in survey	Total food	Expenditures		
Range	Average			Fruit (fresh, frozen, canned)	Bread, rolls, etc.	Total Alcoholic drink
				Shillings and pence		
Under £6	£ 7 5s	63	57/1	2/4	4/5	2/4
£ 6 to under £8	£ 8 10s	289	64/5	3/1	4/–	4/2
£ 8 to under £10	£11	405	71/3	3/9	4/–	6/1
£10 to under £14	£13 10s	568	79/2	4/7	3/9	6/5
£14 to under £20	£17	258	86/7	5/3	3/8	10/5
£20 or more	£27 10s	82	108/2	7/10	3/6	17/–

Source: Ministry of Labour: *Report . . . into Household Expenditure in* 1953-4
(*HMSO* 1957), Table 21.

rounded to the nearest five shillings. For the lower incomes this
figure is greater than the top of the respective range—indicating an
understatement of income by the households in the survey (as the
Report suggests, pp. 15 and 20), rather than recourse to the money
lender.

Draw a scatter diagram for each type of expenditure (e.g. for fruit,
measure average weekly expenditure on fruit on one axis, and average
weekly household income on the other—there are six points to plot).
Compare the forms of the relationships. (There is no need to draw in
the lines describing the relationships when the number of points is so
small.)

Use the *Report* itself to compare the forms of the relationships
between income and the main categories of expenditure, i.e. housing;
fuel, light and power; food; alcoholic drink; tobacco; clothing and
footwear; etc. Which category of expenditure is most responsive to
differences in income? What is the connection between these income-
expenditure relationships and the concept of elasticity of demand?

Note that when expenditure changes with income, two things can
change: the quantity of the good or service, and also its quality. The
Ministry of Labour's *Report* contains no information on this matter,
but some figures are available from the National Food Survey's
quarterly estimates of household food expenditure and consumption,
published in the MDS. In Table 116 of the September 1959 MDS there
are figures of weekly expenditure per head and of weekly quantity
purchases (ounces, pints, etc.), both expenditures and quantities
being classified according to household income. By dividing the

N

quantity into the expenditure an average price is obtained; differences in average price paid by different income groups can be regarded as indicating the differences in quality consumed. What is the form of the relationship between quality and income in the cases of bread and tea consumption?

CHAPTER ELEVEN

The Dependence of the United Kingdom Economy upon Imports

1. INPUT-OUTPUT TABLES

In this chapter our examples of economic relationships are drawn from the dependence of the United Kingdom economy upon imports. Dependence, which is a matter of degree, can be considered from two points of view: first, the economy is dependent upon imports in the sense that the organization and structure of the economy relies upon imported raw materials used in production, and imported goods and services for final consumption (especially foodstuffs); second, dependence can mean that changes in the level of output are so closely related to changes in the level of imports that the blame for the vicissitudes of the economy can in some way be placed on imports—for example, a rise in the price of imports may cause an adverse balance of payments which could engender a foreign exchange crisis of some sort.

In this section we shall consider the extent to which imports affect the structure of the economy.

From Table 11 of the 1959 NIE we find that imports of goods and services (at factor cost) were in 1958 just over 20 per cent of GNP(fc) —they had been 23 per cent in 1957. This means that to produce its 1958 GNP the United Kingdom used up imported goods and services equal to over one fifth of the value of GNP. This is an average for the economy as a whole: obviously in some industries the figure would be greater. What the situation is in different industries is shown in the input-output table for 1954 presented as Table 18 in the 1958 NIE.[1]

The 1954 input-output table shows the dependence of each industry upon the outputs of other industries. For example, in 1954 the metals, engineering and vehicles industry group, whose total output was

---

[1] Input-output tables and their connection with the social accounts were explained in Chapter 5, section 7, above. The only issue of NIE in which the 1954 table is contained is that of 1958; it is also contained in the December 1958 issue of ET.

£4,719 million, purchased £198 million of the output of the chemical industry (column 4, row 3). We say that on the average £100 of the metal, engineering and vehicle group's output required £4 of the chemical industry's output $\left(\dfrac{198}{4,719}=0\cdot04\right)$. But this was only the *direct* requirement. The metal, engineering and vehicle group purchased goods from several other industries whose outputs in turn required the use of part of the chemical output. For example, the metal, engineering and vehicle group purchased £50 million of mining and quarrying output, and mining and quarrying's total output of £797 million required £16 million of chemical's output. But the calculations do not stop there for mining and quarrying themselves purchased goods from other industries who in turn purchased goods from chemicals. In other words, as well as metal, engineering and vehicle's direct requirements from the chemical industry, there are the *indirect* requirements caused by the inter-dependence amongst industries.

The direct *plus* indirect requirements, calculated from Table 18, are shown in Tables 19 and 20 (all in the 1958 NIE). Table 19 gives the information that in 1954 each £100 of final output (output purchased by final buyers) of the metals, engineering and vehicles group required on the average £6 of the chemical industry's output. Table 20 states that each £100 of metal, engineering and vehicle's total output required £1 of the net output of the chemical industry. Table 21 shows the relationships of Table 18 in another form. It starts with final expenditures of persons, public authorities, etc., and gives the direct *plus* indirect requirements of the net output of the industries which the expenditures create. Tables 22-24 rearrange these requirements according to types of income rather than industrial net output.

Let us now return to the economy's dependence upon imports. First consider the import requirements of an industry. The estimates taking into account both direct and indirect requirements are given in the lower half of Table 19 of 1958 NIE. To produce £100 of total output of the metals, engineering and vehicle group required on the average in 1954 £12 of imports. This import requirement varies from £4 in the case of mining and quarrying to £29 in the case of textiles, leather and clothing.

Second, consider the import requirements of different types of final expenditure: the information is given in Table 21 of 1958 NIE. In 1954, on the average, £100 of consumers' expenditure required £20 of imports; £100 of exports required £18 of imports; for all final expenditure the figure was £17. Final expenditure is the same quantity as final output, and Table 24 shows that the average import requirements each year since 1948 have varied between £16 and £18 except in 1951.

The figures we have been quoting from the input-output tables are average figures, i.e. it is assumed that any £100 of A's output requires the same amount of an input from B as any other £100 of A's output. Also, the figures are based upon the transactions actually occurring in 1954. To use the figures to answer a question such as: 'how much more inputs are required to produce an *extra* £100 of A's output?' is to assume that the extra (or marginal) requirement is the same as the average requirement. This may often be the case, but sometimes it will not be so—for instance when the capacity of the coal industry is under-used, an extra £100 of steel probably would not require any coal imports, but if the capacity of the coal industry is being fully used, an extra £100 of steel would require imports of coal.

The distinction between average and extra requirements is clearly an important one (the student will remember the distinctions between average and marginal costs, and average and marginal productivity). Economists and framers of economic policy are interested in the extra inputs of various kinds (including imports) required by increases in output—the construction of a modern steel works will increase steel requirements because of the repercussions of the construction upon other industries; a policy aimed at raising national income will increase imports. In the absence of other information, the average figures in the input-output tables give a rough idea of extra input requirements, but guesses based on these figures must take into account the circumstances in which the extra inputs are required, and in particular the extent to which the capacity of the various industries is being used. We shall refer again to the distinction between average and marginal requirements in section 3 below.

2. IMPORTS AND THE BALANCE OF PAYMENTS

At the beginning of the previous section we pointed out that imports, as well as entering importantly into the structure of the economy, may also through their changes affect the fortunes of the economy— by way of affecting the balance of payments. In this section we shall examine the effect of changes in imports upon the balance of payments. The current surplus—or deficit—on the balance of payments is the surplus—or deficit—of receipts over payments arising from the United Kingdom's current international transactions: receipts from exports of goods and services, and current transfers; and payments for imports of goods and services, and current transfers. If any one of these items change so the current surplus or deficit will change.

TABLE 11.1

Imports and the Balance of Payments, 1948-58

£ million at factor cost

	Surplus on current account	Annual change in surplus on current account	Value of imports of goods and services		Annual change in value of imports of goods and services		
			at current prices	at 1954 prices	at current prices	at 1954 prices	Change in value due to price changes
	(1)	(2)	(3)	(4)	(5)	(6)	(7)
1948	7		2195	2951			
1949	38	+ 31	2407	3163	+212	+212	0
1950	297	+259	2817	3208	+410	+ 35	+375
1951	−419	−716	4077	3590	+1260	+382	+878
1952	227	+646	3548	3285	−529	−305	−224
1953	179	− 48	3452	3472	− 96	+187	−283
1954	211	+ 32	3612	3612	+160	+140	+ 20
1955	− 73	−284	4149	3983	+537	+371	+166
1956	237	+310	4280	4093	+131	+110	+ 21
1957	263	− 26	4433	4199	+153	+106	+ 47
1958	438	+175	4118	4201	−315	+ 2	−313

Source: 1959 NIE, Tables 7, 11 and 13.

In Table 11.1 we show the surplus on current account (column 1) and the value of imports of goods and services (column 3) from Tables 7 and 11 respectively of the 1959 NIE. To show the relationships between changes in imports and changes in the current surplus we calculate the annual changes by taking the differences of successive years. These are shown in columns 2 and 5. The effect of an increase in imports, other items remaining unchanged, is to reduce the current surplus (or increase the current deficit). In 1948-9, and 1949-50, imports increased but so did the current surplus—obviously other items were more than offsetting the rise in imports. But in 1950-1 imports increased by a large amount—£1,260 million: the Korean war commodity boom—and the current surplus fell by £716 million. Some items offset the rise in imports, but not enough to prevent the large swing from surplus to deficit. In 1951-2 imports fell and the deficit was reduced—becoming a surplus—by about the same amount. In 1952-3 and 1953-4 there were small changes in imports which appear to have been offset by changes in other items. In 1954-5 a large rise in imports caused a large fall in the surplus; in 1955-6 another rise in imports was offset by other items because the surplus increased; and in 1956-7 a further rise in imports was again largely offset. The big fall in imports in 1957-8 was associated with a rise in the surplus, although not by the same amount.

It is clear from this examination that the annual changes in imports have frequently been large in relation to the annual value of imports, although due to offsetting changes in other items these large changes have been responsible for large changes in the surplus on only a few occasions—in 1950-1, 1951-2, and 1954-5 in particular. Note however that 1951 and 1955 were the only two years when the current account was in deficit, and these were years of sterling crisis and spectacular changes in Government policy.[1]

To what extent were the changes in the value of imports due to changes in volume (physical quantity) or to changes in the prices of imports? To determine this we use the figures of imports valued at 1954 prices (Table 13, 1959 NIE). The annual change in this volume series is shown in column 6 of Table 11.1. The difference between the value changes in column 5 and the volume changes in column 6 is the change in value due to price changes: this is shown in column 7.[2] It appears that volume changes and price changes contributed differently in different years to the value change, although in all the annual changes except one the price and volume changes reinforced each other. The exception was 1952-3 when a considerable price fall more than offset a rise in the volume of imports—this was the coincidence of the revival of the United Kingdom economy after its brief recession in 1952 with the post-Korean fall in world commodity prices.

It is clear that changes in the value of imports are an important influence on the balance of payments. Can we explain these changes? Can we say why imports rise and fall in the ways they have done? To start to answer these questions we shall consider the *volume* of imports. In what follows we shall neglect import prices, leaving that problem for the student to examine himself. One reason for initially neglecting import prices in this context is that Table 11.1 shows that on average import prices and volume of imports change in the same direction. This suggests that a rise in the volume of United Kingdom imports causes a rise in their price. In view of the United Kingdom's prominent position as an international trader this is a reasonable hypothesis—although the situation of 1952-3 mentioned above shows that this need not always be the case.

---

[1] We have picked out the years when changes in imports were not sufficiently offset by changes in other items to diminish the effect on the current surplus. Clearly, surpluses in some years would have been larger were it not for increases in imports—crisis years are those years when the changes in other items are not sufficiently offsetting.

[2] 'Change in value due to price changes' is the volume of the first year's imports multiplied by the price change *plus* the change in the volume of imports multiplied by the second year's price.

3. IMPORTS AND CHANGES IN OUTPUT

We want to explain the annual changes in the volume of exports from 1948 to 1958. What determines whether the annual change is large or small, an increase or a decrease? We approach the question by examining the demand for imports. The input-output tables discussed in section 1 above showed that each of the components of final expenditure (or final output) required large amounts of imports for their production. It seems likely that an increase in output would require an increase in imports—for instance, an increase in the production of cotton cloth requires an increase in the use of raw cotton which is one of the United Kingdom's important imported raw materials.

Our hypothesis is that changes in imports are determined by changes in output. We measure changes in imports by the annual changes in their volume (column 6 of Table 11.1) and changes in output by annual changes in the volume of total final expenditure. Total final expenditure includes all goods and services produced in the United Kingdom available for consumption or investment, at home or abroad. Both imports and final expenditure are valued at factor cost—we have the choice of factor cost or market prices (both are given in NIE) and we follow the procedure adopted in other volume indexes (such as in the index of industrial production) by valuing at factor cost. The 1959 NIE does not give a separate figure for final expenditure at 1954 factor cost, which can be obtained from Table 13 (lower half) by subtracting 'Adjustment to factor cost' from 'Total final expenditure at market prices'.

TABLE 11.2
Imports and Total Final Expenditure; 1948-58
£ million at 1954 *factor cost*

	Total final expenditure	Annual change in total final expenditure	Annual change in imports of goods and services
	(1)	(2)	(3)
1948	16,006		
1949	16,684	+678	+212
1950	17,195	+511	+ 35
1951	18,024	+829	+382
1952	17,776	−248	−305
1953	18,514	+738	+187
1954	19,326	+812	+140
1955	20,211	+885	+371
1956	20,641	+430	+110
1957	20,968	+327	+106
1958	20,849	−119	+ 2

Source: 1959 NIE, Table 13.

The two series of annual changes are shown together in Table 11.2. We wish to show the form and reliability of the relationship between the changes. The scatter diagram is the appropriate tool. Before we procede with this, some general comments on the use of scatter diagrams in connection with time series are necessary.

4. SCATTER DIAGRAMS OF RELATIONSHIPS BE-TWEEN TIME SERIES

In Chapter 10 our scatter diagrams were confined to measurements taken at the same point or period of time. We are now dealing with time series whose measurements refer to a sequence of dates or periods. Most time series have a trend—a tendency for the values to rise or fall (see Chapter 9). Tables 11.1 (column 4) and 11.2 (column 1) show that both annual imports and annual final expenditures (not annual changes) have a rising trend over the eleven year period. This means that if we plot these two series on a scatter diagram—a point for the pair of measurements for each year—we shall inevitably find a relationship whose form links high annual imports with high annual final expenditure. *This would be a very misleading relationship.* It shows no more than that both series have rising trends (which we know from simple inspection of the tables). The difficulty is that most economic times series of expenditure and output over the period 1948 to 1958 have rising trends—the different parts of the economy are so inter-dependent that most economic quantities over a lengthy period show the same characteristic trends of growth—or of stagnation or decay. *To show a relationship of cause and effect between two economic time series it is nearly always necessary to eliminate the trend first.*

Both imports and final expenditures tended to rise during the period: that in itself proves nothing about the dependence of imports upon final expenditures. But if we find that a large divergence from the trend in imports is associated with a large divergence from the trend in final expenditures then we have some proof of dependence which is not just a coincidental relationship between trends.

The measurement of trend and divergences from it can be a complicated procedure in the case of the time series we are considering. The simplest, and often the best practice, is to go part of the way to eliminate the trend by taking annual differences between successive measurements. Instead of taking the difference between the actual measurement in a year and the trend value of that year, we take the difference between one year's measurement and that of the next year. Thus for imports we take their annual change, and for final expendi-

tures their annual change also. We draw a scatter diagram of the pairs
of annual changes.

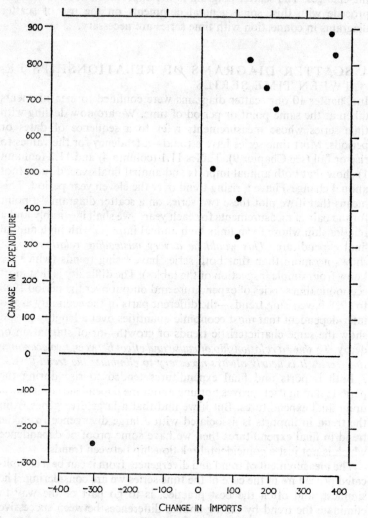

CHART 11.1. Scatter Diagram: Annual Change in Volume of Total
Final Expenditure and of Imports, 1948-58. United Kingdom.
£ million at 1954 prices.
Source: Table 11.2.

The procedure outlined in the last paragraph is just what we were going to do before we interrupted with this digression on the relationship between times series. Our earlier argument had led us naturally to attempt to relate annual changes. The student can take as a general rule—with hardly any safe exceptions—that he should always plot on scatter diagrams the changes rather than the original series themselves.

The scatter diagram of the annual changes of final expenditure and imports is shown in Chart 11.1. Each annual change in imports is plotted against the corresponding annual change in final expenditure, e.g. in 1948-9 imports increased by £212 million; the corresponding change in final expenditure was a rise of £678 million: this is represented by the point (+212, +678). Note that the axes must be numbered from negative numbers (decreases) to positive numbers.

The resulting pattern shows the expected relationship: when final expenditures increase so do imports. A straight line describing the relationship suggests that £100 million increase (or decrease) in final expenditure requires approximately £50 million increase (or decrease) in imports.[1] This high figure for *extra* import requirements is to be compared with the 1954 *average* figure of only £17 of imports for each £100 of final expenditure. This is a striking example of the possible difference between extra (marginal) requirements and average requirements discussed above in section 1.

With the statistics we are using it is not possible to be more precise than we have been in the last paragraph. We would conclude this investigation by saying that there appears to be a strong relationship between changes in imports and changes in final expenditure. The evidence covers only the post-war period during part of which imports were subjected to severe Government controls. The likelihood that extra import requirements are much larger than average requirements must be an important consideration in the framing of economic policy.

5. IMPORTS AND CHANGES IN INVESTMENT IN STOCKS

The features of the relationship between imports and output (or final expenditures) are striking and important enough to warrant much more investigation. One line of approach is the connection between imports and the various components of final expenditure: some of these components may be less important as determinants of imports

[1] The student should plot the scatter diagram from the figures in Table 11.2, fit the straight line, and estimate the reliability of the relationship.

than others, e.g. changes in consumers' expenditure may have little immediate effect upon imports even though consumers' expenditure has a large average import requirement. One item of final expenditure, the value of the physical increase in stocks and work in progress (inventory or stock investment), is likely to be strongly associated with imports because a large part of stocks in the United Kingdom are imported raw materials.

Decisions to increase stocks of raw materials because of expected price increases or increases in demand for output may result in increased imports of those raw materials. We shall examine this relationship here. A word of warning is necessary however. Increases in stocks may be unintended: a fall in sales of output may catch manufacturers unawares so that stocks may rise before production and orders for raw materials can be cut back. Thus instead of a decision to increase stocks causing an increase in imports, a decision to increase imports may cause an unintended rise in stocks if it coincides with an unexpected fall in sales. This uncertainty about the proper interpretation of statistics of stock investment is always present.

The NIE estimates of stock investment are shown in Table 11.3. We have already mentioned the exceptional error likely to be attached to these figures; the volume estimates are to be regarded as even more

TABLE 11.3

Investment in Stocks, 1948-58

£ million at market prices

	Investment in stocks*		Annual change in investment in stocks	
	(1) at current prices	(2) at 1954 prices	(3) at current prices	(4) at 1954 prices
1948	175	235		
1949	65	35	−110	−200
1950	−210	−240	−275	−275
1951	575	565	+785	+805
1952	50	40	−525	−525
1953	125	130	+ 75	+ 90
1954	50	50	− 75	− 80
1955	300	315	+250	+265
1956	275	265	− 25	− 50
1957	360	300	+ 85	+ 35
1958	50	50	−310	−250

* Value of physical increase in stocks and work in progress.
Source: 1959 NIE, Tables 11 and 13.

uncertain and the annual changes (column 4) must be treated as the least reliable economic measurements the statisticians have been able to devise. We must not expect too much from our investigation nor should we read too much into the results.

Stock investment at factor cost is not shown separately in the 1959 NIE; consequently we use the estimates at market prices. The valuation of stocks is such a matter of guesswork and convention that this should not affect our results. We use the same import statistics as before (column 3 of Table 11.2).

The scatter diagram of the annual changes in imports and stock investment is shown in Chart 11.2. Considering the unreliability of the statistics the appearance of a marked pattern is gratifying. Moreover it is a scatter in the direction we should expect, with no errant points. Clearly, an increase in investment in stocks is strongly associated with an increase in imports. If we exclude the highest point (1950-1) the relationship can be satisfactorily described by a straight line. If we take this highest point into account, the relationship appears to be described by a slightly curved line—the import requirement of a small change in stock investment is greater than the import requirement of a large change. This at first sight is surprising—the opposite of what we might expect. The explanation is most likely that there are some special factors pushing the 1950-1 point out of line, i.e. the expected relationship between imports and stock investment is being interfered with by other factors. The change in stock investment in 1950-1 is the largest recorded, and must be ultimately connected with the commodity boom and associated attempt to stockpile at the onset of the Korean war. In view of these exceptional factors, and the unreliability of the measurements themselves, we think it inadvisable to regard the scatter diagram as evidence of anything but a simple straight line relationship with the 1950-1 point out of line for exceptional reasons.

If this interpretation of the scatter is agreed, our line describing the relationship would be drawn neglecting the 1950-1 point, and would suggest that every £100 million increase in investment in stocks is associated with about £100 million increase in imports. If we assume that most of the increases in stocks are intended, we can call this figure the marginal import requirement of stock investment. Obviously it is very high in relation to the average and marginal import requirements of other components of final expenditure, and suggests that the United Kingdom's external position—as reflected in her balance of payments—is extremely sensitive to changes in the level of stock investment.

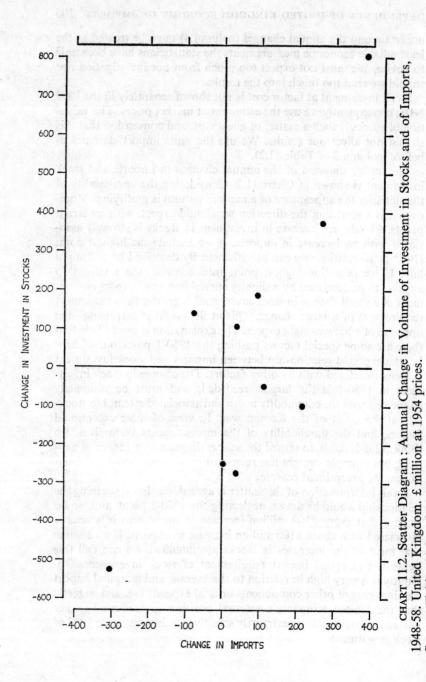

CHART 11.2. Scatter Diagram: Annual Change in Volume of Investment in Stocks and of Imports,
1948-58. United Kingdom. £ million at 1954 prices.
Source: Tables 11.2 and 11.3.

The assumptions involved in the conclusions of the last two paragraphs should serve to warn the student that this investigation into the determination of the volume of imports is intended to be suggestive rather than conclusive. The steps to follow at the next stage of the investigation would be studies of the determinants of the different types of imported goods themselves.[1]

6. EXERCISES ON THE USE OF SCATTER DIAGRAMS

(a) The 'wage drift' and the market for labour. At times since the end of the war there has been observed a tendency for weekly wage earnings (including overtime, bonuses, etc.) to increase more rapidly than weekly wage rates (minimum rates for work during a standard working week). This phenomenon, first called the 'wage drift' in Sweden where it has been also observed, has been thought by some economists to be associated with full employment in the labour market and the consequent competition amongst employers for labour. The competition takes the form of offering rates of pay higher than the minimum, bonuses and overtime opportunities so that weekly earnings inevitably increase faster than the minimum standard rates which are either set by statute or by slowly working processes of negotiation.

The evidence of the wage drift can be examined by comparing the Ministry of Labour's six-monthly estimates of average weekly earnings of wage earners with the Ministry's index of wage rates. Both of these sets of figures are published in the MDS. Table 159 in the September 1959 MDS gives the figures of earnings for all operatives in manufacturing and certain other industries from April 1947. The column alongside the earnings series shows the earnings index obtained by calculating the percentage increases over April 1947, and also an index of wage rates which relates to the industries covered by the earnings figures.[2]

Plot the April values of the earnings index and the wage rate index (both with April 1947=100) on a ratio chart. Examine the graphs to determine at what periods earnings rose more rapidly than wage rates.

To investigate the relationship between the wage drift and the state of the labour market we must first measure these two phenomena. The wage drift can be measured by the ratio of the earnings index to the wage rate index. A rise in this ratio will show that earnings in-

[1] For a recent investigation on these lines the student can consult the article on 'Imports and Expansion' in the *National Institute Economic Review*, March 1959, pp. 26-40.

[2] Wage rate indexes for industries whether included in the earnings figures or not are shown in Table 163 of the MDS.

creased more rapidly than wage rates. The state of the labour market is not such an easy thing to measure. We suggest the ratio of the number unemployed to the number of unfilled employment vacancies. A rise in this ratio will indicate that employment is more difficult to obtain; a fall will show that jobs are easier to come by. Monthly averages of the registered unemployed in Great Britain for each year back to 1947 are given in the AAS (Table 136 of the 1958 AAS); unfilled employment vacancies in Great Britain back to 1947 are also shown in the AAS (Table 137 of the 1958 AAS): use either the December figure or the monthly average.

Calculate these two ratios (earnings over wage rates; and unemployment over vacancies) for each year since 1947, and plot the points on a scatter diagram to determine the form and reliability of the relationship. Also, calculate the annual percentage changes of each of the two ratios for each year since 1947—to avoid allowing the marked trend in the wage drift to influence the results—and plot the points of this relationship on a scatter diagram.

(b) *Liquidity and interest rates.* Modern monetary theory suggests that changes in the supply of money will affect interest rates. This complicated subject can not be treated comprehensively in a single example here, and the following exercise is intended to do no more than start the student on his own investigations.

The appropriate measure of money in these circumstances is the ratio of the stock of money to the national income: what is called the *liquidity ratio* (the inverse of this ratio is the income velocity of circulation). The definition of what is money is inevitably rather arbitrary and should suit the circumstances; we shall take it as notes and coin held by the public *plus* total bank deposits. The 1958 AAS gives these statistics from 1947 in Tables 324 and 325. From them, using national income figures, the average annual liquidity ratio can be calculated. It is the annual changes in this ratio which are likely to be important.

Which rates of interest are affected by changes in liquidity is part of our problem. It is sensible to try, first, the average annual yield on Government $2\frac{1}{2}$ per cent Consols—usually regarded as the typical long-term interest rate. This is given in Table 328 of the 1958 AAS (along with other interest rates—the very short-term rates are shown in Table 329). Determine the relationship, using a scatter diagram, between the annual change in the liquidity ratio and the annual percentage change in the average yield on Consols.

Can you give an explanation of your findings? Can you improve upon the statistical procedure outlined above?

CHAPTER TWELVE

Fluctuations in American Business Activity
1947-58

1. INTRODUCTION: UNITED STATES ECONOMIC STATISTICS

The United States Government and its numerous agencies, as well as many private investigators, collect and publish periodically an enormous quantity of statistical information and economic comment based upon the statistics. Despite the quantity of information it is in some respects more accessible than that provided in the United Kingdom largely because it is conveniently collected into a small number of publications. The main United States statistical sources are:

(1) *Survey of Current Business* (SCB), published monthly by the Department of Commerce, Washington. This is similar in design to the United Kingdom's MDS and ET, but contains also authoritative articles on current economic subjects, including in February each year an annual review. In February, May, August and November the latest quarterly national income statistics are published and discussed, and in July the annual national income statistics are brought up to date. SCB is indispensible for the student of current American affairs.

(2) *National Income* (Supplement to the Survey of Current Business). This is a periodical reference book for national income statistics, containing figures back to 1929 and explanations of methods of estimation. The last edition was in 1954.

(3) *United States Income and Output* (Supplement to the Survey of Current Business, 1958). A special reference book containing quarterly national income statistics at constant prices since 1946, an analysis of the American economy using the national income statistics, and a discussion of methods of estimation and uses of the estimates.

(4) *Business Statistics* (Supplement to the Survey of Current Business). A biennial reference book of annual (with quarterly and

o

monthly over a three year period) figures of the series contained in SCB. The last edition was in 1957. It is similar in design to the United Kingdom's AAS.

These four sources contain most of the statistics the student normally requires. They include statistics calculated by branches of the United States Government which are also published in the journals of those branches such as the Federal Reserve Board's index of production published in its *Monthly Bulletin*, and the Department of Labour's consumer price index published in its *Monthly Labour Review*. A useful summary of economic statistics is contained in the annual *Economic Report of the President*. Most of these American sources are available in large libraries in the United Kingdom, and can also be obtained through booksellers or directly from the United States Government Printing Office, Washington.

We do not intend to describe the peculiarities of American statistics here. That in fact is usually done in the sources listed above. However, two general observations are required. Most American statistics are published very quickly after their collection or estimation. This usually involves a large amount of guesswork, especially in quarterly national income statistics at constant prices. Subsequently these provisional figures are revised, and often the revisions are large. We have already mentioned this problem in connection with some United Kingdom statistics: in the United States this problem is even greater both because of the greater extent of the economy and because of the Americans' daring in the matter of rapid publication. In preparing a series of statistics over a lengthy period of time, the student will find it essential to make certain that the earlier figures being used are not only comparable with later figures but are the revised figures. This is where the periodical supplements to SCB like *National Income* and *Business Statistics* are useful: these sources both give lengthy series and indicate differences in coverage and revisions.

The second general observation refers to comparisons between United Kingdom and United States statistics (or between those of any other group of countries). *In general this is extremely hazardous* unless the student knows how the different sets of statistics have been obtained. In the case of national income statistics the differences are not too great: differences in classification (e.g. what payments are to be treated as transfer payments) can usually be found by consulting the reference books. But in other cases the differences are large and can be misleading. For instance, the United Kingdom unemployment statistics are based upon the numbers of people who register at employment exchanges for work. The United States statistics are based on a sample of people actually out of a job, the sample being then adjusted to the size of the total population. If these figures are then calculated as percentages of the total working population it is quite misleading to compare the percentages of the two countries. Quite apart from the meaning and importance of unemployment in the two countries because of differences in the mobility of labour, the percentages are measuring differing things. The student is warned!

What we are going to do in this chapter is to show how some of the most accessible American statistics can be used to describe and explain the development of the American economy since the war. We do this by studying the fluctuations in economic activity as revealed by the index of industrial production and the quarterly constant price national income statistics. The fluctuations—sometimes called the trade or business cycle—are discussed in relation to the political and other economic events of the times, and also in relation to the long-term growth in American economic activity. Undoubtedly in the short space of a chapter many of the reader's questions will be left unanswered: the remedy lies in the American statistical sources in his own hands.

2. EXPENDITURE AND OUTPUT IN PERIODS OF CONTRACTION AND EXPANSION

Since the end of the Second World War there have been four periods of expanding business activity in the United States (including the most recent revival after the 1957-8 recession) broken by three short but sharp contractions. The peaks and troughs in industrial production are shown in Table 12.1 (and also in Chart 12.1). For the table

TABLE 12.1

Peaks and Troughs in American Business Activity, 1948-58

		Index of industrial production 1947-9 = 100	Number of quarters from peak to trough
Peak	1948/III	104	3
Trough	1949/II	95	16
Peak	1953/II	138	5
Trough	1954/III	123	10
Peak	1957/I	146	5
Trough	1958/II	129	

Note: Roman numerals refer to the quarter of the year. Index numbers are quarterly averages of monthly index.
Source: *Survey of Current Business.*

and the following analysis the peak of an expansion is defined as that quarter after which the index of production ceased to rise, and the trough of a contraction is that quarter after which the index ceased to fall. Monthly data would, of course, show larger proportionate falls during the slumps. No great precision is aimed at in this dating—it is no more than an attempt to classify the main characteristics of business activity over time. Other measures of economic activity— such as quarterly national income figures—may have their peaks and troughs at different dates, but the differences will not be large.[1] The student can consult Chart 12.1 to see the differences between the index of production and GNP.

Production fell by about $11\frac{1}{2}$ per cent (from peak to trough) in the 1948-9 slump, by 9 per cent in 1953-4, and by $8\frac{1}{2}$ per cent in 1957-8. Chart 12.1 illustrates three further features of production: the 'sagging' of activity in early 1951 and again in early 1956; the fact that the gains in production over the 1947-9 level have been concentrated in two short periods—1950, and the three quarters after 1952/III; and the undoubted fact that industrial production over the whole period shows a declining rate of growth (compare with the GNP series).

For the period of each expansion and contraction we have identified, the changes in the main types of national expenditure are shown in Table 12.2. The figures are in constant (1957) dollars, and are the differences between the annual rates of expenditure between the peak quarter and the trough quarter in the case of contractions, and between the trough quarter and the peak quarter in the case of expansions.[2] The presentation in the table, while the simplest, can be misleading to the extent that between any two dates a certain expenditure may change and materially influence an expansion or contraction yet the change may not be shown in the table. We shall consider these

[1] National income estimates are of course the most comprehensive measure of economic activity, but they have the disadvantage in problems of dating economic fluctuations that they contain such a large element of service output. In considering the extent of rises and falls in activity and its effect upon incomes and welfare this is desirable, but in the matter of dating short-period alterations in activity with a view to establishing the causes of such alterations national income estimates will normally show peaks and troughs *after* the index of production because of the strong upwards trend in the output of the service industries and their insensitivity in the short run to changes in other types of economic activity.

[2] These estimates are based upon a new, constant price, quarterly national income series (seasonally adjusted) recently commenced by the Department of Commerce. The user is warned that small changes in the data from quarter to quarter can not be considered significant (unless they fall into some acceptable pattern).

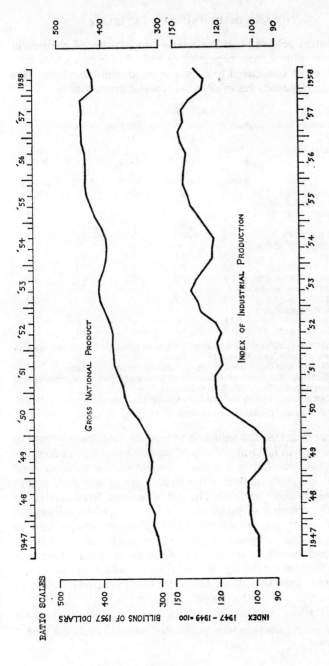

CHART 12.1. United States. Measures of Business Activity, 1947-58.
RATIO SCALES.
(1) Gross National Product: quarterly, seasonally adjusted at annual rates. Billions of 1957 dollars.
(2) Index of Industrial Production: quarterly averages of monthly seasonally adjusted indexes, 1947-9=100.
Sources: *US Income and Output*, and *SCB*.

casual matters below; here, the relative importance of changes in types of expenditure from beginning to end of an expansion or contraction is to be considered to obtain some idea of the quantitative importance of the changes in different types of expenditures.

TABLE 12.2

Changes in Expenditure on Gross National Product, 1948-1958

$ billion

Change in	From 1948/III to 1949/II	From 1949/II to 1953/II	From 1953/II to 1954/III	From 1954/III to 1957/I	From 1957/I to 1958/II
Gross national product	−5·3	+92·1	−13·6	+49·1	−22·6
Personal consumption expenditures (other than durables)	+3·7	+26·4	+ 4·2	+24·4	+ 4·0
Government purchases	+4·5	+43·5	−13·4	+ 2·1	+ 1·5
Inventory investment (other than farms)	−9·5	+ 9·5	− 7·5	+ 3·6	− 8·2
Business fixed investment	−2·8	+ 5·3	− 1·1	+ 8·1	− 8·9
New residential construction	−1·4	+ 3·9	+ 2·2	− 0·1	− 1·1
Personal expenditures on durables	+0·8	+ 7·9	− 1·2	+ 6·6	− 5·0
Net exports of goods and services	+2·1	− 4·6	+ 1·7	+ 4·5	− 4·6
Farm inventory investment	−2·7	+ 0·4	+ 1·4	− 0·1	− 0·4

Notes: (i) changes calculated from seasonally adjusted quarterly figures expressed as annual rates, in constant (1957) prices.
(ii) Government purchases include Government fixed investment.
(iii) Business fixed investment consists of producers' durable equipment and new construction other than residential.
(iv) Net exports of goods and services exclude Government cash grants abroad.

Source: *US Income and Output* (supplement to SCB), 1959.

First, it is clear that the reduction in business investment—both in fixed assets and in inventories[1]—is of prime importance in contractions. In 1948-9 the fall in inventory investment was twice as great as the fall in GNP, in 1953-4 it was as large as one half, and in 1957-8 it was nearly one third. The fall in business fixed investment was—by the criterion of proportion of fall in GNP—significant in 1948-9, of major importance in 1957-8, although insignificant in 1953-4. Two other categories of private investment—residential construction and inventory investment of the farm sector—have had little effect, except for the fall of the latter in 1948-9. In the expansions business fixed investment has contributed relatively slightly to the rise in output, and other forms of investment hardly at all.

Second, it is obvious that the demand for durable consumer goods

[1] We shall use the American term 'inventories' instead of the British 'stocks' in what follows.

(cars, furniture and household appliances, etc.) is an unstable item, although quantitatively it has been important only in the expansion which came after 1954/III, and in the following contraction. Its contribution to the 1953-4 slump was slight, while sales of these goods actually increased in 1948-9.

Third, Government purchases of goods and services increased in

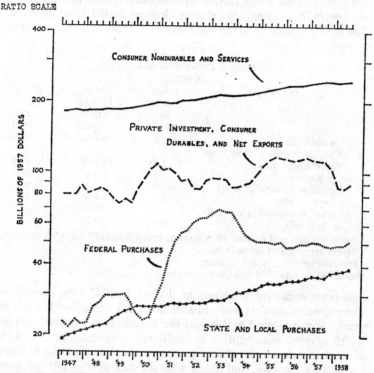

CHART 12.2. United States. Components of Gross National Product, 1947-58. RATIO SCALE. Quarterly, seasonally adjusted at annual rates. Billions of 1957 dollars.
Source: *US Income and Output*.

every period except during the contraction of 1953-4 when their fall was as great as the fall in GNP. In the other two contractions Government purchases moved anti-cyclically (for instance in 1948-9 they offset half the decline in inventory investment). The expansion of the early nineteen fifties was to be attributed mainly to Government purchases (more particularly: military expenditures) although the expansion of the mid-fifties owed little to Government.

Fourth, and most important from the point of view of the severity and duration of the slumps, personal consumption expenditures other than on durables rose in each of the periods, contributing considerably to each of the expansions. The stability of these expenditures in the contractions needs further examination. Table 12.3 shows the changes in the disposition of personal income during the contractions. The table is drawn up in the same way as is Table 12.2 except that the

TABLE 12.3

Changes in Personal Income, 1948-58

$ billion

Change in*	From 1948/III to 1949/II	From 1953/II to 1954/III	From 1957/I to 1958/II
Personal income	−5·9	+1·0	+7·5
[of which transfer income from Government was]	[+1·3]	[+2·5]	[+6·2]
Income taxes	−1·5	−3·0	0·0
Disposable personal income†	−4·5	+4·0	+7·5
Personal saving	−5·3	−1·6	−1·1
Personal consumption expenditures (total)	+0.9	+5.4	+8.5

* Items will not add because of rounding. From seasonally adjusted quarterly figures expressed as annual rates.
† Personal income *less* income taxes.
Source: SCB, July 1958 and December 1958.

figures are in current, not constant, dollars. In 1948-9 the increase in Government transfers and reduced taxes did not offset the fall in production incomes,[1] and it was the reduction in personal savings which allowed consumption expenditures to increase. In 1953-4 increased transfers and reduced tax payments did offset the reduced production incomes, and along with reduced savings allowed consumption to increase moderately. The pattern in 1957-8 differed, but the effects were the same: increased transfers swelled increased production incomes, tax and savings changes being slight.[2] It is obvious

[1] We refer to personal income *less* transfer payments as production income. It is income from employment and self-employment, *plus* rent, dividends and interest.

[2] We refer of course to changes over the entire contraction. Production income reached a peak in 1957/III, after which it fell for two quarters. It rose in 1958/II and in the following quarter surpassed the previous peak. See 'National Income and Product—A Review of the 1957-8 Decline and Recovery', *SCB*, November 1958.

that the automatic workings of the fiscal mechanism together with some positive Government action (reduced tax rates were effective in

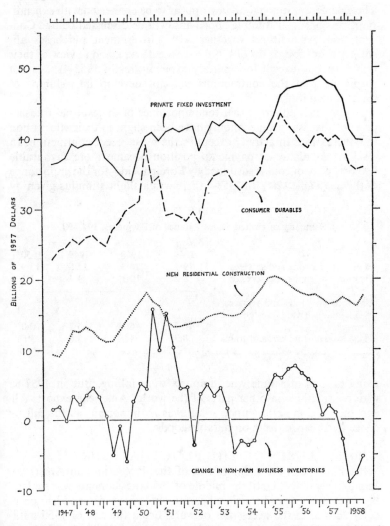

CHART 12.3. United States. Unstable Components of Gross National Product, 1947-58. Quarterly, seasonally adjusted at annual rates. Billions of 1957 dollars.

Source: *US Income and Output*.

1949 and in 1954) largely explain why consumption expenditures have been stabilizing and even expansionary factors in the contractions. The changes in personal savings appear to be connected with expenditures on consumer durable goods and will be discussed below. Consumption expenditures together with Government purchases absorbed about four fifths of GNP over the decade, and in view of their failure to fall (except for military expenditures in 1953-4) it is not surprising that the contractions did not develop into slumps of serious magnitudes.

Finally, it is apparent that the importance of the external transactions of the American economy have been slight in their effect upon the fluctuations in activity except in the most recent contraction. In 1948-9 the balance of payments position became more favourable (exports were of course sustained by Foreign Aid—for the importance of this see Table 12.4). In 1953-4 there was a slight stimulus given by

TABLE 12.4

Summary of United States Balance of Payments, 1947-50

| | $ billion | | | |
	1947	1948	1949	1950
Exports of goods and services	19·7	16·8	15·8	13·9
Imports of goods and services	8·2	10·3	9·7	12·1
Balance on goods and services, including private transfers and capital	+10·7	+6·1	+5·7	0·0
US Government loans and grants	8·7	4·9	5·6	3·6

Source: *Economic Report of the President*, January 1955, p. 196.

rising exports at a time when imports were falling. But in 1957-8, with contractions in other parts of the world, American exports fell and the resulting effect upon GNP was as important as the fall in consumers' expenditure on durable goods.

3. THE CAUSES OF THE FLUCTUATIONS

What have been the main causes of the fluctuations in American economic activity? Until the middle of 1950 the economy was replacing assets—both producers' and consumers' whose demand had been deferred due to the necessities of war.[1] From the end of 1950 until early in 1953 the Korean rearmament programme lifted activity to new heights. After that, until 1957, booms in consumer durables and in business investment sustained a further high level of activity until

[1] Investment had also been exceptionally low for ten years before the war.

the most recent contraction. Each of the three expansionary periods will now be examined in relation to the contractions that followed. The main statistics used in this section are presented in Charts 12.2 and 12.3. Detailed evidence for the statements made about the periods after 1950 is given, but to save space we shall not give detailed evidence for our conclusions about the post-war boom, but shall merely state our conclusions to serve as an introduction.[1]

The post-war replacement boom
The 1948-9 slump was the result of a shifting of demand from those assets whose replacement had been completed to those whose replacement had still to be made. The timing of these different replacement demands was not such as to prevent a contraction in activity but the successions were close enough to prevent a lengthy slump. Also, the easing of inflationary pressure in important sections of the economy in 1948 (largely through the slackening of replacement demands) permitted other pent-up demands to be met—although this caused some slackening in demands susceptible to deflation, such as inventory investment. In particular, total business fixed investment started to fall off at the end of 1948: in many lines investment had been falling off ever since 1946, e.g. machine tools. This fall in fixed investment caused manufacturers of durable goods to reduce their inventories of raw materials and goods in process, the fall in inventories between end-1948 and end-1949 being—the farm sector apart —almost entirely in the durable goods sector. But, to illustrate the point about off-setting demands, investment by the railways did not reach its peak until the end of 1949, while investment by public utilities rose until 1952.

These shifts in the composition of investment did not themselves prevent a fall in the total. What effectively offset the fall in investment was the big expansion in the sales of consumer durables starting in early 1949 and not reaching its peak until 1950/III. Cars in particular became more readily available for private consumers in early 1949 and a large deferred demand was awaiting them. (Hire purchase controls, imposed in September 1948, were relaxed in March 1949 and expired in September.) Television sets came on to the market in quantity in 1949 and 1950. We have mentioned in section 2 that tax

[1] The evidence on which our interpretation of the post-war boom is based can be found in C. A. Blyth: 'The 1948-9 American Recession'. *Economic Journal*, September 1954; and 'The US Cycle in Private Fixed Investment', 1946-50', *Review of Economics and Statistics*, February 1956. See also the *Economic Report of the President* (January 1950), pp. 70-71.

and transfer effects did not entirely offset the fall in production incomes in 1949: what did offset the fall was the decline in savings. It
seems that this fall in savings was a consequence of consumers'
decisions to spend more on durables.

The other factors which offset the fall in activity in 1949 were rising
Government expenditures and a rise in new residential construction.
Military expenditures and foreign aid rose from late 1947 to mid-
1949; other Government expenditures—particularly state and local
—were rising from early 1947 to late 1949; after that Government
expenditures fell until mid-1950. Residential construction started to
rise in the middle of 1949 and did not fall until late 1950—this anti-
cyclical movement was undoubtedly due to cheap money as well as a
fall in construction costs (a part of state and local Government expenditures being also due to these causes).

In conclusion, it appears that the 1948-9 contraction was due to a
shifting of replacement demands, aggravated by the induced fall in
inventory investment, and the revival was fundamentally due to the
same causes which permitted the expansion in sales of consumer
durables and the easing of inflationary pressure which stimulated
construction. Only the increase in military expenditures and foreign
aid can be regarded as economically unrelated in a direct way to these
causes.

The Korean rearmament boom
As we stated above, business investment, residential construction,
purchases of consumer durables—in fact all items of national expenditure—were rising in early 1950. How long the consumer durables
boom would have lasted without the Korean war can not be guessed,
but a wave of speculative buying in the face of fears of renewed
shortages undoubtedly explains the peak in consumer durables expenditures in 1950/III and also the peak in business inventory investment one quarter later. The subsequent fall in these items—and in
residential construction—would explain the sagging of the index of
production during 1951 already noticed.

Government expenditures—especially military—almost trebled between 1950/III and 1953/II. Business fixed investment maintained a
high and stable level during this period, inventory investment fell
back to less abnormal levels, while residential construction after
declining until 1951/III was stable until the end of 1953. Amongst the
controls established after the attack in Korea were those on hire
purchase of consumer durables, and regulations requiring longer
down payments and shorter periods of amortization in the construc-

tion and sale of new houses. The Council of Economic Advisors was undecided about the effect of these controls upon the expenditures they attempted to curb.[1]

Into this plateau of high activity in late 1952 burst another consumer durables boom which lasted until the third quarter of 1953—concentrated mainly on cars.[2] This boom, along with maturing rearmament programmes pushed activity to its peak in 1953/III after which a fall in military expenditures—especially on durable equipment—began the contraction. Inventory investment responded by falling sharply (particularly that of durable goods manufacturers); fixed investment fell only slightly; purchases of consumer durables fell for six months after 1953/III. But before the factors which had initiated the contraction had reached bottom, residential construction had responded to cheap money (starting to rise in 1954/II), and consumer durable expenditures were also starting to rise. The tax and transfer effects in maintaining incomes have already been mentioned; also, state and local Government expenditures increased during 1954.[3]

This was a controlled contraction: initiated by the Federal Government, and minimized by a rapid transfer of resources from armaments to civilian assets. The stability of business fixed investment is to be explained by this transfer, assisted by earlier Government aid in the financing of the facilities to produce armaments.

The peaceful boom

The last four years have been the only period since 1939 when the American economy has not been either preparing for, recovering from, or engaged in war. Not that Government purchases of output are at their pre-1939 levels—for the last four years they have been stable at about one fifth of GNP.[4] But the fluctuating expenditures have been exclusively non-military and non-Governmental.

The boom had two stages. In the earlier, purchases of consumer durables, inventory investment and residential construction rose, the first reaching its peak in 1955/II, the second in 1956/I, and the third earlier in 1955/II. Business fixed investment also rose sharply above its pre-1953 levels. The later stage of the boom was sustained by a

[1] See the *Economic Report of the President* (January 1951), p. 39.

[2] The hire purchase controls were ended in the middle of 1952.

[3] Regarding monetary policy: in May and June 1953 'the Federal Reserve Authorities responded to the incipient, and possibly dangerous, scramble for liquidity with a degree of promptness and vigour for which there is no close parallel in our central bank history'. *Economic Report of the President* (January 1954), p. 50.

[4] One sixth in 1939; one ninth in 1929.

continued—although slower—rise in business fixed investment which did not reach its peak until 1957/I. Expenditures on consumer durables had fallen from their peak for a year after 1955/III; their subsequent movement (this applies both to cars and to furniture and appliances) suggests a definite—although weaker—boom in 1957. They rose slightly in the last quarter of 1956 and during 1957 were actually at a level higher than that of the 1953 boom.[1] Inventory investment fell continuously during 1956 and 1957, as did residential construction. These offsetting forces made GNP high but not expanding, and gave the index of production its irregular appearance from the end of 1955 to the third quarter of 1957.

After 1957/I business fixed investment fell steeply—its largest and most rapid fall since the 1930's. Coming on top of a falling rate of inventory investment it was followed by a sharp fall in purchases of consumer durables in 1958/I (almost entirely cars). While the 1948-9 slump can be described as a consequence of the post-war readjustment, and that of 1953-4 as the post-Korean adjustment, the 1957-8 slump was not an adjustment to any external factor. The fact on which any explanation must hinge is that activity expanded very little—if at all—after the end of 1955. This in itself, which is explained by falls in expenditures on consumer durables and in new construction, would cause a fall in those types of investment which are made when demand is increasing or expected to increase. Thus it is not surprising that inventory investment should be the first to fall. Nor at first sight is it surprising that eventually fixed investment should fall—with a fairly constant level of activity sooner or later further additions to capacity will seem to be unnecessary. The surprising thing is that investment continued at such a high level for so long. For example, from the beginning of 1956 to the end of 1957 consumer expenditures on non-durable goods were almost at a constant level, yet investment by the non-durable goods manufacturers was slightly higher in 1957 than in 1956.[2] It would appear that business confidence was very hard to break.

The rise in wholesale prices which commenced in late 1956 when GNP had risen well above previous levels, was no doubt indicative of high utilization of capacity and the appearance of bottlenecks; and as the inflationary pressure was sustained by a combination of demands in 1956 it would have provided a stimulus to the continuance

---

[1] As is clear from Chart 12.3 it is difficult to date the peak of the weak consumer durable boom in 1957.

[2] If investment by the chemical and petroleum industries is excluded, 1957 is slightly lower than 1956.

of the fixed investment boom.[1] Thus we have the picture of a boom checked by a high rate of use of capacity, 'running along the ceiling' for a time under the pressure of investment designed to increase capacity. The effects on incomes of this high level of investment were absorbed in rising prices, so that no expansion in the *volume* of expenditures was available to sustain activity once the extra capacity had been created. Stringent monetary policies during most of 1957 accentuated these fundamental forces. The 'peaceful boom' and its subsequent contraction thus take on a classic appearance.

4. CONCLUSION

In one sense the American economy has been (and still is) in the hands of the buyer of consumer durables; which is another way of saying that the unpredictables in the economy are the vagaries of the demand for cars. Yet both in 1949 and in early 1953 sales of cars depended to some extent upon the shifting of resources from other production over to cars. Further, vagaries may be too strong a word: the car boom in 1949-50 probably allowed anyone who wanted a car to get one. The succeeding booms of 1952/IV to 1953/III, 1954/II to 1955/III, and 1956/IV to 1957/III,[2] suggest a two year replacement cycle with a surprising persistence. On the other hand, demand for other types of consumer durables does not show this characteristic, and would seem to depend as much on new things as on new looks. The trend of expenditures on furniture and the older-fashioned appliances such as cookers depends of course on the rate of family formation and new residential construction.

But more important than cars is the output of durable goods as a whole—consumers' and producers' durables, and military hardware —in relation to the level of activity. Always regarded as a strategic factor in business cycles, there is no doubt that it continues to be so (and its influence extends to another unstable element: inventories held by manufacturers of durable goods). Fluctuations in new residential construction on the other hand have not in the last decade

---

[1] For example, steel production was running near 100 per cent of rated capacity during most of 1956 and early 1957. This degree of use of capacity is usually considered to be well above the most profitable level. See *SCB*, February and September 1958, S32. Wholesale prices of all commodities rose during 1956 and at a lesser rate after the beginning of 1957: during 1957 the prices of non-agricultural commodities stopped rising. Consumer prices started rising in mid-1956, the prices of durables rising very sharply in the last quarter of that year. See *SCB*, November 1958, pp. 7-8.

[2] Dated from trough to peak: *SCB*, September 1958, p. 24.

been quantitatively important as depressing influences. In fact this type of construction has been stabilizing and anti-cyclical: the first a reflection of demographic factors, the second of the responsiveness of construction to cheap money.

The influence of Government—Federal, state and local—upon fluctuations in activity has been considerable. Rearmament has tempered one slump, and caused another boom and slump. The anti-cyclical effect of falling taxes and increasing transfer payments in stabilizing personal income has been important. Cheap money in the contractions has stimulated state and local Government public construction (as well as private residential construction). From the point of view of the volume of unstable expenditures that Government can influence markedly and rapidly, both directly and indirectly, there is no doubt that the Federal Government and its agencies have been the most important single influence acting upon American economic activity.

It is only in a special sense that we can talk of the *growth* of the American economy in the post-war decade. Growth usually implies a clear trend. Study of the index of production (see Chart 12.1) shows that this is hardly evident: what is most obvious is a series of steps on to floors or plateaus. It resembles the discontinuous growth of an organism, rather than the continuous growth of a population. But if a trend *is* drawn through the steps it is obvious that the rate of growth —even if the 1959 revival persists—is declining. The steps of 1950 and late 1952 lifted the economy to new heights of activity; the step of 1955 did not lift activity much above the 1953 level (although it was sustained for a much longer period). Whether the lowered rate of growth (or declining height of the steps) will make future contractions worse depends whether it affects those expenditures which have been high and relatively stable during the past decade. In particular, it depends whether residential and public construction, and fixed investment in power, communications and transport systems, and in the large sector of the distributive and service trades, are geared to the rate of growth. If the trend in these should be declining in a contraction—which has not been evident since the late 1920's—then without considerably more Government aid than has been required in the past the slumps undoubtedly will be more severe.

It is true that investment in any particular type of house, form of power or method of distribution is likely to be closely related to population growth and levels of income. But it hardly needs saying that Americans are not particularly conservative in the matter of types, forms and methods. The same factors which make the demand for consumer durables to be so unstable can keep the aggregate of growth investment growing.

5. EXERCISES

(1) What types of national expenditure have contributed most to the revival in business activity following the 1957-8 slump? [HINT: use the quarterly constant price national income estimates (seasonally adjusted) in SCB. Compare the changes between the trough of the 1957-8 slump and the peak (or most recent date) in the expansion.]

(2) Compare the changes in the index of durable goods manufacturing production with those in the index of non-durable goods manufacturing production since 1955. [HINT: use the indexes in SCB; take quarterly averages; plot on a ratio chart.] Which index is more likely to give an early warning of changes in business activity?

(3) In the early post-war period the United States had a large surplus on its balance of current payments (see Table 12.4 above). Deficits in other countries' balance of payments and their shortages of gold and dollar reserves were directly related to this phenomenon. In the years since 1957 however, the United States has been losing gold to other countries. Is this due to a deficit on current account, or is it due to movements of capital? [HINT: SCB publishes quarterly estimates of the balance of payments, and there is also an annual Supplement to SCB on the Balance of Payments of the United States. The *National Income* and *Business Statistics* Supplements also give balance of payments statistics. Use recent issues of any of these sources to compile figures for 1957-9. Compare the changes in the current surplus over the period with the changes in capital movements.]

Reference Table of United Kingdom Economic Statistics

The following table is a guide to the most useful and easily accessible statistics that the economics student requires. The classification is based on the information available in the national income accounts. The first column lists the main economic subjects of interest. The second indicates the relevent national income statistics. The third column gives the most useful supplementary or short period statistics (mainly from MDS or AAS); and the fourth shows for what subjects the Censuses of Population, Production and Distribution are useful.

To keep the table short only one source is given for each statistical series, and in the third column the student is referred to either the MDS or the AAS unless other sources are better or give more useful detail.

Two sets of abbreviations are used:

(1) Frequency of calculation
    A annually
    H half-yearly
    Q quarterly
    M monthly
(2) Title of source
    NIE   National Income and Expenditure (published annually)
    AAS   Annual Abstract of Statistics (published annually)
    MDS   Monthly Digest of Statistics (published monthly)
    ET   Economic Trends (published monthly)
    MLG   Ministry of Labour Gazette (published monthly)
    BTJ   Board of Trade Journal (published weekly)

Thus 'Q in MDS' means that the statistical series is calculated quarterly or every quarter, and published in the Monthly Digest of Statistics. In the second column we have omitted reference to sources because A in all cases means calculated annually and published in NIE, and Q means calculated quarterly and published in both MDS and ET.

For descriptions of the statistics, their methods of compilation, coverage, etc., the following reference works will be useful:

1. CSO *National Income Statistics: Sources and Methods* (HMSO, 1956).

2. CSO *Supplement of Definitions and Explanatory Notes to the Monthly Digest of Statistics* (HMSO, annually).
3. Ministry of Labour *Method of Construction and Calculation of the Index of Retail Prices* (HMSO, 1956).
4. HM Treasury *United Kingdom Balance of Payments, 1946-57* (HMSO, 1959).

New statistical series are usually introduced in ET with accompanying explanatory notes.

Reference Table of United Kingdom Economic Statistics

ECONOMIC SUBJECTS	STATISTICS IN THE FRAMEWORK OF THE NATIONAL INCOME ACCOUNTS Annually (A) in NIE Quarterly (Q) in MDS and ET

A. NATIONAL EXPENDITURE

1. *Consumers' expenditure*

   (*a*) durable goods

   (*b*) non-durable goods

   (*c*) services

   both at current and 1954 prices: A and Q in thirteen groups; A in forty-seven sub-groups.

2. *Gross fixed capital formation*

   (*a*) dwellings

   (*b*) other: building and construction, plant and machinery, vehicles

   both at current and 1954 prices, A and Q. NIE classifies by industry, sector and type, and gives separate figures for net investment and capital consumption. MDS and ET by industry group at current prices, and by type and sector at 1954 prices (with greater detail for manufacturing industry).

OTHER STATISTICS   CENSUSES

Indexes of value of retail sales: A in AAS; M in MDS.

Household food expenditure and consumption in Great Britain: Q in MDS

Food supplies per head of population: A in AAS

Hire purchase and other instalment credit: debt and new business. M in MDS and BTJ.

Censuses of Distribution, 1950 and 1957, give value of wholesale and retail sales. Summaries in AAS.

Note: statistics of deliveries or production of commodities may be used as indicators of sales or purchases. (They may need to be adjusted for imports and exports.) A in AAS; M in MDS.

Value of constructional work: A in AAS; Q in MDS.

Censuses of Production since 1948 contain statistics of capital expenditures. Summary in AAS.

Note: statistics of production of commodities, machinery and vehicles may be used as indicators of investment. A in AAS; M in MDS.

ECONOMIC SUBJECTS	STATISTICS IN THE FRAMEWORK OF THE NATIONAL INCOME ACCOUNTS Annually (A) in NIE Quarterly (Q) in MDS and ET
3. *Investment in stocks* (inventory investment)	Value of physical increase in stocks and work in progress: both at current and 1954 prices, A and Q. Change in value of stocks: by industry and type: A at current prices; Q (for manufacturing only) at current prices. Value of stocks held: by industry and type: A at current prices.
4. *Public authorities' current expenditure*	both at current and 1954 prices, A and Q.
5. *Balance of payments and international trade*	Balance of current transactions: current prices, A and Q. Imports and exports: at 1954 prices, A and Q.

B. NATIONAL OUTPUT

1. *Agriculture, forestry and fishing*

2. *Mining and quarrying*

net outputs at current and 1954 prices, A.

OTHER STATISTICS   CENSUSES

Index of retail stocks. M in MDS
Statistics of stocks of industrial materials (e.g. raw cotton, coal, steel). A in AAS; M in MDS.

Censuses of Production since 1948 contain statistics of stocks and work in progress. Summary in AAS.

United Kingdom balance of payments: H and A in *Balance of Payments White Paper*.
Imports and Exports: M in *Trade and Navigation Accounts* and MDS; A in AAS and *Annual Statement of Trade*. (Seasonally adjusted M and Q in BTJ.)
Official gold and foreign currency holdings
European Payments Union   } M in MDS
Foreign exchange rates
Overseas sterling holdings and acceptances outstanding: Q in MDS.
Overseas investments of the United Kingdom: A in AAS.

Gross output of agriculture, at current and 1945/46 prices: A in AAS.
Farming net income: A in AAS
Production statistics of individual commodities: A in AAS; M in MDS.

Index of mining and quarrying production: M in MDS.
Statistics of coal production, consumption and productivity: A in AAS; M in MDS.
Statistics of other mineral production: A in AAS.

Censuses of Production, annually since 1948. Summary in AAS.

ECONOMIC SUBJECTS	STATISTICS IN THE FRAMEWORK OF THE NATIONAL INCOME ACCOUNTS
	Annually (A) in NIE
	Quarterly (Q) in MDS and ET

3. *Manufacturing*

4. *Building and contracting* (construction)

5. *Gas, electricity and water*

6. *Distribution* (*wholesale and retail*)

7. *Transport and communication*

} net outputs at current and 1954 prices, A.

8. *Insurance, banking and finance*

9. *Other services* (*e.g. law, laundering*)

10. *Public administration and defence*

11. *Public health and educational services*

} Expenditures on goods and services: A.

OTHER STATISTICS   CENSUSES

Indexes of production for 18 manufacturing
   groups: A in AAS; M in MDS.
Production statistics of individual industrial raw
   materials and manufactured goods: M in
   MDS; A in AAS

Index of construction: Q in MDS.
Value of constructional output in ⎫
   Great Britain   ⎬ Q in
Industrial building in Great Britain ⎫ MDS
Permanent house building   ⎭
Permanent houses completed: M in MDS.

Index of gas, electricity and water production:
   M in MDS
Statistics of gas production and electricity gen-
   eration: M in MDS; A in AAS.

Censuses of Pro-
duction, annually
since 1948. Sum-
mary in AAS.

Censuses of Distri-
bution, 1950 and
1957.

Public road passenger transport: traffic and re-
   ceipts: A in AAS; M (for British Transport
   Commission) and Q (other) in MDS.
Railways: traffic and receipts: A in AAS; M in
   MDS.
Shipping movement: A in AAS; M in MDS.
Air transport: traffic, A in AAS; M in MDS.
Statistics of postal, telegraph and telephone ser-
   vices: A in AAS.
Insurance statistics: A in AAS.

Broadcast receiving licences current: A in AAS;
   M in MDS.
Cinemas: admissions and receipts: A in AAS;
   Q in MDS.

National Health Service and educational statistics: A in AAS.

| ECONOMIC SUBJECTS | STATISTICS IN THE FRAMEWORK OF THE NATIONAL INCOME ACCOUNTS
Annually (A) in NIE
Quarterly (Q) in MDS and ET |

C. INCOME

1. *Income from employment*

   (a) wages and salaries — for major sectors and manufacturing groups: A.
   for whole economy only: Q.

   (b) pay of the Forces ⎫

   (c) employers' contributions ⎬ A and Q.

2. *Income from self-employment*

   (a) Farmers ⎫

   (b) Professions ⎬ A; total only (together with rent): Q.

   (c) Other sole traders and partnerships ⎭ for major sectors: A.

3. *Gross trading profit of companies* — for major sectors and manufacturing groups, A; allocations to dividends, interest, taxes, savings, A; totals only, Q.

4. *Gross trading surpluses of public corporations* — for industry groups, A; totals only, Q.

   Also *Personal income* — A and Q.

   Government revenue — A, and Q for Central Government only.

   Distribution of income by size — A for selected years.

OTHER STATISTICS   CENSUSES

Index of weekly wage rates: M in MDS.
Average weekly earnings: H in MLG (summary
   in MDS).

Censuses of Pro-
duction, annually
since 1948. Statis-
tics of wages and
salaries.

Farming net income: A in AAS.

Income and Finance of Public Quoted Companies: A in ET (each February).

Annual Reports of Public Corporations.

Distribution of income by size ⎱ A in AAS.
Tax rates   ⎰

ECONOMIC SUBJECTS	STATISTICS IN THE FRAMEWORK OF THE NATIONAL INCOME ACCOUNTS Annually (A) in NIE Quarterly (Q) in MDS and ET

D. LABOUR
   1. *Employment and unemployment*

   2. *Vacancies*

OTHER STATISTICS   CENSUSES

Numbers employed, temporarily stopped, wholly unemployed: M, by sex, for 164 industries, Great Britain, in MLG.

Following summaries in MDS and AAS:

(a) *Civil employment* (including employers and self-employed, excluding wholly unemployed)

α in Great Britain for 11 sectors and 14 manufacturing groups: A in AAS.

β in Northern Ireland for 9 sectors: A in AAS.

γ in Great Britain for 9 major sectors: M in MDS.

(b) *Numbers of employees* (including wholly unemployed)

in United Kingdom for 164 industries, A (for May) in AAS.

(c) *Numbers employed* (excluding wholly unemployed)

α in Great Britain for 14 manufacturing groups: M in MDS.

β in Great Britain for about 64 manufacturing industries, by sex: M in MDS.

(d) *Registered unemployed*

α in United Kingdom for 164 industries: A in AAS.

β in Great Britain and Northern Ireland, by sex: M in AAS.

γ in Great Britain (distinguishing wholly unemployed and temporarily stopped) and Northern Ireland, by sex: M in MDS.

δ in Great Britain, by duration and sex, and by 11 sectors: M in MDS.

Census of Population, 1951, gives figures of occupations.

Censuses of Production give numbers employed *plus* working proprietors.

In Great Britain and Northern Ireland, by sex: placings and vacancies by age, M in MDS; vacancies only, M in AAS.

ECONOMIC SUBJECTS	STATISTICS IN THE FRAMEWORK OF THE NATIONAL INCOME ACCOUNTS Annually (A) in NIE Quarterly (Q) in MDS and ET

3. *Hours*

4. *Turnover*

5. *Ages of Labour force*

E. PRICES
   1. *Retail*

   2. *Wholesale*

   3. *Agricultural*

   4. *Imports and exports*

Indexes of market prices of consumers' expenditure: A.

Indexes of certain prices and costs, e.g. imports, exports, fixed assets: A.

F. MONEY
   1. *Banking*

OTHER STATISTICS   CENSUSES

Average weekly hours worked, by sex, H in
    MDS; A for 14 manufacturing groups in AAS.
Overtime and short-time worked in manufactur-
    ing industries in Great Britain: M in MDS.

Rates of intake and losses, by sex, for manufac-
    turing industries: Q in MLG.

Number of employees, by age: A (June) in MLG.

Index of retail prices: for 10 groups, M in MDS;
    for 33 sub-groups, Q in MDS.

International commodity prices: M in MDS.
Average wholesale prices for selected home pro-
    duced and imported commodities: A in AAS.
Indexes of wholesale prices: M in MDS; A in
    AAS.

England and Wales. Average prices of agricul-
    tural products, dairy cows and feeding stuffs:
    A in AAS.
Indexes of agricultural prices: M in MDS.

Indexes of import and export prices: M in
    MDS; A and Q in AAS.

Currency circulation: M in MDS.
London clearing banks balance sheets: M in
    MDS.
Bank advances by industry: M in MDS.

ECONOMIC SUBJECTS	STATISTICS IN THE FRAMEWORK OF THE NATIONAL INCOME ACCOUNTS Annually (A) in NIE Quarterly (Q) in MDS and ET
2. *Savings*	Savings by sector: A; for persons and Central Government only: Q.
3. *Government finance*	A. Central Government revenue only: Q.
4. *Interest rates, etc.*	
5. *Hire purchase*	

G. POPULATION AND VITAL STATISTICS

OTHER STATISTICS   CENSUSES

Income and Finance of Public Quoted Com-
  panies: A in ET.
Capital issues: Q in MDS.
Insurance and building society statistics: A in
  AAS.

A in AAS.
Tax receipts: M in MDS.
Exchequer financing: Q in MDS.

Security prices and yields ⎫ M in MDS.
Foreign exchange rates   ⎭
Money and bill rates: M in AAS.

Hire purchase and other instalment credit: debt
  and new business, M and Q (more detail) in
  BTJ; Summary, M in MDS.

Reports of Registrars General.   Censuses of Popu-
Summaries available: lation, decennial.
(*a*) total population, births, deaths, marriages,
     age distribution: A in AAS.
(*b*) marital condition, geographical distribution,
     industrial status: A in AAS.
(*c*) migration: A in AAS.
(*d*) births, deaths, marriages: Q in MDS.

Q

INDEX

See also Reference Table, pp. 226–41

GEORGE ALLEN & UNWIN LTD
London: 40 Museum Street, W.C.1

Auckland: 24 Wyndham Street
Sydney, N.S.W.: Bradbury House, 55 York Street
Cape Town: 109 Long Street
Bombay: 15 Graham Road, Ballard Estate, Bombay 1
Calcutta: 17 Chittaranjan Avenue, Calcutta 13
New Delhi: 13–14 Ajmeri Gate Extension, New Delhi 1
Karachi: Meherson's Estate, Wood Street, Karachi 2
Mexico: Villalongin 32–10, Piso, Mexico 5, D.F.
Toronto: 91 Wellington Street West
São Paulo: Avenida 9 de Julho 1138–Ap. 51
Buenos Aires: Escritorio 454–459, Florida 165
Singapore: 36c Princep Street, Singapore 7
Hong Kong: 1/12 Mirador Mansions, Kowloon

THE MINERVA SERIES
OF STUDENTS' HANDBOOKS

1. RUSSIAN POLITICAL INSTITUTIONS

by J. D. R. SCOTT, M.A., PH.D

University of Manchester   *Demy 8vo. 21s cloth. 16s boards*

'. . . the most useful introductory survey of the subject in English that has so far been produced.' Professor MAX BELOFF in *Parliamentary Affairs*

'He has succeeded brilliantly. His succinct, comprehensive, and judicious study, written in an agreebly crisp and lively style, is by far the best survey of the subject yet published, and will be of great use to many others besides the undergraduates whom he had in mind.' *International Affairs*

'. . . thoughtful and thorough textbook, which patiently, and without imparting irrelevant criteria, sets out what can be known about the governmental system, and describes exactly what gaps in our knowledge are the inevitable product of the limitations of the sources.' *Economist*

2. INTERNATIONAL INSTITUTIONS

by PAUL REUTER

Professor of International Law, University of Paris

Demy 8vo. 28s cloth. 20s boards

Broadly speaking institutions are the organizations, the traditions and the basic rules of a particular society. Between nations a similar series of traditions has developed and it is possible to assess the continuity and the variety of international societies as they have existed in recent history and as they exist and work today. Although the study of international institutions is firmly based on a foundation of law, it is also a matter of importance for sociology, history and politics. This carefully prepared book is of prime importance for all deeply concerned with these subjects.

'. . . one could not imagine a better introduction to International Law, and it is much to be wished that Professor Reuter's calm, reasonable analysis will attract and influence many readers.' *Law Journal*

'Part One is concerned with the origins of present-day international institutions and is a cogent historical analysis from ancient civilizations to present times. . . . The most useful part of the book deals with this central problem of the subordination of the state to the international community. . . . Part Two deals with the structure of the day-to-day relations between states and the means of recognizing changes within a state. . . . Part Three is concerned with international organizations.' *Law Times*

3. FREE ELECTIONS
by W. J. M. MACKENZIE, LL.B., M.A

Professor of Government, University of Manchester

Demy 8vo. 15s cloth. 12s 6d boards

'. . . deserves a very warm welcome. For the first time the basic problems about franchise qualifications, methods of voting, and systems of administration have been described and classified in one book.' D. E. BUTLER in *Journal of African Administration*

'. . . an outstandingly able piece of writing, drawing upon a wealth of comparative material presented with critical discernment and in a pleasing style. No teacher of politics or public law can afford not to have this book.' *Modern Law Review*

'*Free Elections* has all the attributes of a good textbook, but students are too rarely offered an introduction which, like this one, provokes discussion as well as providing information.' *Times Literary Supplement*

4. MODERN FORMS OF GOVERNMENT
by MICHAEL STEWART, M.A., M.P

Demy 8vo. 21s cloth. 17s 6d boards

Mr Stewart describes both the formal constitution and the actual working of the government in some twenty countries in all parts of the world: the United Kingdom and the older and newer countries of the Commonwealth; the U.S.A. and the nations of Western Europe; the U.S.S.R. and the smaller Communist countries. While each country is treated separately, the book deals admirably with ideas and principles as well as facts. The chapter describing the Commonwealth countries precedes an examination of the development and potentialities of the unique Commonwealth form of association; the description of the U.S.A., Germany, and Switzerland is followed by a discussion of Federalism; and an inquiry into the Communist conception of politics precedes the description of Communist governments.

'. . . an admirable book. . . . If any intelligent person, with a concern for politics, and stemming from one of the newly developing countries in Asia and Africa, asked me to recommend him one book as a constant, straightforward companion, I would without hesitation choose this.' *Socialist Commentary*

THE BRITISH ECONOMY, 1920–1957

by A. J. YOUNGSON

Professor of Economic History, University of Edinburgh

Demy 8vo. 28s net

The greater part of the book consists of an attempt to describe and account for the course of British economic development since the end of the post-war boom in 1920, a subject which has hardly been tackled at any length or in any convenient form. The coverage is general, but the author pays particular attention to changes in the industrial structure, to international trade, financial policy and fluctuations in the level of activity. The final section is devoted to a fascinating discussion of government economic policy throughout the period, in which the author seeks to trace the relation between policy and the ideas put forward at the time by economists such as Pigou, Robertson and Keynes.

The basic intention is to provide a book which deals with the economic history of Britain since 1920 as fully and as consistently as many books now deal with the nineteenth century. Primarily suitable for undergraduates, the book will also make a strong appeal to the wider public interested in the trends of recent economic development. The author's discussion of economic policy will also interest those who already have some knowledge of the academic writings of the period. The picture which emerges of economic development and policy as a whole in the past quarter century will greatly contribute to our general understanding of current problems.

TRADE UNIONS AND THE LABOUR PARTY SINCE 1945

by MARTIN HARRISON

Demy 8vo. 32s net

Here is a study of the most controversial alliance in British politics. The 'wage freeze', Bevanism, the block vote, nuclear disarmament; these are only a few of the points at which the unions' activities within the Labour Party have aroused hot debate. The much disputed political levy, the money the unions give to Labour (there is fresh insight here into the Party's finances), their role in its work in the constituencies, and their struggle to keep their representation in the House of Commons are all examined. 'Is the link with the Labour Party still important enough for the unions to be willing to make sacrifices?' he asks. Do the unions still pay the piper—and do they still call the tune? This point is considered in the course of a thoughtful discussion of the vexed problem of forming union policy 'democratically' at every stage from the branch to the annual conference of the Labour Party. Fresh light is thrown on the way the unions use their power, and on such thorny problems as the block vote. Finally the author reminds Labour of the challenge of the non-political unions.

ECONOMIC AND FINANCIAL ASPECTS OF SOCIAL SECURITY
AN INTERNATIONAL SURVEY
by PROFESSOR J. HENRY RICHARDSON   *Demy 8vo. 30s net*

This important book by an experienced authority on social security discusses a subject of vital interest to governments and peoples everywhere. In all countries social security is still experimental, its principles and methods are being actively reviewed, and nowhere has a final pattern evolved. In many countries the systems have grown piecemeal with numerous anomalies and gaps. Professor Richardson's survey is timely in directing attention to those basic principles and methods which are essential for sound progress.

Specially valuable is the chapter which considers what proportion of the national income can be afforded for social security, and also that on the alternatives of financing by accumulating large funds or by 'pay-as-you-go' methods. It is clear that the State may become financially overburdened, and may also interfere too much with individual freedom. Professor Richardson concludes that when the State has ensured basic provision, people should be substantially free to make provision for their own special circumstances. He emphasizes the flexibility of private occupational schemes and insurance to supplement basic State provision.

FISCAL POLICY IN UNDERDEVELOPED COUNTRIES
WITH SPECIAL REFERENCE TO INDIA
by RAJA J. CHELLIAH, PH.D   *Demy 8vo. 20s net*

The central thesis of this important book is an application of recent advances in the theory of fiscal policy to the promotion of economic development, while at the same time diminishing inequalities. The author demonstrates why advanced and underdeveloped countries need different policies, and thereby makes a distinct contribution to fiscal theory.

The book will interest those concerned with the theory of public finance, to those responsible for practical policy, and particularly to economists working in underdeveloped areas. What makes it very topical is the growing awareness of economic problems in general, and in particular the desire to employ taxation in the service of economic development. India is a notable case, which Dr Chelliah handles on the basis of his own study, research and personal experience. He analyses and evaluates the recommendations of the Indian Taxation Enquiry Commission (1953–54) and those in Mr Kaldor's recent report to the Indian Government.

Dr Chelliah, formerly on the Economics staff of the Madras Christian College, was a Fulbright scholar at the University of Pittsburgh, where the present study was completed. He is now an economist on the staff of the National Council of Applied Economic Research, New Delhi.

NATIONALIZED INDUSTRY AND PUBLIC OWNERSHIP

by WILLIAM A. ROBSON

Professor of Public Administration, London School of Economics and Political Science   *Small Royal 8vo. 50s net*

Most of the books, articles, and pamphlets on the subject of nationalization are so prejudiced that they are of little value except as ammunition for political warfare. Professor Robson's new book is primarily an inquiry into the working of the British nationalized industries during the past ten years. He examines, with the aid of a wealth of material, the organization and management of these industries, how far they are subject to competition, their labour relations, their financial policies, their research and development programmes, their consumer councils, their relations with Ministers and Parliament, the political influences to which they are subject, and their general performance. He considers also the ideas and proposals which have recently been put forward about the manner in which publicly owned industries should be run and the aims they should pursue. The final chapter discusses some of the alternatives to nationalization which have been advanced.

Nationalized Industry and Public Ownership stands in a class by itself, for although the author makes no attempt to conceal his own views, his main object is to present a fair and accurate account of the nationalized industries. The reader will find here no simple story of success or failure, but an honest account of achievements and shortcomings, of difficulties overcome and of problems still unsolved.

FINANCIAL ADMINISTRATION IN LOCAL GOVERNMENT

by DR A. H. MARSHALL, C.B.E   *Demy 8vo. 32s net*

The financial administration which Local Government demands is as complex as the services are varied and vital. Dr Marshall's book on this important subject is neither involved nor fragmentary. Deftly he explains the internal organization of local authorities, describes the responsibilities with which Councils generally charge their Finance Committees, and then analyses stage by stage the methods employed by Chief Financial Officers and their staffs to implement the Council's policies.

Dr Marshall, City Treasurer of Coventry, past chairman of the Executive Council of the Royal Institute of Public Administration and past president of the Institute of Municipal Treasurers and Accountants, is well known in the world of Local Government finance. With this authoritative book he has earned the gratitude of all Local Government financial officers, of their colleagues in other departments and of students who seek a textbook based on great practical experience. He has also produced a work which will be read with interest by those concerned with the similar functions and problems of financial administration in large scale private industry and the other branches of the public services.

AMERICAN FOREIGN POLICY

THEORY AND REALITY   *Demy 8vo. 25s net*

by LOUIS J. HALLE

Mr Halle, a former member of the State Department's Policy Planning
staff, writes as one who knows from personal experience that government
is people. The book, therefore, is not another recital of selected events in
American diplomatic history. It is a sympathetic but ironic appreciation
of the imperfect humanity that is represented by foreign policy in general,
by American foreign policy in particular.

The birth of America was regarded as a fresh start for mankind. But
the notion that America was Utopia implied an isolation which could
not be maintained. Here are the elements of tragedy implicit in all history
—the sequence of hope and disillusion, of dream and reality. It is in this
context that the current American debate over idealism *v.* realism must
be viewed.

INFLATION AND SOCIETY

by GRAHAM HUTTON   *Demy 8vo. 15s net*

This important and timely book is by an economist for non-economists.
It looks at inflation in societies past, present and yet in process of formation.
In its author's words its theme is 'how inflation as a policy has come
about in modern democracies, how it works, how to avoid it, and at what
cost'. His chief concern is 'to make clear in non-technical terms what inflation does, both to society and to its individual elements, to weaken and
hamper democracy'. Mr Hutton brings to this task a wealth of experience
expressed in striking examples and illustrations of inflation at work in
widely differing communities past and present This work goes with the same
swing as his classic study of productivity also published by Allen & Unwin
(1953) entitled *We Too Can Prosper*. Like that too, it is stimulating,
provocative and hard to put down.

Graham Hutton, born in 1904 in Hertfordshire, was educated at 'every
kind of school'—State, grammar, private and public—and at London,
French and German universities. After a first in economics, he was called
to the Bar, taught at the London School of Economics and in 1933 joined
the *Economist*. During the war he served in the Foreign Office and the
Ministry of Information.

In 1948 he started business as an independent economic consultant,
but continued writing, broadcasting and serving on the boards of several
companies.

GEORGE ALLEN AND UNWIN LTD